KU-604-133

ADRIAN
EDMONDSON

BERSERKER!

MACMILLAN

First published 2023 by Macmillan
an imprint of Pan Macmillan
The Smithson, 6 Briset Street, London EC1M 5NR
EU representative: Macmillan Publishers Ireland Ltd, 1st Floor,
The Liffey Trust Centre, 117–126 Sheriff Street Upper,
Dublin 1, D01 YC43
Associated companies throughout the world
www.panmacmillan.com

ISBN 978-1-0350-1427-9 HB
ISBN 978-1-0350-1428-6 TPB

The picture acknowledgements on pp. 402–3 constitute an extension of
this copyright page.

9 8 7 6 5 4

A CIP catalogue record for this book is available from the British Library.

Typeset in Stempel Garamond LT Pro by
Palimpsest Book Production Ltd, Falkirk, Stirlingshire

Printed and bound by CPI Group (UK) Ltd, Croydon, CR0 4YY

For Ella, Beattie and Freya

‘That’s our story and we’re stuck with it’

Stan Laurel, *Sons of the Desert*, 1933

Contents

PART 3
Finding things funny

PART 4
International rock god

PART 5
Manchester (before it was cool)

PART 6

The accidental comedian

PART 7

We're on the telly!

PART 8

The life and death of a double act

PART 9

International rock god pt 2

PART 10

Where's the berserker?

PART 11

Endings

Introduction

Somewhere in the blood-filled soft tissue of my hippocampus – a part of the brain that looks like a rather stringy chicken fillet in the shape of a seahorse – a mass of neurons and synapses have apparently been sorting out my experiences and stashing them away in various bits of my brain since the day I was born.

I never studied biology and can only imagine these neurons and synapses as being like the Numskulls in *The Beezer* – little men who are looking out through my eyeballs and working me from within. My Numskulls are in constant despair at the antics of their simple-minded 'man': 'He's not going to eat the *entire* packet of biscuits, surely?' 'Why does he waste so much time playing fantasy football?' 'Good Lord, he's moving on to spirits now!' They work twenty-four hours a day trying to keep me on the straight and narrow, and lurch from crisis to crisis, getting tired and making mistakes. Some memories get stashed away in the wrong place or get stuffed in so hard that they get squashed out of shape.

Taking into account that everyone's head is full of Numskulls, each fighting a constant battle to get their man or woman to breathe, to eat, or to have an opinion about whether that was definitely offside or not, it's easy to see how haphazard the memory system might be.

There's a one-act play by Tom Stoppard I love, called *After Magritte*, in which a woman is certain she's just seen a man in a West Bromwich Albion shirt, with shaving foam around his chin and a football under his arm, running down the street; her husband swears it was a man wearing pyjamas, with a white beard, carrying a tortoise; while her mother says it was a minstrel wearing striped prison clothes, sporting a surgical mask and carrying a lute.

At least they can all agree they've seen something. Something happened.

The something in question in this book is my life. Which I'm pretty sure has happened – not all of it, but quite a lot of it. Many people have been party to bits of it but I doubt they could all agree on what they've seen.

Years ago the Wikipedia entry on me used to say that I was born in Bolton, that I'd smash up the piano in any club I went to, and that whilst I was a student at Manchester I shacked up with Viv Albertine, the guitarist from The Slits. Well, I was born in Bradford, I've never attacked a piano – I love pianos and wish them no harm – and I've never even met Viv Albertine, much though I would've loved to have shacked up with her in the mid-seventies.

Back then I tried to edit the page but the Wikipedia moderators – self-appointed guardians of the truth – always took my corrections down. I sent a message saying I actually *was* Adrian Edmondson. Oh, how they scoffed. They said it was obvious from what I'd written that I knew absolutely nothing about him, and they blocked me from editing the page thereafter.

Of course, on one level they might be right – do I really know anything about myself? Really? Deep down? What would my psychiatrist say?

I know I'm not the bloke on the Wikipedia page, which,

amongst the strange emphasis and vague biographical errors, is mainly a list of programmes I've been in. The list is more or less accurate, but I'm not a list of programmes.

I'm not *The Young Ones* – I mean of course I was in it, I was bloody good in it actually, but making the two series of *The Young Ones* took up precisely fourteen weeks of my life. Or to put it another way – less than one half of one per cent of my life.

So far.

In 2016 I adapted William Leith's book *Bits of Me Are Falling Apart* into a one-man play. It took six weeks to do the adaptation, four weeks to rehearse it, and it played for a further four weeks at the Soho Theatre, a small London venue, to a total of around 2,500 people. It took up the same amount of my life as *The Young Ones*. I'm not expecting you to think it's as noteworthy, but the Numskulls in my head have given it exactly the same amount of space.

I know one thing for sure, this is not the most linear autobiography you'll ever read. It doesn't start at the beginning and plod resolutely through to the end. My memory isn't linear – it flits about from one subject to another, back and forth through the years. So this book is not particularly coherent, but then neither is my life. It's all about the tangents.

It's also littered with references to songs that were at some point number one in the charts. Whenever I hear a song it gives me more context about the time I first heard it than any potted history might do – I can see the colour and the shape of cars, the way people dressed and behaved, and I can feel how people were thinking at the time. So every song title in this book is like one of Proust's madeleines to me – it takes me straight back to where I was and what it felt like. I hope they help you in the same way. Or at least bring you joy.

I hope this book is about more than just me, I think it might be about you too, because most of us have lived through the same era. I hope it makes you laugh occasionally, I hope you enjoy the diversions into history, cooking and pop music, because it's basically everything I know about being a human being born in Britain in the mid twentieth century.

My memory is like a misprinted dot-to-dot puzzle – some of the dots are missing but my brain fills them in for me. Which sounds imprecise, but I know that what I remember is true to me. This is how it felt to me. I have lived my life thinking all of the following to be the truth, which in some way *makes* it the truth.

On the other hand I often forget my own children's names, and can never remember where I left the bloody keys – so good luck, and *caveat emptor*.

My daughter Freya says she's always loved this photo of me because I look like a Danish philosopher. If only. I discuss my frustrated claims of Viking ancestry later in the book, and only have a puny degree in drama not philosophy, but you learn the odd thing by simply hanging around for sixty-six years. So perhaps there is some philosophy in here too. And I like the Danes.

Part 1

What's in a name?

It's all a bit woolly

The first problem with pinning down who I really am is that no one even knows my name. No one knows what to call me. Even me. On first meeting people always say, 'Do we call you Ade or Adrian?' and I usually reply, 'Whatever you can manage', because in truth I can't stomach either.

How did this come to pass?

I arrive into this world 'quite quickly' at the bottom of the stairs in a modest, pebble-dashed semi in an area of Bradford called Wrose. It's now BD2, but I'm born two years before postcodes were invented – which is probably why the ambulance can't find us, and why my dad ends up delivering me.

This happens on 24 January 1957 when Guy Mitchell is toppermost of the poppermost with 'Singing the Blues'.

This isn't a conscious memory of course, and Guy isn't at the birth, even though his face suggests otherwise. Is that joy? Or horror? Or a clever mix of the two? One disguising the other? Everything's fine. This is normal. I still love you. Aggghh! The horror! The horror! Hide it for ever! Never speak of it!

It could be the very same expression on Dad's face, because he has no training, no aptitude and apparently no stomach for it, but it's an emergency and he's the only one there, apart from my mum, obviously. And I survive.

The wool rug at the bottom of the stairs doesn't.

My family history is very woolly. It's precise, but it's precisely about wool.

At the time I arrive Bradford is struggling with a decline in fortunes. My earliest memories of the city are of all the buildings being jet black – a thick residue of filth and soot that had built up from all the coke and coal that was burned to keep the machines going in the mills.

Back in 1841 two-thirds of the UK's wool production was processed in Bradford, and the population doubled in a decade. By 1900 there were 350 mills – scouring, carding, gilling, combing, drafting, spinning and twisting to produce yarn and fabric. It was boom time, and despite the amount of muck and grime being chucked out by all those chimneys there was a lot of civic pride in all that industry. To compete with the town halls of neighbouring Leeds and Halifax, Bradford built a town hall with a clock tower based on the Palazzo Vecchio in Florence, and boasted of the city being built on seven hills – 'just like Rome'.

While Manchester was nicknamed 'Cottonopolis', Bradford became 'the Wool Capital of the World'. Not quite as snazzy, but no less true. Worsted – a superior yarn made using only the longest fibres, very popular for making suits – became a speciality of the city and some people tried to adopt the name 'Worstedopolis', which sounds like a bad review for a Greek restaurant on TripAdvisor, and thankfully it didn't catch on.

This constant desire to make a name for itself, to be better than Leeds and Halifax, to be on a par with Manchester, or even Florence and Rome, has the whiff of an inferiority complex. Can a city have a collective consciousness? All my immediate forebears were born in Bradford, and while I don't think they felt inferior exactly, they certainly seemed to 'know their place'. I was brought up to think that other people probably knew better than me. I've always struggled with the idea that I'm not good enough.

My mum is called Dorothy and her maiden name is Sturgeon, a name that comes originally from Suffolk, which was once a great sheep-rearing county. It seems the Sturgeons must have followed the sheep to Bradford because they ended up in the Wool Capital of the World by the middle of the nineteenth century.

Her dad, George Sturgeon, worked on the shop floor of the dark satanic mills and died of a heart attack three years short of his retirement, and a year before I was born.

Her mum was Doris (Grandma Sturgeon), though her maiden name was Luscombe – a name that comes originally from Devon, where I now live in a bizarre case of reverse migration. There were, and still are, a lot of sheep in Devon – I've raised a few myself – but the Luscombes too followed the sheep, and the work, to Bradford. Doris worked in a weaving mill until she got married when she was apparently sacked for . . . getting married. She took up moaning as a full-time occupation. And cheating at canasta with a young boy, namely me. If she were alive today I could happily tell her that you don't have to shout 'I'm in Meredith' when you produce your first meld, that putting the first red three on the table doesn't entitle you to all the red threes as they appear, and that you can't play the game with just two people anyway.

My dad was Fred Edmondson. That was his full name. Not Frederick, not Alfred, not Manfred. And no middle name. No nonsense. Just Fred. He's one of the very few of my extended family not to be born in Bradford. Oh yes – this is the fruity part of the plot – he was a foreigner, born in Liversedge, a full seven and a half miles from the centre of Bradford. Virtually . . . Dewsbury.

Dad's dad was Redvers Edmondson (Grandad Ed) – named after the great general of the Zulu and Boer Wars, and heroic winner of the Victoria Cross, Redvers Buller. Grandad was a market trader. And no, he didn't wear a pinstripe suit and a bowler hat and gamble with people's pensions, he worked in actual markets, with his hands, on actual market stalls, selling, you've guessed it, wool.

He was married to Ruth (Grandma Ed), who died in the summer of 1977 when 'I Feel Love' by Donna Summer was top of the charts. Nothing could be less like Grandma Ed than 'I Feel Love'. I never hear her say anything nice about anyone. She is dismissive of everyone and everything. In the 1960s Billy Smart's Circus is on the telly every Easter. We'll sit there watching some trapeze artist shoot through a hoop of fire and land on an elephant's back, all whilst juggling actual lions, and Grandma Ed (a short dumpy woman with thick ankles – she looks like the grandma in the Giles cartoons) will say: 'Oh, I could do that with a bit of practice.'

They're very big in the church, Grandma and Grandad Ed. Which might explain the lack of love and compassion. Except it isn't the church, it's the mission. The Sunbridge Road Mission. I haven't set foot in it since the late sixties but at that time it was an evangelical Methodist enclave that, if it were in another country, might be called fundamentalist.

The Bible is everything. It's God's word or nothing. Except the rude bits, obviously. Not the bit in Genesis when Lot's daughters get him drunk and have sex with him; or the bit in Deuteronomy about not being allowed to go to church if you've damaged your testicles; or the bit in Judges when a woman gets gang raped, dies, and is cut into twelve pieces which are sent to the twelve tribes of Israel. Mention them and you're in trouble. And it's surprisingly easy to get into trouble when this stern Methodist God is watching you.

One Sunday, Grandad, who's one of the 'elders', gets me and my cousin Kevin out in the corridor for some misdemeanour – perhaps we've been smiling – and bangs our heads together so hard that half of Kevin's front tooth breaks off and lodges itself in my forehead. I can still feel the dent. Kevin has a lifetime of dental problems. Praise the Lord.

It's a tough religion to go with the tough life of working in a tough industry in a tough city in tough times. And it's all in decline!

Even Dad's faith is in decline. When I get to the age of seven Dad stops going to the Mission.

'Hurrah,' I think, 'that's surely the end of it for me, as well? No more sitting in that fusty room with the other bored kids taking it in turn to read the Bible aloud.'

But no. Every Sunday my sister and I are now picked up by Grandma and Grandad Ed and are dragged along – *on our own* – to have all the joy sucked out of us. Our parents and our two younger brothers are allowed to stay at home and hang on to their joy. Despite asking for an explanation for this over the years none has ever been forthcoming.

It must have been a moment of high rebellion on Dad's part, and I'm rather proud of him – though it seems odd he then couldn't accept the rebellious streak in me further on down the line. His mum was the sternest woman I ever knew, and standing up to her must have taken some bottle. Although there was obviously some form of negotiation which must have gone along the lines of:

> *Grandma Ed*: There is only one true path to salvation.
>
> *Fred*: I can no longer see the path, Mother.
>
> *Grandma Ed*: Then you are lost to me but I will take your first- and second-born children, that they may become truly miserable, like me.

Grandma Ed must be aware that there's a world beyond the Mission because she's a cousin of Thora Hird, the famous actress – one of Alan Bennett's muses.

Well that's where you got the acting bug from then – it's in the blood!

But no, we never see Thora or any of that side of the family. Partly because they're from Lancashire, anathema to Yorkshire folk, but mostly because of Thora's decision to become an actress. The Bible bashers on our side of the Pennines think it's tantamount to becoming a prostitute. There's a rift. They don't speak. Neither do they turn the other cheek. Or love their neighbour as they love themselves.

'Ooooh, I feel love, I feel love, I feel love, I feel love, I feeeeeel love.'

Although Thora very definitely wins the argument in my view. First by appearing in the TV show *Hallelujah!*, a sitcom about the Salvation Army, set in the fictional town of Brigthorpe which looks suspiciously like Bradford, and which incidentally features the fantastic Patsy Rowlands, who goes on to play Mrs Potato, Spudgun's mum in *Bottom*.

And second by going on to present *Songs of Praise* and beating them at their own game.

I eventually meet Thora at some awards do in the nineties, mention our family connection, and she gives me the oddest look before simply saying, 'Oh.'

But back to the wool industry before it dies out completely.

How does this relate to your name? You were right about tangents.

It's coming, I promise you.

Uncle Douglas also works on the markets, driving out before the crack of dawn to set up his stall in South Elmsall, Scunthorpe or Doncaster. He's also – well guessed again – selling wool. I sometimes go with him and help set up the stall, but my main job is to wander around the market and keep a steady eye on how much his rivals are selling for, so that he can adjust his prices accordingly. There's a bloke on a neighbouring stall selling crockery, he's brilliant at the patter and can display an entire dinner service along one outstretched arm. I want to push him over at the moment of greatest peril but never summon up the nerve.

And Uncle Colin, well he's a step up – he works for a wool-importing business. He goes around the world, looking at sheep. When he comes back he has a slide show and we all go round to his house and look at the sheep he's looked at. Please don't judge us too harshly – remember, we'd only recently gone from two to three channels on the telly.

But of course there isn't room for everyone in the wool business, especially as it's in steep decline. So rather like those aristocratic families where the eldest inherits, the next becomes a priest, the third a soldier and so on, my family diversifies. Dad becomes a teacher, my uncle Tom becomes a missionary in the Cameroons (I'm not making this up), and my uncle David becomes an air traffic controller at Yeadon airport. Now called Leeds-Bradford airport. Because it's neither in Leeds nor Bradford. It's in Yeadon.

But they all do time on the wool stalls at some point in their lives.

So the bulk of my family history is tied to wool and wool production in a grimy, industrial, northern town; they don't mind getting their hands dirty, they get stuck in, and they have no-nonsense names to match – Fred, Douglas, George, Colin – unless they happen to be named after a Victoria Cross winner, like Redvers. And amidst all that northernness, grit, and war heroics, my parents decide to give me a girl's name: Adrian.

I told you we'd get there!

A boy named Sue

Why do you call it a girl's name?

Because in the 1960s everyone in the playground tells me it's a girl's name: 'It's a girl's name, it's a girl's name, you must be a girl, you've got a girl's name!'

And people wonder why my most famous characters are so psychotic and violent . . . Well, there's a start. It's compounded by the fact that up until the age of twelve I go to a different school almost every year and have to explain my stupid name all over again.

A different school every year?

Yes.

Do you keep getting expelled?

No.

Dad's 'diversification' sees him become a geography teacher. It's understandable – he has a real passion for geography and for maps in particular. He spends a lot of time looking at his atlas and wondering what it might be like in all those far-flung places.

I've inherited this love of maps. I collect the educational maps that used to hang on the walls of classrooms in the fifties and sixties with titles like 'The Rise and Fall of the Ottoman Empire', 'The Unification of Italy', 'Europe After the Peace of Utrecht'. Apart from being colourful and decorative I find them intriguing. I know where Pomerania, Swabia and Wallachia once were, and, interestingly in terms of modern-day international argy-bargy, I can see that the borders within Europe have never been fixed for long – they move about like the last few strands of spaghetti on an oily plate.

Dad's love of maps transforms into a kind of permanent wanderlust when he discovers there are opportunities to teach in foreign places. He's first offered a post in Egypt but turns it down because the Suez Crisis is still fresh in his mind and he deems it 'too dangerous'. So in 1958, when I'm a mere toddler, we move to Cyprus, living variously in Nicosia, Famagusta and an army camp just outside Limassol. He's teaching the kids of British Army personnel stationed out there.

…ch in trouble spot

NEWSPAPER reports of continued unrest in Cyprus do not worry Mr. Fred Edmondson, a Bradford teacher, and his family. This week they leave their home at Plumpton Gardens, Wrose, and on Sunday fly to Nicosia, where, for three years, Mr. Edmondson will teach the junior children of English army personnel. His last post was at Whetley Lane Secondary School and he has also taught at All Saints' Secondary School, Little Horton Lane, Bradford. Mr. and Mrs. Edmondson are looking forward to their new life, although they will be sorry to leave Bradford. "It's something completely new," said Mr. Edmondson yesterday. The couple are pictured with their two children, Hilary (four) and baby Adrian.

The reason they're stationed out there is because Cyprus is going through the usual violent transition from former British colony to independent state. You'd have thought Dad would have noticed this? He's issued with a handgun – a teacher with a handgun – that he keeps under the driver's seat of the car in case we're attacked by EOKA paramilitaries. We stay six years but a few months after the 'Bloody Christmas' uprising in 1963 we're advised to leave.

Should have gone to Egypt . . .

Evacuated from Cyprus

MRS. DOROTHY EDMONDSON and her children Hilary (10), Adrian (7) and Matthew (1), who have been evacuated from Cyprus. They are now staying with relatives in Stayhrite Avenue, Cottingley. Mr. Edmondson is still in Cyprus teaching RAF children at Limassol.

We return to Bradford but he gets itchy feet again and a year or so later, when I'm aged about seven, we move to Bahrain, where he teaches RAF and navy kids.

By a stroke of luck we get there just in time for the 'March Intifada' of 1965, a general uprising against the British presence in Bahrain. The bus that takes us to school looks like one of those American school buses but the bodywork is made of wood, and is designed to have no glass in the windows – an early form of air-conditioning. It's basically a charabanc with a roof. These glass-free openings also provide the perfect opportunity for disgruntled Bahrainis to leap up and try to hit the British schoolchildren within. After two years of intimidation we leave.

Should have gone to Egypt . . .

I mean, all right, they do have the third Arab-Israeli War during this period, but it only lasts six days.

We return to Bradford once more but in 1969, when I'm twelve, we move to Uganda, where he's part of some kind of British aid package teaching local children.

A couple of years into our stay Idi Amin stages a coup and

starts killing everyone who doesn't agree with him. My family hang on until 1973 but things get so bad that Dad eventually sends everyone home by plane and dashes over the border into Kenya with as many of our belongings as he can cram into the car.

Should have gone to Egypt . . . we'd have got out just before the fourth Arab-Israeli War.

The world is a violent place, isn't it? I've always had the impression that the trouble was following Dad around, like he was a magnet for conflict, but I think we'd have encountered it wherever we went.

But each of these moves means a new school for me – although in Bradford I end up going to the same school twice, albeit with a gap of two years – and each time I have to defend my stupid bloody name.

Turning up at Swain House Junior School in Bradford, a much bigger boy called Gary starts punching me to prove that I'm 'a girl'. The fury of indignation is so strong within me that moments later I find myself on top of big Gary pushing his head into the gravel and I have to be dragged off by a teacher. Victory!

At the next school the same thing happens – a much bigger boy says I must be a girl because I've got a girl's name. Emboldened by my recent success I offer to fight him after school, out of sight of the teachers. A large crowd gathers on 'the rec' – our name for the patch of mud and grass which is deemed a 'recreation ground' by the Bradford City Council. The recreation for the crowd in this instance is to watch me get beaten to a pulp.

Increasingly fed up with fighting my way through the 'you've got a girl's name' routine I eventually rebel and ask the extended family to call me Charlie instead, Charles being my second name. Adrian Charles Edmondson. Named after Prince Charles, of course.

My sister is born a month after Edmund Hillary conquers Everest and is named Hilary Edmondson. What are my parents playing at?

Needless to say, my attempts to be called Charlie meet with indifference from everyone. Except for Uncle Douglas – who gamely keeps the idea alive while I help him shift wool from the space above his garage into the van, but gives up fairly quickly once we've finished loading.

Like the character in Johnny Cash's song 'A Boy Named Sue' I sometimes wonder if they give me the name just so I '*get tough or die*'.

Things aren't helped by developments in the world of wrestling, which in the sixties is a staple of Saturday afternoon telly. When we're living in England I'll be sent off to the local sweet shop to fetch half a pound of chocolate chewing nuts and we'll sit round as a family watching Mick McManus grapple with some other bloke in a swimming costume whilst some old ladies in the front row try to clobber him with their handbags. Pretty straightforward stuff and we think it's real!

But things take a turn for the worse when a new wrestler arrives on the scene. He's a flamboyant, androgynous character, 'effeminate', as we say in the sixties, who dresses in satin and sequins. He wears glittery make-up, has dyed blond hair, and his signature move when pinned to the floor is to kiss his opponent until they let him go. He develops the role because, in his own words:

'I was getting far more reaction than I'd ever got, just playing this poof.'

His name, of course, is Adrian. Adrian Street. The self-styled Sadist in Sequins or Merchant of Menace.

I'm so pleased on reaching secondary school to find that most people are called by their surnames alone, so I become

Adrian Street and his dad

Edmondson, or Edmonster, or Eddiemonster, which shortens to Eddie, and rather alarmingly to Teddy Edward for a brief period, but by the sixth form this in turn transmutes to Ted. Ted! Result! Ah – blissful two years . . .

Then comes university and things change again. Though at university *everyone* is trying out a new version of themselves. People are much more friendly, more generous, and they're not looking to score points off your girl's name. And it's a *drama* course – luvvies, darlings – so perhaps Adrian fits in a little better; isn't it just a little bit artistic? After all, there are the poets Adrian Henri and Adrian Mitchell. Yes, maybe at last I'm coming into my own name. Maybe this is nominative determinism?

But the film *Rocky* sends everything spinning back to the beginning again. I don't know if you remember the second-highest-grossing film of 1977, in which a small-time boxer played by Sylvester Stallone gets a chance to fight the heavyweight champion of the world simply in order to prove himself to his girlfriend. But if you do you might remember him at the end of the fight – badly bruised and bleeding, having been severely beaten up and having had his swollen eyelids lanced with a razor in order to see – yelling at the top of his voice: 'Adrian! Adrian!'

Because, of course, dear reader, that is his girlfriend's name. And that brutal, primeval, guttural scream – 'Adrian!' – becomes the accepted way to pronounce my name.

Life carries on, there are bigger problems in the world, and a slowly growing career in a comedy double act (four gigs in the first year out of uni!) brings us to London, where the pavements are paved with . . . well, thanks to the poor quality of pet food at the time, they're mostly paved with white dog poo.

We manage to elbow our way onto a late-night TV chat show *Friday Night Saturday Morning* as 'the entertainment', which offers an elusive but all-important Equity contract, which in turn will help secure entry into Equity, the actors' union, which at the time is a closed shop. You can't work as an actor if you aren't in Equity, and you can't get into Equity if you aren't in work as an actor. Catch 22.

But variety contracts are a loophole, and we are at this point, for want of a better description, a variety act. Here's the chance to join the union – and also here's a chance to change my name for good.

Your Equity name does not have to be your legal name – I can call myself whatever I like and that will be my official professional name for the rest of my life. Rik and I drink late into the night discussing our names. He's already changed his as a teenager from Richard to Rik, spelled R I K – no square 'c' in the middle for this dude – and he's very happy to be called Rik Mayall. John Mayall, the blues guitarist, giving his surname a bit of street cred – and Rik sometimes does a small circle instead of a dot over the 'i' in Rik to be just that little bit . . . cooler.

We talk about my troublesome name. The whole thing is a mess: Adrian Edmondson. It never comes out of anyone's mouth sounding right, even my own. There's a sort of trip in the middle where the 'n' on the end of Adrian runs into the 'Ed' on the front of Edmondson. Adria Nedmondson is how it comes out quite frequently. And what about that second 'd' in Edmondson? Is that pronounced? A-dri-an Ed-mond-son? This is how hotel receptionists in Italy and Spain say it. Six syllables and none of them go together.

We come up with the notion that Edmondson is a bit like Ed Monsoon, and with a little tweak it suddenly becomes Eddie Monsoon. **Eddie Monsoon!** What a name! What a perfect name! I love it!

The next day I go into the TV studio and I tell the production assistant that I want my contract to be in the name of Eddie Monsoon, but she tells me it has already been sent off to Equity . . . and that's it, I'm officially Adrian Edmondson, for ever.

So here I am. Adrian Edmondson. Although some people find the whole thing so daunting, such a mishmash of troublesome sounds, that they use only the first syllable, and call me Ade.

Despite the Equity ruling someone mistakenly writes my name down as Ade Edmondson in the credits to *The Young Ones*. How can this be? What was all the palaver about? Surely this is impossible? But it turns out it is possible. It's corrected by the second series but the damage is already done.

And of course some people don't know how to pronounce it – it's written A D E – is that Ada? Or Adey? West African minicab drivers are always confused when I get in the back of the car – 'Your name is Ade?' – expecting it to be pronounced in the same way as King Sunny Ade: A-day.

I use Eddie Monsoon as the name for a character in an episode of *The Comic Strip Presents*, 'Eddie Monsoon: A Life?'. And then my wife uses it as the name of her character in *Absolutely Fabulous*. So it lives on. Some might say it's had a better career without me – people can be very cruel.

Is that a Viking surname?

Between the ages of twelve and eighteen I find myself in a boarding school in the small market town of Pocklington in East Yorkshire. I'm at the epicentre of the Viking incursion into Britain – fourteen miles from York, or 'Jorvik' as we call it, the Viking capital. So many place names of nearby villages are Viking in origin – Kexby, Foggathorpe, Bubwith, Cawkeld, Wilberfoss, Wetwang. I'm not making these up.

I study medieval history for A-level at school. For the first year it concentrates almost exclusively on Vikings, and the Danelaw. It's full of great names like Ivar the Boneless and Erik Bloodaxe, not to mention that great typing error who becomes King of a United England, King Cnut, and his somehow even funnier son, King Harthacnut – try it in a Cockney accent, turning the *th* into an *f*. Half-a-cnut.

Me and my classmates love the Vikings – not only do they seem very good at fighting but they have great-looking boats, cool weapons and nifty hats with horns. Modern archaeologists are keen to debunk this idea, but it's such an iconic one that I'm prepared to hang on until some future archaeologist debunks the debunkers.

They also have *berserkers*, an elite fighting corps who are off their tits on henbane – a hallucinogenic drug – and large quantities of alcohol. This makes them fight with a furious and senseless abandon which is still evident in many Scandinavian heavy metal bands to this day.

The etymology of the word 'berserk' is disputed. Some think it means bear-shirted (wearing a shirt made of bearskin), others think it means bare-shirted (naked) like one of those big-bellied Leeds United supporters in the Lurpak stand. In Norse sagas they're often described as so wild-eyed and frenzied that they bite into their shields. The rook from the Lewis chess set depicts such a fellow.

My school is eight miles from the site of the battle of Stamford Bridge, where the last English king, Harold Godwinson, finally saw off the last of the Vikings, Harold Hardrada. One Sunday afternoon I cycle there to look at the battlefield. I'm singing 'See My Baby Jive' by Wizzard as I pootle along the gloriously named Hatkill Lane between Fangfoss and Full Sutton. I'm not wearing a hat, so I figure I'm safe.

Once I get to Stamford Bridge I find the original bridge disappeared centuries ago and there are no archaeological remains of the battlefield at all. There's an uninspiring monument in the village, but no buildings older than 1591, so you have to conjure up everything yourself. There weren't even any embroiderers from Bayeux, like there were at Hastings three weeks later, to quickly stitch down the salient details. The current thinking is that the bridge crossed from the present-day caravan park on the west bank to the Co-op on the east bank.

But whose side are you on? Are you a Viking or an Anglo-Saxon?

That's what I'd like to know.

Edmondson is a patronymic name – the father's name with 'son' added. In Scotland the patronymic is 'Mac' or 'Mc'; in Ireland it's 'O'. . .'; in Wales it's 'Ap' usually contracted to a simple 'P' in names like Price and Prichard. But the 'son' patronymic, whilst in use in England, is more particularly associated with Scandinavia.

As a young schoolboy historian this gives me the idea that I *am* in fact Scandinavian.

I join the school Local History Society and get a closer understanding of the waves of Viking invasion and settlement – their origins, their destinations, their movements – and conclude that I am, more precisely, Norwegian. It's a harmless fantasy, but it takes hold of me. Forever after when anyone asks me about my family history I say, 'I'm originally Norwegian – I came over with the Vikings.'

By the time I have children old enough to be interested in genealogy I tell them the same story: 'Yes, we're definitely Vikings. Norwegians to be precise.'

It's not a lie as such. It's based on circumstantial evidence. No one would like to be convicted for murder on circumstantial evidence, but in terms of carving out an identity for yourself it's fairly harmless.

As an adult I visit Sweden and Iceland and discover something truly brilliant. Although I had white-blond hair as a child, what's left of it is now a fairly dull fairish/brown, and I find that only a few Scandinavians look like Ulrika Jonsson: there's a more common, much uglier underclass, that look like they're descended from trolls – these people look like me!

My birthday is in January, and one year my lovely wife Jennifer organizes a trip to my homeland Norway as a birthday surprise. It's an odd time to go on holiday to Scandinavia unless you're going skiing. We fail to see the Northern Lights in Tromsø because it's just *snowing all the time*. We shiver around Bergen looking at the port and the fish market, which is mostly closed because it's *the middle of winter*. We get the train from Bergen to Oslo across the mountains, where the visibility is so bad it's like a scene from that Kirk Douglas war film *Heroes of Telemark*.

The person sitting opposite us, a Norwegian, studies us for a while and eventually asks what we're doing on the Bergen–Oslo train in the off season. I tell him I have this bee in my bonnet that I'm of Norwegian heritage.

'What's your name?' he asks.

'Edmondson,' I reply.

'No!' he shouts, rather too angrily for comfort. 'You're not Norwegian! You're *Danish*!'

It's only later that I find that the Norwegians have always felt bullied by the other Scandinavian countries, and have a particular antipathy towards the Danes. So perhaps he was angry with them rather than with me in particular. Still, if he was angry with me it meant *he* thought I was Danish? *He* thought I was Scandinavian, right? I mean, talk about hearing it from the horse's mouth.

Eventually, of course, with the growth of the internet and data banks full of old birth, death and marriage certificates, the genealogy craze kicks off big time. In the late nineties my niece Clare does her family history as a project at school. She gets back as far as the generation before my grandparents before she leaves school to go to university (and get a social life).

But my sister takes up the study and delves back further. It becomes a minor obsession. Then a fairly major one. She visits gravestones in Yorkshire, Suffolk and Devon and discovers that somewhere along the line some bloke changed the spelling of our surname from Edmonson to Edmondson for no apparent reason.

FOR NO APPARENT REASON!

Perhaps he just spelled it wrongly.

An Edmondson spelling his own name wrongly!

Dad is already slipping into dementia by the time Hilary uncovers this, which is a blessing, because one thing that really got his goat was people missing out the second 'd' when writing our name. He successfully passed this splenetic fury on to us and it used to bother me a lot until I learned that there are only six existing documents on which William Shakespeare wrote his name, and that he spelled it differently on each one. There are eighty different spellings of his name from contemporaneous sources, ranging from Shappere to Shaxberd. I told Dad. He wasn't impressed.

I don't care. Edmondson, Edmonson, Edmundson, Edmunson, Evanson, Evinson, Amundson, Saunders . . . I've had them all.

Perhaps Dad was feeling residual anger at the comparative feebleness of his name, Fred Edmondson, and was keen to protect every letter he had.

He'd had apoplectic fits when as a teacher at Tong Comprehensive in Bradford pupils would elide the two words Mister and Edmondson, and he would be addressed as Mr Redmonson.

'Blood and stomach pills!', as Dad would say.

But are the Redmonsons Danish or Norwegian?

By the 2010s DNA tests become ever cheaper, more sophisticated and supposedly more accurate. Eventually I spit into a small plastic tube, send it off, and sit back to await the results. I'm 90% certain that my results will show strong Scandinavian heritage. Most probably Danish with a hint of Norwegian.

The results come back. They are very disappointing. I am overwhelmingly British. I am 72% 'British'. 'Europe West', an alarmingly nebulous group to be in, comes in second with 16%.

Then trailing in third place, in the bronze medal position, is 'Scandinavia' at a miserable 10%. Further analysis says I'm most probably from Yorkshire and the Pennines, with a possible connection to Devon and the South West.

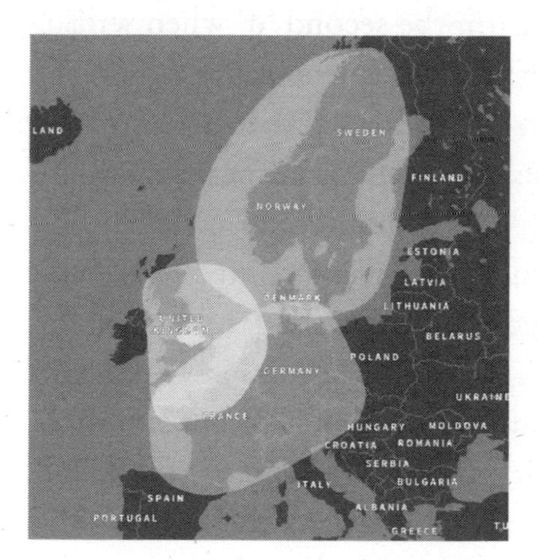

Europe	100%
Great Britain	72%
Europe West	16%
Scandinavia	10%
Low Confidence Region	
Ireland	1%
Iberian Peninsula	<1%
Other Regions Tested	
Europe East	0%
European Jewish	0%
Italy/Greece	0%
Finland/Northwest Rus...	0%

It takes a while for me to process the disappointment and cancel my application for a Danish passport. But I eventually turn it into a vague positive – at least the idea I have of myself made the podium, I am partly Scandinavian, I have *some* Viking blood in me.

Through her grandparents' heritage Jennifer is confident she's three-quarters English, and a quarter Scottish. But she turns out to be only 9% British (most of which is Scottish). She is 38% Irish, and – get this – **37% Scandinavian!** She also has other odds and sods in her report, including 5% Italy/Greece, 2% Finland/Northwest Russia, and 2% South Asian.

But although she is such a mongrel she is still almost four times more Scandinavian than me.

At least our children are pleased, the idea that they have some Viking blood in them – the idea I've been selling them all these years as their birthright – is corroborated on their mother's side.

And at least I'm married to a Viking. I'm half hoping she'll drag me off by what's left of my hair and pillage me.

Some years later I uncover more research about the name Edmondson and its geographical spread. Someone has researched all the Edmondsons that ever existed in Great Britain. Turns out 98 per cent of them were from the West Riding of Yorkshire. Not only am I not an adventurous Viking setting off bravely in my longboat for lands unknown – Britain, Normandy, Sicily, Greenland, the Black Sea, Constantinople – I've barely made it out of my own front door.

For balance, it's worth pointing out that my brother Alastair sends off a sample to a different DNA testing company and they tell him he has a lot of Native American in him. So, either my mum was playing the field in a way that we never knew, and that I frankly find quite impressive, or we have to take these test results with a pinch of salt.

Or with a pinch of salted liquorice as they might say in Finland. Though this is perhaps a clue to the amount of Scandinavian blood in me, because salmiakki is one of the very few things on this earth that I find truly disgusting and impossible to eat. The same can be said for the Icelandic delicacy hákarl – a fermented shark dish. A common misconception is that they dig a hole in gravelly sand, put the shark in, piss on it, fill in the hole and come back a year later when it has rotted. In fact, the Greenland shark doesn't have a urinary system so releases urea through its own flesh. It smells of urine even if you don't piss on it. Either way, it's not my cup of tea.

And yet – isn't there something of the berserker in my character Vyvyan Basterd from *The Young Ones*? And Sir Adrian Dangerous from the Dangerous Brothers? And Eddie Hitler from *Bottom*?

The dictionary defines 'berserk' as: out of control with anger or excitement; wild or frenzied. A 'berserker' is: an ancient

Norse warrior frenzied in battle and held to be invulnerable; one whose actions are recklessly defiant.

This seems to describe a lot of what I am and a lot of what I go on to do. For a child brought up in the Mission where does this seemingly inherent anger, frenzy and defiance come from?

Part 2

The making of a berserker

A cataclysm

My parents are of the 'smacking' generation. The further the notion of casual violence against children recedes into the past, the more ridiculous it seems – but throughout my early years it's a constant threat.

It's frequent, and usually unplanned. It comes out of the blue. I'm seldom even aware of the crime, but suddenly feel them holding one of my hands high in their left hand, as a rudimentary tether, whilst their right hand swipes indiscriminately at my nether regions.

It's such an imprecise manoeuvre – perhaps its saving grace – and allows me to squirm about like a badly behaved puppet. This presents a moving target which makes it difficult for them to deliver the killer blow. They want to hear the 'smack'. Only the sharp smacking sound will convince them that justice has been done. They want to say, 'Let that be a lesson to you', and they can't say it until they hear the smack.

So all my writhing about, all my jumps and side steps, my running round in circles, merely prolong the agony.

It's hard to know whether standing still and just letting them hit me would make the sorry business end sooner. Part of me fears that if they could get the smacking sound more easily they might just do more of it. So perhaps wriggling about is the best policy.

Dad's decision to swan off to Uganda comes in January 1969, when I'm turning twelve. He leaves suddenly. On his own. I sometimes wonder if Dad wasn't running away from something, rather than to something: From his mother? From Bradford? From the Mission? From us?

Because the rest of us – Mum, Hilary, Matthew, Alastair and me – are left in Bradford. We're to join him in six months. This is supposedly because Hilary is in her final O-level year and it's considered important not to interrupt her studies.

No one suggests it might be important not to interrupt family life by buggering off to Uganda. No one thinks it might be important not to leave Mum looking after four kids on her own. No one mentions that he's off to live the life of Riley while the rest of us are off to live in a grim council flat in Thorpe Edge because Dad has already sold the family home in Highfield Road.

While Dad is off on an adventure to equatorial Africa, joining the expat club in Jinja, learning golf, playing squash, and swimming in the outdoor pool, we're travelling up to the seventh floor in a lift that reeks of Greenland shark, to a landing with an open rubbish chute that stinks of the same shark twelve months later. Whenever the lift breaks down – most days – with me and my younger brothers in it, they both scream in panic and fury like young berserkers in the making.

I don't know exactly what I say to upset my mum so much on the day Dad leaves for Uganda: I hope it's something along the lines of 'what a wanker', or 'I shall endeavour for the rest of my life never to treat my own family like this' – and I have to acknowledge that she's under great pressure – but I make some kind of twelve-year-old's version of the above comment and . . . she tries to throttle me.

To be fair, there's not much 'trying' about it to begin with, she gives it a bloody good go. In fact I'd say her chances of success are high and that I might be on my way to Valhalla. She's got both her hands clamped around my throat and is shaking me so hard that my brain feels like it's detaching itself from the inside of my skull. This is different to smacking. She's *very* angry. Perhaps she's transferring some of her anger towards Dad onto me. If so, she's furious with him too, and it occurs to me that she wants to kill him.

Puny twelve-year-old me is no match for this raging grown woman – she seems to have a touch of the berserker about her as well – besides which I quickly begin to feel quite woozy. Is she shouting? Is everyone shouting? I can't tell. Maybe. Her hands have formed a ligature round my neck and my ears are pumped so full of blood I can only hear my own heart thumping. Then I become aware that her grasp is loosening. Maybe she's too tired to finish me off. Maybe my siblings have cried out in my defence. Maybe not. But it ends with me being told to go to my room and I trudge off feeling faint though strangely exhilarated. Of course, it's not 'my' room, it's a room I share with my brothers, and they will follow on and do some casual taunting.

'*Ob La Di Ob La Da, life goes on,*' the group Marmalade are singing in the number one spot at the time, and so it does, though second in the hit parade is 'Albatross' by Fleetwood Mac, which might be a more fitting metaphor for the Coleridge fans amongst you.

Six months later we all make it to Uganda, but almost immediately I'm sent back to start at the boarding school in Pocklington in East Yorkshire.

Mum said the plan was for all four of us kids to go to school in Uganda, but once we get there Dad changes his mind. My two young brothers are sent to the local international primary (mostly white), and my sister is enrolled in a correspondence course to do her A-levels, but I get sent to boarding school in England. The first person in the history of my extended family to do this. Years later I summon up the courage to ask why and they mumble something about the standard of teaching not being good enough in Uganda. But surely that's my *Dad* they're talking about? What? He wasn't good enough? All those colleagues that become his best friends, the Steggels, the Pidcocks – they weren't good enough either?

It's obvious in hindsight – he didn't want me going to a school where I would be the only white boy. It was fine for him to teach black pupils, but not fine for me to be their equal.

My only defence is that I was twelve and had no power, and no learned ability to form an argument. Especially with my dad. I grew up in a house where politics were simply never talked about. Ever. There was never any discussion about left or right, about race, about social justice, about how the economy works, about rich and poor. *The News* was listened to in silence and then not commented on. I once asked Dad which side he voted for in one of the 1974 general elections and he said it was a secret ballot and that I had no right to know. Which I think meant he voted Conservative. I think when people won't tell you it always means they've voted Conservative.

Of course the other reason they sent me away might be that they just wanted to get rid of me? Maybe I was 'trouble'?

Either way, it turns out to be the most cataclysmic moment of my life.

My mum still makes the defence that she *asked me* if I wanted to go, and that I said 'yes' – so it was my decision, not theirs. If that's true it was the only time my opinion was ever sought, or indeed acted upon. Aged eighteen I once told my dad I was 'off to the pub', and he said, 'No you're not – not while you're living under my roof.'

I can imagine that if I was asked I did say 'yes'. Back in the grotty flat in Thorpe Edge I'd borrowed the entire series of Jennings books, by Anthony Buckeridge, from Eccleshill Library. They follow the adventures of JCT Jennings (only ever known by his surname) at Linbury Court School. They have the same basic set-up as the Harry Potter stories which follow: boarding school, kids allowed their own agency, and lots of japes and scrapes. But Jennings is more parochial, with less wizardry and more jokes. There's a lot of speaking French incorrectly and setting fire to things – I remember laughing *a lot*.

So in September 1969, as Creedence Clearwater Revival are top of the charts, rather prophetically, with 'Bad Moon Rising', I'm off-loaded at the school by my Aunty Margaret and Uncle Colin, and I cry solidly for two weeks. It isn't nearly as much fun as Anthony Buckeridge suggested.

The initial scene as they drop me off is a fair enough portent; it doesn't look at all like the joyful cover of *Jennings Follows a Clue*. A small seven-year-old boy is screaming 'No' at the very top of his voice, and red-hot tears are burning welts down his face, which is a picture of absolute blind terror. Whenever I see a horror film and watch an actor screaming in fright I think back to that kid's face and remark to myself that actors never get anywhere near it. He's clinging onto his mother's wrist while she's trying to pull away from him. A teacher has hold of the boy's other hand and is himself hanging onto a cast iron radiator.

A couple of years later I play one of the lawyers in a school production of Bertolt Brecht's *The Caucasian Chalk Circle*. Two women are in dispute over a young boy: one is his actual mother, who abandoned him as a baby but who now needs him in order to claim some land, the other is the woman who took him in and has cared for him and loved him. The judge draws a circle on the ground, puts the boy in it, and tells the two women to take a hand each, saying that whoever can pull him out of the circle will get the boy. The one who loves the boy fears they will tear him in half and lets go of his hand.

The parallel with the mother, the boy, and the teacher hanging onto the radiator is striking – except in this version the real mother doesn't want the child, and the school wins. The school always wins. Principally because they've got sticks, and they're not afraid to use them.

My first dormitory is directly opposite Matron Brown's little dispensary. She's very kind to me in those first two weeks while I bawl my eyes out. She comes into the dorm and strokes my head and shushes me to sleep. It's an act of such absolute kindness, and I like to imagine she does it only for me, but she probably does her rounds of the dorms every night at the beginning of each term, soothing all the troubled boys to sleep. And of course, like most boys who are sent to these institutions in the sixties and seventies, I learn to be emotionally cold and maladjusted-without-showing-it-too-much, and finally stop crying.

And that's the cataclysm really. The definition of cataclysm: a sudden disaster or a violent event that causes change.

It is sudden, and violent, and it does cause change. By the end of my time at Pocklington I have a different accent to the rest of my family and feel I no longer belong. They're more or less strangers to me. I don't really know much about them. I go home twice a year – at Christmas and for the summer holidays – and they come back to England once I reach the sixth form, but we share too little time to really connect. And because I'm learning to repress my emotions so effectively, I don't bloody care!

The only emotions I don't repress are anger and a desire for excitement that borders on frenzy. I am a novice berserker, and the masters try to beat this out of me. Idiots – little do they know they're actually beating it *in* to me.

'The rules!' shouted Ralph, 'you're breaking the rules'

As a young 'specky-four-eyes' I identify with Piggy in *Lord of the Flies* when his glasses get broken, but there's a lot of Jack in me too. I've always thought rules weren't for me. It occurred to me fairly early on in life that rules were generally arbitrary, were designed to suit the people that made them, and were mostly prejudicial to the people they were made against, i.e. me.

There was an experiment in the Netherlands recently: they removed the traffic lights and all the road markings from a few busy junctions to see what would happen, and the answer was 'less than usually happened' – people used common sense, caution and even politeness, and there were fewer accidents than usual.

When I get to Pocklington we're given a little booklet at the beginning of every term. It's blue, and is simply called the Blue Book – it holds details of who's in which form, sports fixtures, exam schedules, even the dates the barbers are coming to make us look more like convicts – and at the back there's a list of rules, two pages of them, and it becomes a game really, to see how quickly we can break them. 'Boys may not use or possess chalk or a board duster', tick. 'Boys will be clean and tidy and conform to the dress regulations laid down by the headmaster', tick. 'The following are forbidden: smoking, gambling, chewing gum, eating in the street', tick, tick, tick, tick. If the rules weren't there, we might be better behaved.

43

SCHOOL RULES

These Rules are laid down:
For the good of the individual,
For the good of the School as a whole,
To maintain good relations between the School and the town.

Bounds

House Regulations (Boarding and Day) lay down the times at which boys may leave the School premises and the circumstances in which they may enter places of refreshment. There must be no departure from these rules without a Master's permission.

Within the School, the following places are out of bounds (unless special permission is given by a Master):

Music Rooms; The Assembly Hall Block.

Classrooms

a) Classrooms may be entered only by boys whose form rooms they are, or for the purpose of a lesson or supervised study.

b) Boys may not use or possess chalk or board duster, and may in no circumstances open another boy's desk.

c) During Break boys will be outside the buildings unless the Duty Master orders otherwise.

d) At the beginning of each period boys must be sitting quietly at their desks with books open.

e) Books are to be collected from form rooms only before school and at the end of break.

44

Dress

Boys will be clean and tidy and conform to the dress regulations as laid down by the Headmaster from time to time.

Cars and Motor Cycles

These may be used only with special permission of the Headmaster, and in accordance with the special rules laid down for them.

Bicycles

May not be ridden in the School grounds except on the open part of the Dolman drive.

General

The following are forbidden:

Smoking and the possession of smoking materials.
Betting and gambling.
Chewing gum
Eating in the street.

Boys may not possess medicines, alcohol, explosives or dangerous implements; and electrical apparatus, only with the Headmaster's permission.

No boy may borrow or possess another's property including clothes without permission.

N.B. Any offence against common sense or good manners is a breach of School rules.

Then I discover that all the lessons are full of rules as well.

When I arrive at Pocklington Grammar School for Boys I'm a year behind in practically everything. I've spent a year at Hutton Junior High in Bradford but they haven't taught me anything that the boys at Pocklington have learned. Principally I don't know any grammar. It's a grammar school and I've never been taught any of it, in fact I don't know what it is. Everyone else has had at least a year, some boys who've been in the prep school have been learning grammar for five years.

I'm suddenly thousands of miles away from my parents, and the new people in charge of me – and my new schoolmates – are basically speaking a different language. It's quite alienating, and I begin to feel rather alone.

The Blue Book is not only full of school rules and sports fixtures, in the list of boys in each form there is a handy number printed beside your name. This is your academic ranking based on the previous year. Printing this in a book handed to every pupil makes it much easier for everyone else to see that, after my first year at the school, I'm 27th out of 29. Though in fact one boy doesn't have any ranking at all, because he was in hospital for a long period, so I'm 27th out of 28. Second to bottom. I am officially thick. The indented names indicate day boys – non-boarders – and it's interesting to see that the non-abandoned boys hold all the positions from 1 to 5.

17

THIRD FORM

Mr. Aubrey

X

3	Ainley
1	Allison I M
18	Atkin A J
2	Barrett
19	Bird
16	Brimblecombe R E
13	Clarkson
23	Cowley
17	Dorsey
27	Edmondson
7	Ellison
15	Greenwood P J
11	Harbot
4	Harrison A D
12	Heartshorne
5	Hirst
21	Hollinson
6	Hunston
—	Jones
9	King P J
20	Morgan J C D
24	Munns
14	Pyle
25	Sampson G E
22	Spencer
8	Telfer
26	Whybray
9	Woodhouse
28	Wright A J

29

I don't know how we were taught French at my previous school. I remember a tape machine, and some slides, and repeating things parrot fashion. I'm pretty sure that the bakery is next door to the church and that the grocer's is opposite the butcher's – though I'm aware that this will only come in handy if I go to a town where the geographical layout precisely matches my French.

I've never heard the words *verb*, *noun*, *object* or *subject*, and the words *pluperfect* and *transitive* fill me with fear to this day.

Luckily I've scraped through life without ever having to explain the difference between a *gerund* and a *gerundive*.

It should come as no surprise that grammar schools *love* grammar – and that they use it in *everything*. They use it most particularly in English, French and Latin, but even my history and geography homework is littered with red pen underlinings from the teachers and *GRAMMAR!* written angrily in the margin.

Latin is a complete mystery – I was going to say it's all Greek to me, but that would have been a vast improvement in my skill set. My Latin teacher uses the 'intimidation method'. He thinks I will learn if he shouts loudly at me, but this doesn't work. 'Conjugate!' he will yell, apropos of nothing. I am nonplussed. 'Decline!'

I do eventually decline. I decline to pay much attention. In one lesson he catches me threading a conker and brings me out to the front. He makes me finish threading it and insists I secure it with a good knot. Then he takes the conker and asks me to either decline or conjugate a verb – whichever – and every time I get it wrong he swings the conker on its string in a long arc and brings it down on my head.

It hurts. It hurts a great deal. It only takes a few blows before I start to cry. He thinks this is hilarious . . . but my classmates don't. It's an odd moment. He expects them to be on his side. Bullies do, don't they? But they look at him with distaste. They think he's gone too far. They know how much a conker can hurt. They daren't voice their contempt in case he then picks on *them*, but he soon becomes aware of the lack of support. It unsettles him. He gives me a final clonk, not quite as hard this time, as if it's just a bit of fun, and sends me back to my seat.

'Let that be a lesson to you,' he grins.

I learn nothing except hatred, and a lifelong fear of declining, or conjugating, whichever it is. But here's a thing – why is the first verb I learn 'amare'?

Amo	I love
Amas	You love (singular)
Amat	He/she/it loves
Amamus	We love
Amatis	You love (plural)
Amant	They love

The verb TO LOVE! Oh, the irony. It's still the only Latin verb I know.

Years later when I take my Latin O-level – I cheat. I smuggle in a crib sheet and do a near-perfect translation of part of Julius Caesar's *De Bello Gallico* – his account of the Gallic wars. I'm not stupid, I put in a couple of mistakes so that it doesn't look too suspicious. I'm expected to fail completely but I get a three (one is excellent, seven a pass). When the results are posted, the bully teacher finds me in a corridor and expresses surprise but also delight that his harsh teaching methods have borne such fruit. I hate him even more, but I'm pleased to see that I've successfully pulled the wool over his eyes. '*Veni, vidi, vici, twatface!*' Decline that.

How did you get in to Pocklington Grammar if you didn't know any grammar?

Good question.

Imagine the scene. It's 1968, we're back in England having returned from Bahrain the year before, and I'm sitting the 11-plus. I'm in a classroom. Serried ranks of desks. It's some kind of multiple-choice booklet and I've finished. I look around – no one else has finished. I look at the clock – there's still twenty minutes to go! God, I must be brainy. Much brainier than these other thickos, one of whom is my cousin Kevin. Well, this must finally settle the question as to which of us is the brightest. Look at him, toiling over his answers. You can almost see the beads of sweat springing from his forehead, like an illustration in Tintin.

I'm bored. I flick my pen about. I use it like a drumstick on the desk. The invigilator tells me to stop. I lean back, hands behind my head, making exaggerated sighs of boredom. With about a minute to go the invigilator says 'there's about a minute to go', and that we ought to make sure our names are written clearly on the front. I check the front, there's my name. Duh! Course it's there. I idly flick through the booklet. Look at all those answers – I'm pretty sure they're nearly all correct, and that the ones I've taken a punt on are damn good guesses. Hang on . . . What's this? Two of the pages seem to be stuck together. I prise them apart. What? Two pages of questions I haven't answered? Two pages I haven't even seen? They were stuck together! Two pages out of a total of eight pages. That's a quarter of the entire exam I've missed (good at maths, you see). I panic. I feverishly reach for my pen. I look at the first question . . . and that's when I'm told the exam is over. Kevin gets into Bradford Grammar. I don't. I go to Hutton Junior High. Quite rightly. I mean what kind of arrogant thicko thinks he can answer all the questions twenty minutes quicker than everyone else?

Of course, as you know (do keep up 5C), Dad gets the job in Uganda soon after – if you're having trouble keeping up with my family's movements around the globe let me tell you the feeling's mutual.

When they decide to pack me off to boarding school I sit another exam, an entrance exam, and get in to Pocklington, a very minor public school halfway between York and Hull – or, as the joke went, halfway between York and Hell – a school which seems to take a lot of expat and army 'brats', as we are charmingly called.

It's a direct grant school, which in 1969 means that they give free places to a quarter of their intake as long as they've been at state schools up to that point. And I qualify! This is social mobility in action; a definite move from lower middle class to upper middle class. I've looked it up and 3.1 per cent of secondary pupils go to direct grant schools in the late sixties, which means I'm one of the 3.1 per cent of the socially mobile! Where's my top hat?

But no, nobody has a top hat at school. Nobody has anything much. We're sent to school with one trunk – basically a large suitcase. In this we have our school uniform, our sports kit, and some regulation 'casual wear': a sports jacket, a pair of 'slacks', and a shirt. We then have a satchel or briefcase with pencils, a geometry set and an Osmiroid fountain pen with blue ink and an italic nib. Everything is precisely stipulated, everything is named, and everything has a place. There's a locker for clothing, a boot room for shoes, and a shared study for stationery items.

Everything at school is designed to stop you thinking for yourself. You never have to worry about what to wear because you don't have any choice. Even the colour of our underwear is prescribed. You never have to worry about your *things* because you don't have any *things*. The plan is to mould us all into exactly the same person: a well-educated, upper-middle-class empire builder who isn't worried about being transported 6,000 miles away from his family to live with 600 strangers, none of whom will ever love him.

Of course, it takes some boys longer to become cold-hearted bastards than others.

The school knows this and they've developed their pastoral methods for dealing with it; which are a) never to mention it, and b) to fill in all the time so that there's absolutely no chance to reflect.

Weekdays are taken up with lessons, then supervised home-work, supervised baths, supervised bed and supervised lights out. There's a lot of supervision. And the weekends are no different. On Saturday there's school in the morning, games in the afternoon, and compulsory 'TV' in the evening, and on Sunday there's compulsory church, compulsory 'writing letters home' after lunch, and a compulsory 'nap' in the late afternoon. There's a lot of compulsion. This is why public-school boys do quite well in the armed forces and in prison.

During our 'nap' some of us listen to the chart countdown on small transistor radios hidden under our pillows. My first year there is the year when the chart is truly eclectic. In 1969 the top spot is shared between The Scaffold, Marmalade, Fleetwood Mac, The Move, Amen Corner, Peter Sarstedt, Marvin Gaye, Desmond Dekker, The Beatles (with Billy Preston) – that's some billing – Tommy Roe ('Dizzy'), Thunderclap Newman, The Rolling Stones, Zager and Evans (you think you don't know – 'In the Year 2525'), Creedence Clearwater Revival, Jane Birkin and Serge Gainsbourg getting all steamy and suggestive, Bobbie Gentry, Rolf Harris and . . . oh. Not allowed to mention Rolf.

It's 1969! It's the end of the sixties! But while the rest of the world is flailing around in an orgy of free love, self-expression and hallucinogenic drugs – I'm listening to Radio 1, at very low volume, wearing a sports jacket and casual slacks. I'm trapped in a small prison learning to repress my emotions. Turns out I'm bloody good at it. If the 11-plus had been about repression I would have passed no problem.

Repression is good for trainee berserkers. It builds up like a pressure cooker until you don't know what you're thinking. And as the teachers know – thinking is dangerous.

Don't give them time to think

Like endlessly pointing the cracks in a large patio, the school has to fill in the small gaps which appear in the timetable to stop the boys thinking for themselves. To this end they develop the idea of 'clubs'. In 1969 those of us at the younger end of the school are offered forty minutes of 'clubs' in that tricky gap between the end of school and teatime, and the boys in the first and second forms of senior school, like me, are allowed another forty minutes of 'clubs' in the gap between homework and bath.

This basically means Model Making Club or Glee Club.

Being behind by a year, not only in grammar but also in friendship groups, is a difficult gap to close. I try to do this by joining the Glee Club.

Glee Clubs were originally formed in Britain in the eighteenth century. They concentrated on songs arranged for male voices only. This is why we have one at our *all boys* school – though to be honest there are still a lot of sopranos in the first and second forms.

The concept is taken up in America and transformed in a way only the Americans know how, so that by 2010 there's a famous TV show called *Glee* which runs for 120 episodes. Set in a fictional ordinary high school it's nevertheless full of extraordinarily talented and good-looking singers of both sexes – it's very glossy, with high production values, and their recordings regularly hit the top ten.

Our Glee Club is not like that. Our Glee Club is set in a real secondary school with real boys who smell and are covered in spots. It takes place in a dusty room above the assembly hall; we sit on broken chairs, none of us have any gloss, few have any value, and we will never trouble the top ten. There are about two dozen of us and we murder several songs, the standout being 'Ol' Man River', the song made famous by Paul Robeson in the musical *Show Boat*.

It stands out not because we sing it so brilliantly but because it's such a peculiar thing. Our sheet music is from the original show staged in 1927, and the lyric is written in the dialect of an impoverished black stevedore working on the Mississippi in the late nineteenth century. It's written phonetically, so we sing *Ole Man Ribber* and about being *skeered o' dyin'*. And we sing the N-word. Twice.

People try to excuse these things by saying it was of its time or we didn't know back then, but even in 1969 this is an aberration. There can be no excuse for not being aware of how incongruous it is for a bunch of privileged white kids to be affecting the accent of a black man who was little more than a slave. Even when Frank Sinatra released it in 1945 he dumped the patois, sang *river* not *ribber*, and changed *N*****s all work* to *here we all work*. Even Robeson had been on a journey with the word, changing *N*****s* to *darkies* then to *colored folk* and then finally to *here we all*.

If these people knew it was dubious, demeaning or wrong more than twenty-five years before we sing it, how come our Glee Club leader doesn't know?

It's not the only thing that puts me off Glee Club. The other people turn out to be unlikely friend-material, and I can't read music. The rest of them can. I have to guess at how much higher or lower one note is after the other until I've learned it by heart. I give up.

Luckily there is another club. On Thursday evenings, for the forty minutes after homework, and after much petitioning by the boys, we have Disco Club.

Disco Club! Disco Club is not a real disco. Disco Club is like this: the desks in one of the classrooms are pushed loosely to the side leaving an open space in the middle, the Dansette school record player is produced – maximum volume 0.5 watts – and the boys, there are only boys, let their short hair down, and dance with each other.

And this is the thing that seems strangest of all, thinking back on this first year at boarding school. We don't just dance with everyone else at the same time – you know, a free-for-all, some kind of melee in the middle – we actually dance, one on one, with another boy. Everyone does this.

Twelve is an odd age. We're on the cusp between being children and being teenagers. Puberty is slowly wrapping itself around us like ivy colonizing a tree. We don't know who we are or what's happening to our bodies, and we have absolutely no one to help us. Some of us, myself included, are still somewhat in the dark about how humans reproduce. I've read a page in 'that' book that another boy directed me to in the library, but it seems too fantastical to be true. And rather messy.

I remember very distinctly dancing to 'Sugar Sugar' by The Archies, a song that was top of the charts for eight weeks in a row, with a boy called Martin.

So what is this dance?

My memory of it is vivid. It feels very primitive. It's very intense, and physical – we gyrate a lot. It involves a lot of eye contact. We don't touch – we're doing the kind of dancing we've seen Pan's People do on *Top of the Pops*. But we're doing it *at* each other. You couldn't do this on your own. And it feels like we're breaking the rules.

It's as if we're practising for some time in the future when we might do something similar to what's written in that book in the library. It isn't about sexual orientation, it's about the whole idea of sex. Of being with someone else. It's just electrifying. In our small world where normal emotional responses are being systematically beaten back there's this sudden release which defines itself in movement and real connection with another human being. I'm no longer looking back towards my family, I'm looking forward to a life with other possibilities, and other people, some of them possibly girls, that I haven't met yet.

As we get older we're put in different boarding houses, and I haven't seen or heard of Martin since leaving school in 1975. But I've looked him up (marvellous thing, the internet), and I see he's now a captain of industry. I remember in the last years of school – while I was captain of daydreaming about being a roadie for a rock band – he was pretty much captain of everything else. And I remember that dance with him at the age of twelve, because it's a real moment of change. It's the first proper dance I ever have with anyone. And it signals that my childhood is coming to an end.

The slippery slope

Another thing that can drag you out of the age of innocence and nudge you towards a berserker frame of mind is institutionalized violence.

The violence at Pocklington School is much more organized than the parental smacking routine. Of course there is some rough and tumble between the boys, but the real brutal stuff is inflicted on the boys by the teachers. One or two of them find corporal punishment distasteful and don't participate, but the vast majority a) think beating boys is a perfectly wholesome form of discipline, and b) seem to enjoy it.

I get beaten a lot.

As with my parents, I'm still pretty much in the dark about my actual crimes. It would be churlish to imply that they're spuriously dreamed up by the teachers, but the fact that I can't remember much about them until the later years – when they generally centre around fags and booze – suggests they're mostly minor misdemeanours. I think the word 'cheek' crops up a lot. I'm 'too cheeky'. I'm 'showing too much spirit'. I don't show enough deference. I don't fawn upon them enough.

The teachers are quite high maintenance in terms of the respect they feel they should be paid.

My first formal punishment is a slippering. I'm twelve, I've only been there a few weeks. I'm called into an assistant housemaster's 'flat' just before bedtime. It's more just a bedroom, with a desk and an easy chair crammed into one corner, and it smells of liniment – a kind of all-purpose embrocation, garishly pink in colour, used to massage aching limbs and joints, with a lingering odour of camphor and menthol. It's the snake oil of the seventies, and the rugby players of the school like to rub it in all over. The sight of them massaging it into their inner thighs after a game has a slightly homoerotic charge.

The assistant housemaster tells me the punishment for my crime is 'four', and asks me to bend over. He then feels my bottom through my pyjamas to make sure I'm 'not wearing any padding'. This check takes a long time. Once he's satisfied (!) he picks up one of his size twelve slippers – he's a big man – and hits me with it, very hard, four times. My parents would have been very pleased with the smacking sound. Justice is definitely heard to be done.

It hurts a lot but I am determined not to give him the satisfaction of crying. Once the fourth blow has been delivered I stand up straight, holding in the urge, and wait to be dismissed.

'Not crying?' he asks.

I don't make a reply.

'I can't have done it hard enough,' he continues.

There's a silence. He stares at me. I try not to look at him, but some errant flicker of curiosity causes me to glance at him for the briefest of moments. This quick look must have some measure of defiance or 'cheek' in it, because he then says: 'You're an insolent boy, aren't you? I think I'd better give you four more. Bend over.'

There's absolutely nothing you can do in these situations, which is precisely the point – complete subjugation. And humiliation. Even in Lindsay Anderson's film *if. . .* about insurrection at a public school, when Malcolm McDowell's character is getting caned by the prefects in the gym, he stands when the 'four' have been delivered without being asked to stand, and this provokes the prefects to make him bend over again and take four more. And he *does* it. It's so disappointing. Just when you think the revolution is about to begin he backs down, and takes four more.

Of course – spoiler alert – at the end of the film Malcolm McDowell's character, Mick Travis, finds a stash of weapons belonging to the cadet force and goes berserk, shooting most of the bullies dead from the rooftop.

There but for the keys to the armoury go I . . .

In the assistant housemaster's liniment-reeking bedroom, I bend over again. He hits me four more times, harder than before, but I still don't cry. He makes me stand and stares into my face. He can see that my eyes are smarting, that my bottom lip is starting to quiver.

'Nearly there,' he says, grinning. 'I'm going to hit you until you cry. Bend over again.'

And he keeps on hitting me until I cry.

Once I'm crying properly he comes over all avuncular. He drops the slipper.

'There you are, you see – not too hard, is it?'

He puts an arm around my shoulders to comfort me and *tousles my hair*! Then pats me on the bottom and sends me on my way.

I'm aware that I've described this in a rather matter-of-fact way, while an obvious question might be:

Are you a victim of sexual abuse?

I don't think masters should feel boys' bottoms in that way, or hit them until they cry, but I certainly didn't feel like a victim at the time. Mostly because this form of 'mild' sexual abuse was the way of the world back then, in that school and many others. It was happening to so many people.

Consider the routine that's followed at bath time in that first year at school. There's a communal bathroom with eight large baths in it. It's three boys a bath, and we get into the water that's been used by the previous batch of boys. We have to soap ourselves all over, then stand up and raise a hand. The master will come over and check that we are soaped all over. We will then rinse, stand, and raise a hand again, and he will check that we are rinsed. Then we get out and dry ourselves, and he will make sure we are dry. Each of these inspections involves varying degrees of 'touching' and 'checking'. Some teachers are known to be more thorough than others. They don't grab our genitals as such, it's a sort of fluttering of the hands down the front and back that might accidentally brush against your penis.

We are mostly pre-pubescent, and pre-sexual. It's only in hindsight that we get an understanding of what might be going on. As we move up the school system to the next boarding house these bath checks are dropped, but we've decided who the 'pervs' are. We learn to avoid them as much as possible.

It's society that lets the predators operate in plain sight. For instance, we hear stories in the early seventies of Jimmy Savile fiddling with dead bodies in a Leeds hospital, but he doesn't get 'outed' for another forty years. We know we wouldn't let ourselves be alone in a room with Jimmy Savile. We know he's a wrong'un back then, and if *we* schoolboys know, then *everyone* must know. They're just not saying – because they've got vested interests. People must know about Rolf Harris and Stuart Hall and Gary Glitter too.

Are you damaged by the experience?

If we are the sum of everything that happens to us, then the answer is probably yes, but working out the various weights of all these experiences is not an exact science. We're ground down by so many things at school – chiefly harsh discipline and poor pastoral care – but I'd say the most damaging thing is a lack of love. Love definitely isn't mentioned in the school prospectus.

Some boys 'thrive' under these conditions, others, like me, go gently berserk.

The film *if . . .* is made in 1968, the year before I go to Pocklington. The school depicted is a bit posher than ours, but the studies, the dormitories, the cadet force, the cold showers, and the lack of love, are all very familiar.

Our local fleapit, The Ritz, in Pocklington, generally turns a blind eye to age restrictions, and has a strangely progressive attitude to programming. It often shows art house films, classics, and occasionally porn (or what passes for porn) on Sunday evenings. Praise the Lord. Many of us get to see *if . . .* a couple of years after its release. I would say young public-school boys are the perfect audience for this film, and perhaps the owner of The Ritz has spotted this.

'Violence and revolution are the only pure acts,' says Travis, sitting in his study with his two pals. 'One man can change the world with a bullet in the right place.'

Oh, the pipe dreams I have. Travis and his mates are so hard slash cool. If only I could be more like them.

Sixty-six of the best

From the age of thirteen the slipper is discarded and the cane is introduced.

Many people think canes are made from bamboo, they're not, they're made from rattan. Both have those horizontal notches (nodes), so you can see how the mistake is made. But bamboo is a type of grass, whilst rattan is a climbing palm. They have different properties. Bamboo is hollow and rigid, whereas rattan has a dense, strong and flexible inner core. To process the rattan they strip away the outer layer and leave it to soak so that it becomes more pliable. This is important because you need 'whippiness' – you want the cane to flex as you use it. With a big enough back swing, and a long enough cane, your arm movement is amplified, so that the end section of the cane, at the point of impact, is travelling many times faster than your hand.

I'm basically caught up in an arms race – the slipper is more powerful than the hand, and the cane is more powerful than the slipper. They'll probably shoot me next. Unless I get to the armoury first.

One of the masters is either perverse, stupid or penny-pinching, because he uses a bamboo cane. Anyone who has done any gardening will know how easily bamboo splits and breaks under pressure. When caning one boy the brittle cellulose structure gives way as it whacks against his tiny, malnourished buttocks. The tip of the cane flies off and knocks an ornament from a shelf onto the floor, where it breaks. The master charges the boy for the cost of replacement. Sometimes you just can't win.

During my school career I receive sixty-six strokes of the cane on my arse. I get 'six of the best' eleven times. That's roughly twice a year.

Twice a year! But that's hardly anything, ya big Jessie! That's six months between each beating – what are you moaning about?

I can see where you're coming from. It probably takes less than a minute to deliver six strokes, so that's two minutes a year, why don't I just forget about it? It's over in a flash. Let it lie.

But it isn't over in a flash. There's a long, drawn-out ritual. Whenever you're sentenced to a caning you have to suffer two weeks of waiting before the punishment is delivered. This is deliberate – it's meant to fill you with fear and foreboding. And it does.

My sister-in-law Judy (an ex-teacher) tells me of an ancient colleague who bemoaned the banning of corporal punishment in state schools in 1986 – it wasn't banned in independent schools until 1998, ironically just as the Britney Spears single 'Hit Me Baby One More Time' was released – he thought 'making them wait' was the most effective part of the punishment, besides which he 'didn't like to hit them when he was angry'.

What? He had to wait until he was perfectly calm? Happy? Joyful?

Taking into account the number of weeks I'm at school during a year (forty) and the number of weeks per year waiting (four), I spend 10 per cent of my school life waiting for a sufficiently cheerful adult to hit me with a stick. One more time. Baby.

Over six years I spend twenty-four weeks waiting to get caned, which is ten weeks more than I spend making *The Young Ones*. This is the kind of thing that confuses the Numskulls.

The canings are mostly given by the headmaster, a former officer in the Royal Artillery, who played cricket for Derbyshire in the 1950s. He scored 8,325 first-class runs, so his hand–eye coordination is pretty damn good. His first name is Guy, and he has bushy eyebrows, so we call him Guybrows. His study is very large but sparsely furnished so that he can get a decent run up.

I expect a summons at any moment towards the end of the second week, but it always comes as a surprise. We'll be in the common room wearing out the grooves of David Bowie's LP *Ziggy Stardust & the Spiders from Mars* when a prefect will come in and tell me the headmaster wants to see me in his study.

'Now!'

A hush will come over the room and they'll watch me go. The condemned man.

'*. . . He was the nazz, with God-given ass . . .*'

I get one last chance to fiddle with my ass as I cross to the main school buildings: I've been wearing two pairs of underpants for the last few days – constantly adjusting them so that the two seams are aligned and look like one pair of underpants. It's no wonder I eventually get into university with thinking like this.

The walk there never gets any easier. The fear of the pain never dims. Why would you willingly walk to a place where you know you will get physically beaten?

I knock on the door to his study. A voice comes from within.

'Enter!'

Guybrows wears a schoolmaster's black gown. All the older teachers do. This is the 1970s, we've been through the Swinging Sixties and now we're into glam rock. Slade are top of the charts with 'Mama Weer All Crazee Now', and Noddy Holder is wearing cut-off tartan trousers with bright yellow braces, platform boots, and a top hat covered in mirrors, but the teachers are still dressing up like Robert Donat in that overly sentimental 1939 film about an impossibly genial schoolmaster, *Goodbye, Mr Chips*.

Guybrows solemnly rakes over the details of my heinous crime.

I feign contrition.

He invites me to hold onto the side stretcher of a heavy chair placed at the far end of the room. The stretcher is about four inches from the floor and leaves my arse tilted up into the air, making an inviting target. He gently lifts the flaps of my jacket out of the way so that they won't cause any impediment. He gives my arse a cursory feel to make sure I'm not wearing any padding. This isn't the paedophilic groping of the slippery housemaster, and I think he's even slightly embarrassed at having to touch my bottom. More fool him, because I get away with the two pairs of underpants trick *every time*. Yes, all right, it's only a minor victory, but you start clutching at straws when the dice are loaded so heavily against you.

He then walks back to his starting position, which is a good five paces back. I watch his approach – I'm bent double and can see him through the gap between my legs. Like the first-class cricketer he is, he strides forwards with purpose and speed, as if to meet a spinner's delivery that has pitched short of a length and deserves smashing over the boundary for six. His voluminous gown flies up around him as he raises his cane-wielding arm, his narrow-set eyes are full of righteous fury and vengeance.

In fact he looks like a drawing by Ronald Searle – the man who illustrated the Molesworth and St Trinian's books, whose art has a humorous cruelty to it, influenced by the three years he spent in Japanese prisoner of war camps during the Second World War.

Whack!

The cane whips against my buttocks.

It hurts like fuck.

The instinct is to rise up instantly and rub the pain away, but you know that will only bring further punishment – additional strokes. You become glad of the heavy chair because you can squeeze it tight: like a cowboy in a western chewing down on a piece of leather as some quack removes a bullet with an impossibly large knife – except that the cowboy gets to drink a bottle of whisky as an anaesthetic. Whisky is possibly why I'm here in the first place.

He calmly walks the five paces back to his starting position, turns, composes himself, then rushes forward once more.

Whack!

Walk back, turn, compose, rush.

Whack!

Walk back, turn, compose, rush.

It would be nice to think that you become numbed to it as the beating continues, but every strike hurts just as much as the one before. Every delicate nerve sings out in new pain with every blow. But hang on, we're only halfway through the over.

Whack!

Walk back, turn, compose, rush.

Whack!

Walk back, turn, compose, rush.

Whack!

After the last strike he walks back to his desk, lays the cane upon it, and looks purposefully out of the window. This is to allow you a little time to compose yourself. (He's not a monster!)

Your arse hurts to varying degrees as you rise slowly, the muscles and the skin finding out where the damage has been done. A close grouping, where all the strokes land more or less in one place, hurts less than a wide one. A rogue near miss across the top of your legs can cause severe discomfort. You're permitted to sniffle for a short while and gingerly rub your bottom. It always feels like you must be bleeding, though you seldom are.

Once your personal damage report has been concluded, you wipe your nose on your sleeve and shuffle round to face him. His study is so quiet that he can hear you turn and he does likewise. He holds out his hand for you to shake. You have to thank him! You move forward, each step a discovery of new areas of pain as your buttocks flex. You shake his hand.

'Thank you, sir,' you say.

'Don't let it happen again,' he says.

You leave, walking very oddly.

As you close the door behind you, you might see the next victim waiting. You give him as cheery a smile as you can, trying to hide your desire to blub like a baby. You have to tough it out, grin, give him the thumbs up – there is a camaraderie amongst the convicted – you might whisper:

'Missed!'

And get a rueful smile in return.

Back in the dormitory you will be expected to drop your pants so that everyone can get a good look at the grouping and check for blood. You're hoping for a single line – where every strike landed in exactly the same place – but mostly you get something that looks like the British Rail logo. There's very rarely blood on the actual day, this usually comes later as the welts and weals first form dark black, purple and yellow bruises, then gradually scab over. If you've never picked the scabs off your own arse . . . well, lucky you.

We keep a tally of our canings as we progress through the years and a bizarre kind of league table emerges. The longer I stay at the school the higher I climb, and during my last year I'm one of three way out in front vying for top spot. I finish second. European qualification.

I don't feel significantly more badly behaved than the rest of the inmates, and part of me wonders if I'm singled out, not just for the perceived 'cheek', but because I'm a direct grant boy. Maybe they think I shouldn't really be there, that I've somehow cheated. Maybe it's part of an attempt to make me 'know my place'?

For some reason the league table is based solely on arse canings, we don't bother counting canings of the hand. I don't know why – they hurt a lot too. Possibly because these punishments are meted out summarily. Our housemaster at the 'big school', whose nickname is The Führer, patrols the corridors cane in hand, ready to strike. The crime is committed and the punishment given almost in the same moment.

'What are you doing out in the corridor during study time?'

'I . . . er . . .'

'Hold out your hand.'

Whack! Whack! Whack!

'. . . needed the toilet.'

Hand canings are generally delivered in threes. Again, I don't know why, but I'm not complaining. And there's no run up. But there is something completely absurd about standing next to a grown man, the man who is *in loco parentis*, and holding out your hand at arm's length to let him hit it with a stick. You can see their eyes. You more or less stare at each other as it happens. No wonder so many public-school boys get into S&M.

They always ask for the hand you don't write with and the trick is to give them the wrong one, because once your hand swells from the beating you'll be unable to write with it for a couple of days. No more homework! Result!

'Sorry, sir, I meant right, not left.'

It only works in the early days – the more you get beaten the more they learn which hand you write with, and to be honest it's usually fairly obvious from the ink-stained fingers.

Part 3

Finding things funny

Slapstick

To be hit so regularly, for so many years, with such careless abandon, makes the violence almost meaningless. Is this what berserkers felt as they slashed their way through the enemy ranks with no regard for killing or being killed?

It obviously had a major impact on my life because I'm able to recall it here with such clarity. I think there were only two ways to deal with it: to buckle, and become a gibbering wreck; or to find it funny. Laughing at it somehow negated the ignominy, somehow belittled my tormentors.

But it's weird that things happened to me on a regular basis which less than twenty years later are made illegal.

What's not weird, perhaps, is my obvious delight in gratuitous violence in all the comedy programmes I've been involved in ever since. The glee in The Führer's face as he gives me three on the hand is the same as the glee in Vyvyan's face as he hits Rick between the legs with a cricket bat.

In 2005 the heads of some Christian independent schools (those fun-loving Christians again) appeal against the ban on corporal punishment, claiming it's a breach of their religious freedom. They drag it through various courts trying to assert that their vision for modern corporal punishment won't even hurt like it used to; they say boys will be hit with 'a thin, broad flat paddle to both buttocks simultaneously in a firm controlled manner'. Whilst, 'girls could be strapped on the hand and then comforted by a member of staff and encouraged to pray'. Seems odd that girls should get the stiffer penalty. But the 'broad flat paddle' sounds so amazingly like the slapstick from *commedia dell'arte*.

Commedia dell'arte is a name given to the raucous touring theatre companies popular in Italy from the sixteenth to the eighteenth century. I do my thesis on *commedia dell'arte* in my final year at university. The comedy was broad and often quite violent, and a slapstick was a device – a kind of paddle made of two wooden slats – that made a slapping noise when you hit someone with it. Like a large slim castanet. It meant you could get a satisfying sound without inflicting any major damage. If only my parents had had one.

By the time Rik and I make *The Young Ones*, the Dangerous Brothers and *Bottom*, we replace the actual slapstick with 'spot effects' – a soundman sits watching us and as we pretend to hit each other he plays in various thwacks and smacks. But it's still essentially slapstick. We make a pretence of hitting each other, and it sounds like we've hit each other, but we don't inflict any major damage. Well – that's the theory.

Slapstick has always had a poor reputation, even in the days of *commedia dell'arte*. People call it 'puerile'. Puerile comes from the Latin word for boy – *puer*. Which, rather curiously, is an anagram of the word pure. People only ever use puerile in a derogatory way to suggest slapstick is the kind of humour that would make a young boy laugh, which they think is unworthy. I call it pure. Young boys are a tough crowd. I've got two grandsons. I know.

The reviews for *Bottom* when it's first broadcast in the early nineties are mostly scathing, and often use the word 'puerile' as an insult. Perhaps reviewers fear that enjoying slapstick might make them appear lacking in intellect.

I'm furious when Ken Loach's film *Raining Stones* comes out in 1993. I love Ken Loach films. I love *Raining Stones*. But he uses slapstick in exactly the same way we do: watch the scene as Ricky Tomlinson and his mate go out rustling sheep, slipping about and falling over to a Benny Hill-type soundtrack; or the scene where the toilet backs up violently and he gets covered in shit. Does Ken Loach get censured? No, he doesn't.

I'm happy to admit there's a lot of bad slapstick too, which doesn't help. We've grown up watching the awful custard pie nonsense on the knockabout kid's show *Crackerjack* – unthought out, unstructured and unfunny. They're not even custard pies, it's just shaving foam on a paper plate.

I direct an advert in the early 2000s for some now defunct TV satellite dish. It features Phil Cornwell getting a custard pie in the face. I spend most of pre-production working with the designer Lez Brotherston to get the correct consistency for the custard, and the base, and end up throwing the pie myself because no one can get it to land correctly – breaking on the nose and dropping to reveal the eyes.

And I'm not trying to claim our work is highbrow, but you can't dismiss the urge to laugh at slapstick as simply puerile or lowbrow. Especially when we put so much bloody adult effort into it.

And our slapstick has a vicious streak to it that is perhaps new. It's often mean-spirited, never accidental, and it's meant to look painful. It's the pain we find funny. The more it hurts, the funnier it is. It isn't cosy. It's not Benny Hill slapping the bald bloke's head. It's not the classic wallpaper routine at the panto. It comes from a new strain that we've noticed in Monty Python's Fish Slapping Dance; and in John Cleese's abusive treatment of Manuel in *Fawlty Towers*.

All the work Rik and I create is chock-a-block with violence, disorder and brutality. The most frequently used stage direction in our scripts is 'they fight'. Any argument between our characters, any dispute, will always end in some form of ruckus: punching, kicking, slapping; a dart in the eye, a pencil up the nose, a fork in the testicles; stapling hands to tables, sawing off legs, beating a gas man with a frying pan seventeen times; explosions, electrocutions, being fired out of a cannon. It's relentless. It's frenzied. It's out of control. It's berserk.

Of course, it's not all related to being beaten at school.

A lot of it comes from American cartoons, particularly *Tom & Jerry* and *Road Runner*. These are from the 1940s and '50s respectively. We're also indebted to Bob Monkhouse, an aficionado and avid collector of black and white shorts from the twenties and thirties, whose TV show *Mad Movies* introduces us to Charlie Chaplin, Buster Keaton and especially Laurel & Hardy – the unexplained attachment between these two (why did they stay together when they fought so much?) is a big driver in the relationship between Eddie and Richie in *Bottom*. When I say 'big driver' I mean 'something that we steal wholesale'. Mind you, the same could be said for Galton and Simpson who created *Steptoe & Son* and *Hancock's Half Hour*, and Clement & La Frenais who created *The Likely Lads*.

When *The Young Ones* is conceived the idea is to create four truly horrible characters. It's a kind of reaction to *The Good Life*. We don't want lovable, we don't want comforting, we don't want 'ah', we want what we see around us – spotty, selfish, violent bastards. We don't have an intellectual mission, we just like jokes about what we see. Making jokes about violence is perhaps a way of processing it.

Violence is everywhere in the seventies – our formative years. We're bang in between the Moors Murderers and the Yorkshire

Ripper. Football hooliganism is at its peak – rival 'firms' are busy hospitalizing people and throwing darts from the back of the terraces. The Troubles in Northern Ireland are headline news most days, and spill over onto the mainland in a series of indiscriminate pub bombings. Control of the unions always breaks down into the police giving the workers a bloody good kicking. And in Vietnam the Americans are fighting an enemy they can't see with napalm, Agent Orange, and carpet-bombing.

Army, art, German or droogs?

We think about killing a lot at school. Not just the Charles Manson serial killer type thing, and the missing estate agents and the hitchhikers who always end up being murder victims, but we spend an inordinate amount of time thinking about the Second World War.

At school everything about me screams 'arty fucker', I do all the plays, I build sets, I decide on costumes, I have poetry painted on my guitar, I am crap at the sciences, and languages . . . so how come I don't do O-level art?

Because as a fourteen-year-old schoolboy, like many of my classmates, I'm an avid reader of books by Sven Hassel.

World War Two ended twelve years before we were born but we're obsessed with it. *The Legion of the Damned* is a particularly gruesome (and fictional) account of life as a German soldier on the Eastern Front. Full of a salacious, graphic brutality. We lap it up.

It shares the premise of *The Dirty Dozen*, which followed. A group of convicts is formed into an army unit with the vague promise of being let off if they do all the dirty work. It's basically war porn – summary executions, rape, battles, insurrection.

Sven Hassel is apparently the most widely read Danish author after Hans Christian Andersen, though Andersen's oeuvre is also jam-packed with casual violence.

Us Danes!

There's also a dog-eared copy of *Skinhead* by Richard Allen doing the rounds of the dormitories. Our hero is Joe Hawkins, a skinhead from the East End. He is forever 'kicking off'. He'll pick on anyone: rival football fans, old-age pensioners, hippies, coppers, anyone in a pub, or at the church youth group. Not even having a broken bottle pushed into his face will make him reconsider.

It comes out around the same time as Stanley Kubrick's film of Anthony Burgess's novel *A Clockwork Orange*, which features our favourite actor Malcolm McDowell again. Not only do we enjoy the shocking violence but we love Nadsat – the slang language Alex and his droogs use. Some of us even read the book! We try and use Nadsat, saying *droog* instead of friend, *horrorshow* instead of good, *cutter* instead of money.

It's a mix of Cockney rhyming slang and Russian-sounding words and in our school uniforms and caps we probably don't appear as hard and *ultraviolent* as Malcolm McDowell. We probably sound more like Julian and Sandy – the two camp, Polari-speaking characters from *Round the Horne* played by Hugh Paddick and Kenneth Williams.

The papers are full of stories about 'juvenile delinquents' and 'disaffected youth', but at the same time we're watching bog-standard comedies like *Are You Being Served*, *On the Buses* and *Man About the House* on TV, so perhaps it all evens out.

We like to buy bubblegum, not because we particularly like bubblegum, but because it comes with cards depicting scenes from the war. Despite the fact that they lost, the Germans always look more heroic. We just love the shape of their helmets. Peter Sellers even wears one when he goes on the chat show *Parkinson*.

The very word stormtrooper sounds so much more *Lord of the Rings* than Household Cavalry.

The cards are collectible and swappable, the favourites being pictures of a Stuka, or a soldier throwing one of those grenades shaped like a baked bean tin on the end of a stick. The German uniforms were made by Hugo Boss, so of course they look sharp. Though having played an officer of the First Order in *Star Wars*, whose uniforms were based on the Nazi ones, I can tell you they're incredibly tight. After a week of wearing it I come to the conclusion that the real reason the Nazis were so argumentative is because they were so bloody uncomfortable.

And so it comes to pass that a whole bunch of us, when asked to make our choices at O-level, and finding art and German in the same column – opt for German. Little do we know it's just glorified Latin, full of verbs, gerunds and reflexive pronouns. At no point are we offered a German helmet or a decommissioned grenade.

In an age when a lot of us are wearing greatcoats – the thick woollen coats issued to soldiers – those that can find a German greatcoat are considered the coolest.

And we need greatcoats in order to drink.

What?

Yes.

The Canal Head pub is a mile away from the town. An often-rainy walk down a country lane for us fourteen- and fifteen-year-olds. Sixteen-year-olds can get away with drinking in establishments closer to the school, but us youngsters have to put in the extra mile. Quite literally.

We're lucky enough to live in an age when nobody has any ID and underage drinking is so common that the law barely exists. Even so it's ridiculously obvious that we are underage with our smooth chins and high-pitched voices requesting vodka and lime – the tiny sixth of a gill shot of vodka and the thick sweet cordial making it the alcopop of its day. We generally send our friend Jim up to get the first round in because he has sideburns and his balls have dropped.

Our logic for the greatcoats is that our regular, prescribed casual wear inescapably marks us out. 'Sports Jackets'? Which other kids are wearing sports jackets in the early seventies? So the greatcoats *must* make us look like proper adults.

However, none of the proper adults in the Canal Head are wearing greatcoats. They're wearing anoraks and Bri-nylon car coats. And smirks on their faces.

Perhaps we're just too young to recognize that we've got a fetish for the war, but the long, heavy coat with its deep pockets is considered the height of chic. We purloin as many as we can from the cadet force stores which are chiefly Second World War relics. When rained upon, the heavy woollen fabric has the habit of releasing the odour of previous occupants. We walk to the Canal Head and back and smell like men who've tramped from the Normandy beaches all the way to Berlin with limited bathing facilities.

We are forced to join the CCF, the Combined Cadet Force. Though in truth there's no 'combined' about it, there's no air force wing, no navy section; we don't have any planes or ships. We don't have any tanks either, we just have the infantry, the expendable part of the army, the part with the First World War rifles – no artillery, no bazookas.

And actually, we are not 'forced' – it's compulsory but we go willingly; like underage boys signing up for a war, we're eager to get a gun in our hands and start taking pot shots at people. Everyone's got a *bit* of berserker in them. When we find out that it's mostly marching up and down while some sixth former shouts at us the whole idea loses its appeal fairly quickly.

They're obsessed with shiny boots. The boot room is full of young boys whose parents have paid handsomely for a private education, endlessly polishing their boots. The toecaps in particular have to be so shiny that you can see your face in them. I never learn how to do this. Even at the daily inspection for our 'normal' shoes as we head over to the main school buildings, I simply give my shoes a cursory rub against the back of my trousers.

The boot polishing is called 'bulling your boots' and involves some kind of alchemy which eludes me. You have to wrap a duster around your finger, dip it in black boot polish, then make small circular motions on the toecap for hours and hours and hours. After three days of a constant circular motion the toecap will become vaguely shiny – good start, keep going, another six weeks should see it through.

I try the supposed short cut which involves mixing the shoe polish with some methylated spirit, smearing it on, and setting fire to it. I destroy my boots. Maybe the army isn't for me.

Thankfully, one of the few masters who is not an ex-serviceman takes pity on me, and I am drafted into his 'Pioneers' unit, where shiny toecaps aren't as important. In the regular army the pioneers dig the latrines, but we already have something not too dissimilar to latrines at the school, they are called 'the bogs', so in the Pocklington CCF Pioneers we make . . . canoes! Out of fibreglass.

Despite not needing to go on parade with shiny boots any more, I patch up my burnt toecaps with resin and achieve a permanent shine which is the envy of other boys. Suckers! And making canoes is actually good fun. At one point, once the top and bottom have been stuck together, we turn them on their ends to pour in two chemicals which will create 'buoyancy foam pockets' – a honeycomb structure which will trap air and make them float even when full of water. It's only when I've emptied the contents of both tins into my upended canoe that I hear the master say, 'You only need half a capful of each compound at the most.' I've used a full pint of each. It's quite spectacular.

The two compounds meet and react instantly, frothing up like one of those bicarbonate of soda mixtures used to simulate a volcanic eruption at a primary school – the foam rises up at speed and spews out of the cockpit like an enormous sausage. I end up with a deep understanding of how much people enjoy things that go completely wrong. I can't remember seeing so many people so helpless with mirth as we stand there in the 'technology centre' – an extended portacabin – watching the reaction go on, and on, and on, and on.

Unlike at primary school the 'lava' dries very quickly into a solid honeycomb so I end up with a solid canoe. It's like a giant Crunchie bar only with a fibreglass rather than a chocolate coating. It takes me the rest of the term, working away like Michelangelo with a hammer and chisel, to chip out enough of the hardened foam in the body of the canoe to make way for my legs, but I name her *HMS Unsinkable*. On seaworthiness trials in the Pocklington Canal my canoe sits much higher in the water than other boys', which makes it quite unstable – it tips over quite easily but will never sink.

There's a man who takes us canoeing who's not the kindly teacher who helped us make the canoes. He's a specialist canoeist, I don't know what his link is with the school, he's not one of the teachers. He takes us two at a time. He has an estate car which is handy for strapping the canoes on top of. He says it's also handy for getting changed. He puts the heater on and says we can all get in and wriggle out of our wet things. He puts the radio on to make it more enticing – 'Feel the Need in Me' by The Detroit Emeralds is playing. We don't get in. We get changed on the freezing cold canal bank. We can tell he's a perv. We watch him wriggle about in the back on his own, 'accidentally' flashing his penis at us.

They're everywhere.

• • •

When the cadet force is sent on yearly manoeuvres to Allerthorpe Common we're fed on surplus rations from 1946. Many of the labels have fallen off and we never know whether we're getting bully beef or custard for breakfast. Sometimes we find a bar of chocolate inside a sealed tin. It's developed a white sheen, not mould, just a creeping change in colour, a patina, but we eat it just the same. We're so pissed on the illicit bottles of cider we've smuggled into our backpacks that we can't tell whether it tastes good or bad.

We're carrying our World War One Lee Enfield rifles and have been issued with ten blanks each. The rule sternly issued by our teacher-officers is never to point our guns at anyone, but the half-cut game is to see if you can hit each other with the wad of fiery hot cotton that flies out of these things at 100mph whenever you pull the trigger. I'm surprised no one is blinded or worse, especially given our attempts at making home-made bombs from weedkiller poured into almost empty tins of golden syrup. The yearly weekend out in the wilds of the common is more akin to a *Lord of the Flies* re-enactment society than army manoeuvres. But perhaps that's what real war is like anyway?

The most genuinely military part of these 'let's play soldiers' weekends is the advance on the Plough Inn in the village of Allerthorpe – crawling up to it through the surrounding vegetation to avoid being seen by any teachers – in order to resupply ourselves with cider.

Violence as comedy

The archaeological evidence suggests the Vikings did a lot of drinking, and we are similarly inclined. We're lucky we live in such a backwater because if drugs had been more available we might not have survived. We try smoking nutmeg and grated dried banana skins, and almost get hernias trying to draw on these densely packed roll-ups, but none of the promised effects materialize, so we concentrate on the booze: Newcastle Brown Ale, Watney's Party Seven, Woodpecker cider, Dubonnet, Advocaat, Babycham, Harvey's Bristol Cream – we drink anything we can get hold of.

Aged about sixteen, my friend Wilf and I go to see the band Curved Air at the Student Union in Bradford. Sonja Kristina, the lead singer of Curved Air, is our number one hot crush. We can't believe we're going to see her sing 'Back Street Luv' right in front of us, in the flesh, and we're already a little giddy.

Besides being in love with her I'm also aware of her Scandinavian heritage, and if by some miracle I should get to talk to her, once she learns that I'm Scandinavian too I'm sure we're going to hit it off big time.

This is called magical thinking.

Sonja Kristina, my number one hot crush

The beer in the Student Union is incredibly cheap and we drink a lot of it. We're not very good at it, but practice makes perfect, so we keep practising. We become fairly stocious, fairly quickly.

I am wearing my new light blue denim jacket that I've bought from the back pages of *Melody Maker*. I think Sonja will like it. It's covered in embroidery – little hummingbirds and flowers – and has a jolly hippy vibe that I'm very pleased with.

At school we buy ALL our clothes from the small ads in the back of *Melody Maker*, it's our chief source of groovy clothing, but not all purchases have been this successful. It's the days before trading standards are a noticeable thing. Most of the stuff is extremely badly made. The green satin loons I buy fall to pieces on the second wearing. They don't even have a waistband, just a thin strip of cotton webbing. The only positive is that they fall apart before they need washing.

I'm not sure I'd be who I am without *Melody Maker*. More than any book I read, more than any lesson I'm ever taught, *Melody Maker* is where I read about a different world that I long to join. It's full of people experiencing much more freedom than me. People having much more fun. I read it from cover to cover every week. Ian Hunter, the lead singer of Mott the Hoople, who always seems to be having 'a right lark', becomes a beacon of insouciance – he's the flame to my moth. I want to be him.

But at this point I haven't even got the right trousers.

Clothes are expensive and the only stuff I get free is the stuff my mum buys me from the Grattan catalogue. This stuff is even worse, at least stylistically. I beg her repeatedly for a pair of Levi jeans. Instead she gets me some 'jeans' from the catalogue. They're not even made of denim, they're made of cotton and are printed with a pattern to look like denim. From across the road I might get away with them, but come one step closer and you'll see the red stitching. No real jeans have red stitching. It only invites people to inspect them more thoroughly and then they'll see the true horror of how uncool they really are.

But at the time they're the only jeans I've got and they might impress some girls, at least from a distance. I wear them at every opportunity, even on a geography field trip to Malham Cove. I reckon any girl hikers won't be able to spot my ersatz jeans from a distance, they'll just think: 'Hey, there's a cool guy in jeans.'

On the trudge over from Malham Cove to Gordale Scar I trip and land knee first in an enormous cow pat. A fresh one. I don't know whether it's the acidity of the cow pat or the cheapness of the fabric dye, but this is catastrophic. I scrape the shit off with a dock leaf immediately but some chemical reaction is already taking place. I can see it happening before my very eyes. I wash the knee in a stream but I can see the 'denim effect' disappearing. When the reaction finally stops I'm left with a permanent dull brown/purple patch that makes it look like I've just fallen knee first in a cow pat. Now the girls will be thinking: 'Hey, there's a guy who's just fallen knee deep in a cow pat. And look – he's wearing fake jeans!'

I never wear the jeans again.

Grattan catalogues are one of the major success stories of Bradford-based businesses after the wool industry declines, but I take against them from this point. Even the pages of young ladies modelling bras and pants lose their thrall.

And speaking of young ladies not wearing very much, we don't get to meet Sonja after the gig. We search for the stage door only to find ourselves locked out of the Union building altogether because the tickets don't allow re-entry. She was brilliant though.

Our passions inflamed, we roam the streets of Bradford looking for girls to chat up. We don't know how to chat up girls, but we're hoping to give it a bloody good go if we can find some who'll let us try. We go into a pub and are immediately thrown out, not because we are obviously underage, but because we are in that kind of loud, young, drunk state that draws unnecessary attention to itself. We are wild-eyed and chewing on our shields. The licensing laws are only ignored as long as you sit quietly in the corner with half a pint of shandy.

We spy a cafe down a back alley and figure we might try our luck there. It's one of those grim places that stays open for night shift workers and people who've missed the last bus home. There's a group of 'lads' in the queue before us at the counter. The last one orders a tea, the proprietor puts it on the counter and passes him the sugar in one of those dispensers with the metal tube inside that's supposed to limit each tilt to precisely one teaspoon of sugar, but never works. The lad has trouble with it. Each tilt only produces a few grains. It takes him an age to get the requisite amount of sugar into the cup. I sigh exaggeratedly.

'Where are the spoons?' he says, finally.

'Don't worry – I'll use my finger!' I say, hoping to speed the process up and be amusing at the same time.

I stick my finger into his tea and stir. It scalds my finger, but Wilf laughs, so it's worth it.

The lad looks at me like I'm an idiot.

'I *am* an idiot,' I say, reading his mind.

He looks narked, and Wilf, spotting the potential for argy-bargy – which he likes to avoid because he is on the puny side – apologizes for my behaviour and immediately buys him another tea. The potential for unpleasantness is avoided. Wilf is a whizz at maths – he'll go on to work out the odds for betting companies for a living – and he informs me that if I drink the fingered tea we will be none the worse off.

I know now how annoying sixteen-year-old drunks are, and I apologize if you were there. I imagine I was loud, and obnoxious, and found myself terribly amusing. Luckily there were no girls to disappoint.

The lads leave before us, scowling at us as they go. As we return our empty cups to the counter – see how beautifully well-mannered we are – the proprietor looks at us and says under his breath, 'I'd be careful when you go outside.'

We're too drunk to understand what he means – has there been a sudden snowfall? But as we exit it becomes crystal clear. The lads, all five of them, are in a semicircle around the door. *Grease* hasn't come out yet, so perhaps they're channelling *West Side Story*, but this is definitely the seventies Bradford version of gang warfare. Except that we don't have a gang. There's just the two of us. And they're a lot bigger than us. And there are no songs. And no dancing. And I doubt we'll be falling in love with beautiful girls and doing the kissing thing.

It's amazing how quickly you sober up when you're suddenly confronted with real danger. It's as if drunkenness is just a pretence that you can switch on and off. The one whose tea I stirred starts to air his grievances . . . but barely gets a word out before I shout 'Run!'

At least being smaller makes us more slippery to catch. We jink through them, side-stepping and twisting – who knew being forced to play rugby would ever come in useful – we tear ourselves away from their flailing fists and grasping hands, before hightailing it down the alley. They chase after us but the adrenalin rush of fear gives us an advantage. We've never run so fast.

As you know, Bradford is built on seven hills – just like Rome – and we run up and down them getting the distinct impression that we are faster than them and that they are dropping behind. We turn the corner into Sunbridge Road and would you believe it – there's the 16 bus at the bus stop! The very bus that will take us up the Thornton Road to safety!

We quickly climb aboard, clamber up the stairs to the top deck, and crouch low to the ground so we can't be seen through the windows.

The bus doesn't go.

We hear the running footsteps of the following pack as they come out into Sunbridge Road. They stop running. They must be looking about.

Why won't the bus go?

We can hear them walking up and down trying to find our trail.

It's the terminus! The terminus stop. This is where the 16 waits until its scheduled departure time. It's late at night. It could be stopped here for ages.

We listen out for our tormentors. The sounds seem to be receding. They must have moved on, or given up.

'They must have moved on, or given up,' I say.

'Let's just lie low,' says Wilf. 'Let's just keep out of sight until the bus goes.'

We lie low for ages. The bus doesn't move. Eventually I risk a little sneaky peek – I raise only the top of my head and my eyeballs above the bottom of the window, look out, and find

I'm staring straight into the eyes of one of the lads on the other side of the street.

'They're on the bus!' he shouts.

There's no time to escape. We are doomed. They bundle up the stairs and rush towards us. It's me they want most. They pull Wilf out of the way so they can get closer to me, and then they start punching. I try to protect my face with my arms, and rather like being smacked by my parents they have to keep going until they feel the right number of blows have connected properly. And they each have to have a go. There are two main punchers but as I'm stuck in a seat and curled up they have to keep swapping positions so that they each feel they've made a proper contribution to the beating. Sometimes there's a gap in the punching and I think they might have stopped, but it's just a pause while they change places.

When they finally leave I have an eyebrow that is split open and gushing blood, my nose feels like it's on sideways, and my lips look like I'm a female contestant on *Love Island*.

I have to say, it hurts getting beaten up, but I take away a piece of comedy gold – the beauty of unexpected repetition. There's an episode of *Bottom* called 'Bottom Gas' in which we attack the gasman who's come round to read the meter (that we have bypassed). We try many ruses to prevent him reading the meter but eventually resort to violence.

I hit him once with a frying pan and he falls unconscious to the ground. I then keep hitting him with the frying pan, and when I get tired Rik takes over, punching him with his fist. We swap hitting duties five times, sometimes taking a breath to regain our strength. I hit him a total of seventeen times with the frying pan, Rik punches him twenty times. All with the gasman's body lying inert on the floor. It takes an unexpected amount of time.

The first hit is conventionally funny, but then the sequence dips into a kind of psychosis where the laughter trails off a bit. However, the longer we keep it up, the longer we keep our nerve, the more berserk it becomes, and hysteria starts to build, and the laughter gradually gets louder and louder.

This is what I learn on the top deck of the number 16 bus. There comes a point in repeatedly punching someone in the face when it's just ridiculous. And possibly funny.

On the negative side, my lovely light blue denim jacket with the hippy embroidery is covered in bright red blood that will never wash out. Even after repeated washing with miracle powders advertised on the TV it is still mostly a dull, muddy brown. And I can't afford to get another one sent from the back pages of *Melody Maker*.

The first frying pan

At school the post is delivered at breakfast. Whoever's on 'post' collects the bundle from the top table and walks up and down the lower tables handing it out. I can always see if the pile contains letters from abroad because they're very distinctive.

They're made of the flimsiest blue paper (for weight, obviously) and stand out a mile. They even have their own name – aerogrammes. The Martin brothers, who are in my house, have parents in Zambia, so once they've got their blue slips it's easy to see if there are any others in the pile.

Things are complicated by Idi Amin's military coup – there's a lot of argy-bargy for a while, and amongst all the death and summary executions the postal service is thrown into disarray.

These are the days when intercontinental phone calls are the preserve of presidents, or the results of the Eurovision Song Contest, so for people that rely on the mail, it becomes a trying time. There's a period of several months when I don't receive a single letter from home.

I know that Uganda is a dangerous place. I know that the last time I was out there people were taking pot shots at each other. People had seen bodies being dumped in the Nile. There's a seven-mile stretch of dual carriageway that runs from Jinja to where my family live in Mwiri – and the Ugandan army like to prove they have the biggest cohones by driving their trucks down the wrong carriageway at top speed.

On another occasion, we're driving along this same road which runs between two lines of hills, and adversaries on either side start shooting at each other over our heads.

Yet another time, we're driving back from a trip to see the hippos at Murchison Falls when we get a puncture. We're travelling with two other families in convoy. Dad tells them not to worry and that he will change the wheel and we'll catch them up. He changes the wheel, but we catch them up sooner than expected: a couple of miles down the road we find they've fallen foul of a strange checkpoint where un-uniformed men have got into an argument with the lead driver and are now pistol whipping him on the bonnet of his car. The un-uniformed men come to check us out and stick their guns into our car to show that they are in charge. After some lengthy negotiations, and much shouting on their part, we're finally taken to an actual army camp, held for a few more hours, made to sign some statements, and allowed on our way.

So I know it's a volatile place, and as the weeks without a

letter turn into months, a part of me wonders if my family have been murdered.

It's an odd thing to feel as a fourteen-year-old boy. The school is no help – their way of dealing with things like this is not to mention it. And in all honesty, I learn to adopt the same approach. For nearly everything. 'Don't mention it' would be emblazoned on my coat of arms if I was a toff. In Latin, obviously. *Non Mentionare.*

I write my weekly letter home during the compulsory letter-writing hour on one of the blue flimsies. The good thing is that they're of a finite length – basically a page and a bit, which you then fold over so you can stick down the edges. But a page and a bit can be very hard to fill when there's no back and forth. It's like writing to an imaginary friend every week. I have imaginary parents. As such I become a kind of imaginary boy. I'm sure my previous letters would have been economical with the truth, but now I can just make shit up about how brilliant I am, and perhaps deserving of a raise in pocket money given galloping inflation (and the price of fags).

The mail I receive consists solely of my *Melody Maker* purchases: a leather cowboy hat, tie-dyeing equipment, *Camembert Electrique* by Gong – chiefly bought because it was Virgin's first album and was being sold for the price of a single, 59p. I listened to it again quite recently and it triggered many memories, amongst them the thought I had at the time that I might be alone. Bizarrely there's a lyric in the first song on the album that goes '*You can kill my family, my family tree.*'

My family tree is quite large.

Even when Idi Amin isn't kicking off I only get to go to Uganda twice a year during my early teens because flights are expensive. So I'm often shunted off to live with various members of the family tree during half-term breaks and the Easter holidays. On few occasions is it apparent that they're overjoyed to have me interrupt their lives, and why should they be? They're not unfriendly, or uncaring, but it's a huge imposition. Who would want a slightly damaged, rather smelly boy who's just discovered masturbation, forced on them for as long as three weeks at a time?

On one half term I'm forced to live with Dad's parents, Grandma and Grandad Ed, the God-fearing Bible bashers of the Sunbridge Road Mission. They are teetotallers. My mum accidentally gave Grandma Ed sherry trifle one Christmas and she didn't speak to Mum for a year, so you can see how much fun staying with them might be.

But one night something happens. I think Grandad Ed might have had a titanic struggle with his faith and succumbed to the wicked depravity of Beelzebub . . . or as anyone else might put it – I think he's gone for a pint.

I might have to commission an independent inquiry into my Numskulls here – though that would take years and obviously be inconclusive – because what I remember happening seems so unlikely, and so out of character from anything I'd seen before. But this is my memory of events:

Grandad Ed is 'out', and Grandma Ed is agitated. Grandad Ed is very rarely 'out', in fact I'm not aware of it happening before. Grandma Ed keeps going to the window, pulling back the net curtains, and scouring the street. She's muttering. She's increasingly angry. She paces up and down.

I sit peacefully in the corner reading my Bible – oh, now, you see that bit *is* made up!

Eventually I hear the front door open and Grandad Ed comes into the room. He is not by any stretch of the imagination drunk, he may have had half a shandy, but he has had a drink. And Grandma Ed – this is no word of a lie – rushes in from the kitchen brandishing a frying pan . . . and clobbers him.

In the fantasy biopic of my life – directed by Federico Fellini with Marcello Mastroianni as me – this moment would be seminal. Fellini would anchor all my work to this single moment in the past. It's in black and white, obviously, but then my grandparents are pretty much in black and white anyway. And in the film they've converted to Catholicism to make the costumes a bit more exciting. But here's the scene:

Young Adrian, pious and cherubic, looking like a young Alan Bennett, sits in the corner dressed in the simple robes of a postulant. He is gently flagellating himself with a cat o'nine tails whilst reciting Psalm 23.

'The Lord is my shepherd; I shall not want. He maketh me to lie down in green pastures . . .'

Grandma Ed paces the room. Every thick-ankled step makes the crockery on the dresser clatter and shake. A teacup falls from its hook. She picks it up and throws it at young Adrian. It smashes against the wall just above his head and showers him with broken shards.

'Pray harder! Whip harder!' she cries.

Adrian redoubles his efforts whilst lighting the incense in a thurible and desperately waving it around. The thick smoke billows forth and catches the yellow rays from the streetlight pouring in through the net-curtained window.

There is the sound of a key in the door. It creaks open. Grandad Ed's face peers cautiously round. He thinks he's got away with it but a sudden movement makes him look sharply left. His blood runs cold as a shadow flashes across his face.

Young Adrian cowers in the corner. We see the violence only as shadow play on Adrian's grief-stricken face. The frying pan landing on Grandad Ed's head time after time with the trademark 'clanging' sound. Young Adrian cries tears of blood – the only colour in the black and white picture. As the camera creeps ever closer to him it focuses first on his eyes, then on one eye, until we see the miniature reflection of Grandma and Grandad Ed in his glasses.

We see them punch, kick and slap. He gets a dart in the eye, a pencil up his nose, a fork in his testicles; she staples his hand to the table, saws off his legs, beats him repeatedly with the frying pan. The *Psycho* soundtrack from the shower scene gradually cross-fades with studio laughter. The more she hits him, the more they laugh, and the happier Young Adrian becomes. The tears dry up, he smiles, then laughs. The hitting continues. Young Adrian is now rolling about laughing.

Cross-fade to a television studio many years later. Rik and Ade are punching, kicking, slapping; darts, pencils, forks; staples, saws, frying pans. They've gone berserk. All cut with shots of the audience laughing like maniacs. Some of them look like they might die laughing. 'Cut,' shouts the director. Rik and Ade hug each other. The audience go wild. This is the success they were craving, and it's all thanks to Grandma and Grandad Ed.

Too silly

It's also thanks to Spike Milligan.

In 1972, aged fifteen, I acquire a book of *Goon Show* scripts. I was only three years old when the original radio broadcasts came to an end, so The Goons are a sort of mythical entity to me in 1972. Mythical in the sense that I know they existed but I've never really heard them. I know what they are – an anarchic group of comedians doing a kind of absurdist radio sitcom with musical interludes. But we don't have the internet, or iPlayer, and even cassette tapes don't really take off until the mid-seventies, so I've only ever heard vague clips.

Then, in October 1972, Spike Milligan, Harry Secombe and Peter Sellers reconvene to make 'The Last Goon Show of All'. This is broadcast on Radio 4 and on the telly a few weeks later, though the TV show is just a couple of cameras filming them as they make the radio show. It's a bit self-congratulatory to be honest, and I now know it wasn't their best work, but it ignites a spark in fifteen-year-old me.

There's quite a lot of hoo-ha about it, and a book of scripts is published to cash in on this sudden interest. I buy the book and take it back to Uganda with me for the Christmas holiday.

Dad doesn't like it. Spike Milligan's humour is too lowbrow for Dad. And he doesn't like Welshmen, so that's Harry Secombe out. I'm not sure what he thinks of Peter Sellers, but Dad likes to assert his highbrow credentials by looking down on popular culture in general. As a family in Uganda we go to watch *Carry On Camping* at the cinema in Jinja. When Barbara Windsor's bra pings off during the exercise routine Dad stands and says 'right, we're off', and we file out of the cinema.

Like Graham Chapman's army officer character in *Monty Python*, Dad takes a look at the book of scripts and pronounces them 'too silly'. He says those actual words.

'They're too silly, Adrian.'

When the family returns to England several years later he won't let me watch *Monty Python* for the same reason.

'Too silly.'

Dad has an account with the Folio Society – a publishing business whose aim is to produce the most beautifully bound editions of the world's greatest literature. Every three months a new book arrives, like *The Brothers Karamazov* or *Don Quixote* or *The Odyssey*. They each come in their own decorative slip case, the spines are lavishly tooled and inlaid with gold leaf, and they look very lovely on the shelf. Whether he ever gets round to reading them all, I don't know.

My book of *Goon Show* scripts is not beautifully bound. It's printed on cheap paper and the covers are just thick cardboard. There is no intricate tooling or gold leaf, just a mess of scrawly cartoon figures scribbled all over it which hint at the anarchy within. I love it.

We don't have telly in Uganda, and we have to listen to the BBC World Service on long wave, which is basically white noise with some voices that sound like they're half a mile away shouting into a storm. We try going to the cinema again to watch *The Italian Job* but my brother Matthew gets car sick watching the initial car sequence through the Alps and we have to file out once more. So we spend a lot of time making our own entertainment. I hide myself away and read the *Goon Show* scripts over and over again. It's like the Bible. Like a mantra. I'd have become a very good evangelical Methodist if the Bible was funnier.

Seeing jokes written down is very different to hearing them being performed. Each rereading opens up another insight into how they work. How they're constructed.

I've only seen 'The Last Goon Show of All' once, and heard a few clips of the radio programme at this stage, so I don't know exactly what all the different characters sound like. To help get a feel for them I make recordings of the scripts on Dad's old Grundig reel-to-reel tape recorder. I have to do it fairly quietly because I fear Dad's ridicule should he hear me doing it, but I do *all* the voices. And they're *my* voices, not copies of Spike, Harry and Peter's voices – I invent the characters anew.

Some years later when I get to hear the original programmes of these particular scripts I'm profoundly disappointed, because the voices sound so wrong. They aren't the proper voices. They're not the funny ones *I* invented. They've spoiled it.

Cunts.

Rude word, next question

It's not that kind of book. I'm just dropping the C-bomb there to demonstrate how effective it is as a weapon of surprise. And surprise often brings laughter with it, or at least nervous excitement.

When I'm about eight or nine I'm playing round at a friend's flat, in Bahrain, and we begin to discuss a new word we've learned in the school playground – booby. It's such a funny word. And breasts are such a mystery to us.

There are other boobies, of course: there's the Booby bird, famous for its inability to land without crashing, like a Second World War bomber with its undercarriage shot away; the booby prize, given to someone who comes last by an embarrassing distance; and the booby trap, an unpleasant and possibly lethal surprise. But obviously the thrill of the word to *us* is that it pertains to a part of the female anatomy that is, in the mid-sixties, strictly off-limits.

And it's such a funny *sound*. Especially when it's repeated: booby, booby, booby, booby! The more we say it, the funnier it becomes, until we get frankly hysterical, shouting it out at the top of our voices: **booby, booby, booby, booby!** We laugh so hard we can't breathe, but every time one of us gets enough breath back we shout it out again: **booby, booby, booby, booby!** And roll around on the floor clutching our sides.

Suddenly his mother appears at the door with a face like the wrath of God. She shouts, she hits, she slaps, and she drags us to the bathroom where she washes our mouths out with soap. Actual soap. I can still taste it as I recall the memory. And I am sent home, never to darken her door again.

Ruddy Nora – this naughty word malarkey can be quite provoking, can't it?

I don't hear any conventional swear words at home as a young boy. My parents do not use 'foul language'. Throughout my childhood Dad's three favourite phrases in times of extreme provocation are: 'Hell's bells', 'Blood and sand', and 'My conscience'. Though 'Blood and stomach pills' often creeps into the charts. I hear these frequently – always delivered in extreme anguish – railing at a world that has forsaken him. The things that occasion these outbursts are generally avoidable, which makes them all the funnier to me and my sister.

For instance, he repeatedly knocks his head on the boot catch of our Citroën ID 19.

I was about to say that he does it every time he loads something into the boot, which sounds implausible, but it's not far from the truth: it genuinely happens more than 50 per cent of the time, which by the law of comedic repetition makes it hilarious. He does it so regularly that the skin on the top of his bald head has become paper thin, like some ancient fragment of the Dead Sea Scrolls. The slightest brush against the protruding catch brings fresh blood and misery. 'Hell's bells!' he shouts, long before AC/DC use it as the title of the first track on *Back in Black*, and though Dad's vocal range is an octave below Brian Johnson's, it has almost the same intensity.

Dad never invests in a conventional tool kit. In 1975 when he decides to install central heating into our three-bed semi in Bradford he cuts the copper pipes with a serrated bread knife. It's barely good enough to cut three-day-old bread, so hacking away at the metal tubes unleashes the beast within him. 'Blood and sand!' he rages, as the bread knife slips and scrapes across his knuckles.

The same year he builds a garage from a kit and uses me as his labourer. We're about halfway through when I glance at the instructions and suggest he's forgotten to install the internal bracing rods. 'My conscience!' he spits.

He forges ahead without the bracing but as we finish putting the roof on, the walls buckle slightly. 'Hell's bells and buckets of blood!' he exclaims, allowing himself the full phrase in the face of this fresh test from the universe.

He tries to fix the bracing retrospectively but the ominous bulge is always there, the walls splaying by a few more millimetres every year. I don't go into the garage much, and when I do I don't stay long.

All Dad's quasi-expletives are religious in origin. He's picked them up at the Sunbridge Road Mission, that Bible-bashing fun palace: where Hell's bells ring out to welcome sinners; where the blood of Jesus stains the sand on Calvary; and where 'My conscience' comes from Romans 9: verses 1–2, and goes on to proclaim that 'I have great heaviness and continual sorrow in my heart.'

Those Methodists really know how to enjoy themselves.

Despite his close ties to the Mission, Dad did have a sense of humour. His favourite joke was about peeling onions. He told it every time he made stew – about once a week. And every time he made curry (stew with curry powder in it) – about once a month. His joke went like this: 'The way to stop crying when you're peeling onions is to peel them underwater – but I can never hold my breath long enough . . .'

And he did have a Flanders and Swann record – *At the Drop of a Hat* – a live recording of their musical revue, recorded at the Fortune Theatre in London.

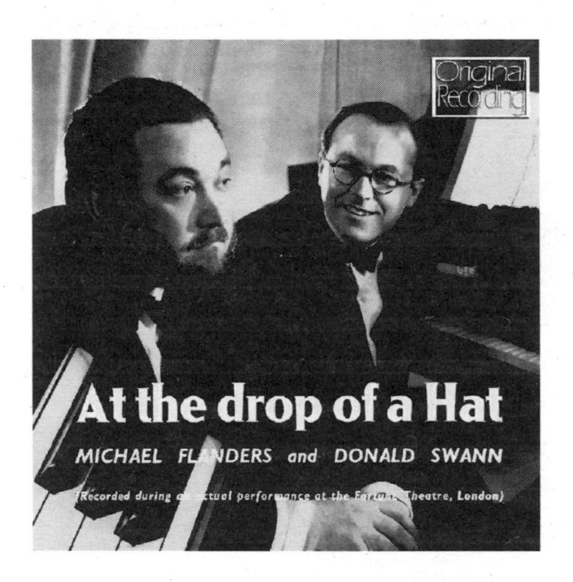

Michael Flanders and Donald Swann were a double act who wrote comedy songs; some about animals, some pure nonsense songs, and some satirical ones that poked fun at the social attitudes of the time. They were unashamedly upper middle class, which pleased my dad as this was something he aspired to, and presented themselves as the kind of jolly guests you'd love to have at a posh dinner party (if you had those sort of things, we didn't). Their songs were, and still are, hilarious.

Somewhere in the liner notes, or on the back of the album cover, it was written that the show had opened at the Fortune Theatre on 24 January 1957. My birthday! This coincidence has always filled me with a sense of personal connection, possibly unwarranted, but sincerely felt nevertheless. More magical thinking.

There were songs about a gnu (and a *gnother gnu*); about the potential moral perils in drinking Madeira; and about redesigning the interior decor of a house to such a ridiculous extent that they actually have to sleep next door, but the most exciting track to me was 'A Song of the Weather'.

It's a series of twelve couplets, one for each month, describing, in a very English way, how terrible the weather is at that particular time of year. There's ice in February, wind in March, and frost in May. The summer months are blighted with non-stop rain, and a lack of sunshine. Autumn brings mists and the occasional hail storm. And winter descends into mud, gales, fog and snow, until we get to the final, shocking line – *'Freezing wet December, then . . . bloody January again!'*

He says 'bloody'!

The B-bomb!

Michael Flanders says the word 'bloody'!

Well in fact they both join in for that last line. Flanders and Swann, both saying 'bloody'. Two grown men, wearing dinner jackets and bow ties, saying, almost shouting, the word 'bloody', and they don't get told off! Even my dad laughs. In fact *he joins in*. This in a house where swearing is most definitely not allowed. Not at all. Not a bit.

We've got one of those tiny mono record players that comes with us as we travel the world. It's like a small suitcase, and the lid detaches to become the speaker. 'Can we listen to Flanders and Swann?' my sister and I will ask, and the record will be gently removed from its sleeve, Dad will carefully wipe it with a lint-free cloth, and reverently place it on the record-stacking spindle – his actions priest-like, as if this is some kind of sacrament. He'll push the lever, the record will drop onto the turntable, and the tone arm will jerk across and fall onto the record with an alarming scratchy thump.

'A Song of the Weather' is the opening track of side two, but we can't ask to play side two first – this would be morally reprehensible, as if we were only in it for *that* word. So we have to listen to side one first. We don't mind too much, there's the song about various forms of public transport, another about record players, the gnu song, the one about interior design, another in French which we don't really understand but sit through patiently, and a song with a nonsense chorus ('*Weech-pop-oooh!*') which Michael Flanders encourages us to sing along to. And we do.

Side one is a little over twenty minutes long, and only serves to heighten the sense of expectation and excitement. When it comes to an end Dad removes the record from the deck. Everyone knows what's coming but no one's allowed to mention it. *Non Mentionare.* The ritual somehow purges him of any guilt. He wipes side two with the lint-free cloth and the procedure is repeated: onto the spindle, push the lever, drop, tone arm, jerk, scratch, thump – and it will start to play.

The song only lasts about a minute and a half, but as it plays my sister and I gradually lean in as we sing along. To make sure we hear it properly? To make sure, once more, that it's true? Who knows, but here it comes . . .

'Freezing wet December, then . . . ***bloody*** *January again!'*

Boom!

It's taken almost half an hour to get here, but we've arrived. Mum, Dad, Hilary and me, all singing together at the tops of our voices. It's as close as I ever get to a religious experience.

Rudeness. I think that was the start of it. Some might say the end of it, as well.

Once I get to boarding school I can indulge myself in rude language as much as I like. We're all new to this freedom and some of us are better at it than others. One poor soul drops a catering-sized dish of baked beans onto the floor as he carries it to one of the long dining tables.

'Bloody God!' he exclaims, getting it fabulously wrong. Everyone laughs and the poor kid will never live it down. He is doomed to have it shouted at him for the next seven years until he leaves school. Who knows, it may have even followed him on to university or the workplace. Maybe his grandchildren still taunt him.

'Bloody God!' lives on with me and Rik. I tell him the story, and thereafter, whenever we want to sound amusingly uncool, we shout 'Bloody God!'

But it's not until I get to university that the real power of swearing becomes beguilingly apparent. The Sex Pistols' appearance on the Bill Grundy *Today* show is probably only watched by a handful of people – the Grundy show is a fairly tedious programme, and Bill Grundy must have been one of the main references for Alan Partridge, and perhaps *Viz*'s Roger Mellie 'The Man on the Telly'. It plays in the London region to a teatime audience. On 1 December 1976 it goes out live, as usual, but the number of people who claim to have seen it rivals the trillion people who claim to have been at Woodstock.

I don't see it live. But it's a seminal TV moment for me.

What's that? A seminal moment of TV that you don't even see?

Keep reading, don't be so impatient.

There's no social media, no Facebook, no Instagram, no Twitter, no TikTok, the 'internet' is a thing no one much outside NASA and the US military has heard about. These are the days before home video recording. Days when we watch everything live and the only 'recording' is made in our minds. The biggest computer any of us has is a Casio calculator. Or maybe a digital watch.

We have to rely on the *actual* media. In this case the *Daily Mirror*. And I have to say they do us proud: under the banner headline '*THE FILTH AND THE FURY*' they repeat the entire interview verbatim. It's printed out like dialogue from a script except that none of the Pistols are referred to by name, it just says 'PISTOL:' or 'GRUNDY:' The swear words are all redacted but they helpfully put the first and the last letters down so that we know exactly what's been said.

Daily Mirror

BRITAIN'S BIGGEST DAILY SALE

TV's Bill Grundy in rock outrage

?!✱!

THE FILTH AND THE FURY!

THE GROUP IN THE BIG TV RUMPUS

When the air turned blue . .

A POP group shocked millions of viewers last night with the filthiest language heard on British television.

Uproar as viewers jam phones

Shocker

WHO ARE THESE PUNKS? PAGE NINE

These are words we use every day, but it's thrilling a) to imagine them being said on teatime telly, and b) to see the outrage they cause. Who would have thought that saying fuck or shit could make you front page news? This is the kind of power that intoxicates Rik and me.

Looking back at the actual TV recording now, it's surprising how tame the language is. Steve Jones is the main potty mouth, but he starts off fairly gently. Bill Grundy, who looks half-cut, letches over Siouxsie Sue, who's standing behind the band, and Steve says: 'You dirty sod. You dirty old man.'

He could be channelling *Steptoe & Son* at this point – Harold's constant rejoinder to his dad Albert is 'You dirty old man!'

'You dirty bastard,' Steve Jones continues.

When we record *The Young Ones* five years later, bastard is still a taboo word, and there is a strict limit on how often we can use it. We use purposely childish words like 'ploppy pants' and 'farty breath' instead. In fact, they work better than swear words because they're so pathetic. It's not until the 1990s and *Bottom* that we're allowed more or less as many bastards as we like.

But no sooner has Steve Jones broken the bastard duck when he tops it:

'You dirty fucker. What a fucking rotter.'

What? A fucking rotter? What kind of language is that? Rotter? ROTTER? He sounds like some ne'er-do-well from an episode of *Dixon of Dock Green*, that homely police drama that ran from 1955 to 1976, but always felt like it was set in some mythical England back in the 1940s.

The cleverest Pistol, of course, is Johnny. He's always very eloquent, a proper wordsmith, knows the power of words and knows what he's saying. His only expletive in the interview almost slips out under his breath. Bill Grundy is making some asinine point about some people preferring Mozart and Beethoven and Johnny says:

'That's just their tough shit.'

'It's what?' asks Grundy.

'Nothing, a rude word, next question.'

This is probably the rudest line in the whole show. There's no expletive, but the underlying lack of deference, the total disdain for Grundy, the feigned politeness, the obvious awareness that he knows more about what's going on than the seasoned host, and doesn't particularly care – this is the real revolution. It's so exciting.

It's the kind of anti-authoritarian sneer that Rik's character Rick in *The Young Ones* adopts, though with Rick it becomes comedic because whenever he comes up against real authority he backs down and shows his middle-class deference – he's a wannabe anarchist, not a real one.

But the Johnny Rotten sneer becomes shorthand when Rik and I write together – for jokingly expressing that feeling that you have no respect whatsoever for what the other person has just said.

'Well, that's just your tough shit,' one of us will say, doing the Johnny Rotten head wobble and eye swivel.

'It's what?' the other will reply.

'Nothing, rude word, next idea.'

On Bill Grundy's show in 1976 there are a total of seven rude words: three fuckings, one fucker, two shits and a bastard. Admittedly that's quite strong for teatime telly. But by the time Richard Curtis's generally wholesome film *Four Weddings and a Funeral* comes round in the early nineties there are ten fucks and a fuckity in the first minute.

Seven years later, in *Bottom Live 2001: An Arse Oddity*, we take swearing a little bit further.

On learning that the bar has disappeared, instead of saying: 'What the fuck happened there?' I say: 'What the fucking fuckity fuck fuck fucking fucking fuck . . . fuckity fucking fuck fuck . . . fucking fuck fuckity fucking fuck fuck fuckity fucking fucking fuck . . .' and so on, and so on, for about three minutes.

Or until people stop laughing. Each false end sounds like '. . . happened there' is finally going to land. And therein lies the potential laugh – defying expectation. It's also funny to say any word over and over again. Like 'booby, booby, booby, booby'. And then it just becomes nonsense. In the end it's just a noise.

When my kids are small I make a conscious effort not to swear in front of them. It's perhaps one of the few things I inherit from my father that I like. Though I do it for a completely different reason – I want them to enjoy their swearing when they get older. Swearing is no fun unless it's naughty. And now, as grown-ups, my girls really enjoy their Anglo-Saxon. And I too have Dad to thank for the thrill I get from a well-placed 'cunt'. If he hadn't made the rules so strict I might never have enjoyed breaking them.

Running away

School is relentless. It goes on and on and on. Perhaps because it's such a fundamentally damaging experience, the Numskulls have stashed away more memories of school than anything that follows, which is why I'm writing so much about it in this book. At the time it feels like it will never end, like a life sentence. It seems the only way to prove that I am not forgotten, that I'm not just a name and number – *A. C. Edmondson 138* – is to constantly rail against the system.

Then as a sixth former I'm actually suspended from school.

My favourite entry in the school punishment log – yes, they keep a book – is 'attempted asphyxiation of a chemistry master' (which in truth was nothing more dramatic than a tussle over a bottle of ammonia), but the official reason for my suspension is 'throwing up in the prefects' waste-paper bin'. The eagle-eyed amongst you will recall that in *Bottom Live: The Big Number Two Tour* Richie and Eddie get sentenced to 350 years in prison for 'attempted asphyxiation of the entire population of West London'.

But back to the plot.

I never make prefect, so it's not my waste-paper bin to throw up in, though I think actually hitting the bin should be a mitigating factor. But hell hath no fury like someone your own age with a prefect's badge; I'm dobbed in. My peers are always dobbing me in. On another occasion I'm eating a Caramac in a bus shelter and a passing young autocrat sees the glint of the gold foil wrapping paper and dobs me in for smoking. That's another six of the best for me. There is no camaraderie, just nastiness, it's like living with the Hitler Youth.

Throwing up in the young Gauleiters' waste-paper bin appears to be the final straw, and on a totting-up basis, which takes into account an 'ongoing laissez-faire attitude to school rules', the headmaster thinks it best to immediately suspend me pending a decision on my expulsion.

He wants to expel me! For throwing up!

How was I to know that several bottles of Newcy Brown and sniffing the dry-cleaning fluid from matron's office would make me a) never hear Lou Reed's 'Sally Can't Dance' without seeing multiple white circles round people's heads, and b) quite bilious?

Guybrows delivers the verdict in his study the next afternoon and as I walk out of his office – now wearing two pairs of pants for no reason at all – I take immediate and complete responsibility for my actions, and run away.

There are only two options really – go back to Bradford and face the wrath of my parents who have recently returned from Uganda, or run away. What's a young berserker to do?

I hitchhike the twenty-six miles to Hull and make straight for the docks. A keen reader of Tintin books as a child, my idea is to find a cargo ship, shimmy up the anchor rope under cover of darkness, stow away in the hold until the ship reaches international waters, then present myself to the captain as a willing and capable deckhand. Surely by the end of the journey he'll see what a stalwart fellow I am and offer me a permanent job on a decent wage?

I've recently read *Heart of Darkness* by Joseph Conrad too – it's set on a steamship on an unnamed river that is obviously the Congo, and follows a young man's journey into a living hell – so this dream is confused at best. But who knows where I might end up: New York, Buenos Aires, the Congo? It's the start of a new life as a working, paid adventurer!

Unfortunately, Hull docks are closed. I climb a lamppost and look over the wall into the docks; they're empty, there isn't a single ship – how can that be? It's 1974, I know it's a recession, I know we've had the Winter of Discontent and the three-day week, and that they haven't been able to bury the bodies, or clear the rubbish, or turn the electric on at night – but no ships at all? What kind of country can we be without any ships? An island with no ships? Are we stranded? It's a brutal way to learn about economics – but possibly more enlightening than doing PPE at Oxford.

Bloody oil crisis, bloody stock market crash, bloody double-digit inflation – I should be on my way to a new life in Africa or South America. I'd be the guy in the panama hat, the hard-drinking fixer who's in with everybody. I'd be adored by women, they'd find me irresistible – the ambassador's wife, the oil magnate's daughter, the local chieftain's entire harem.

I've got nothing with me except a small amount of loose change and two pairs of underpants, both of which I'm wearing. I survive the night on a bench in the bus station and the next morning spend 2p on a phone call to Wilf, the friend who helped mop up my blood after the Curved Air gig. He's a day boy, not a boarder, and lives near Goole. He has to talk quietly so his dad can't hear. He'll bunk off school. He'll come and meet me. We'll have fun. It'll be like the bit in *if . . .* when Mick and Johnny steal a motorbike and drive out to that cafe and have sex with the unnamed girl played by Christine Noonan. Except we probably won't steal a motorbike. Or have sex with Christine Noonan. And I'll just hitch to meet him.

The next morning I wake up in a chicken coop near a farmhouse just outside Beverley. I say 'wake up', but I've had no sleep at all. My brain is fried. Is that what they call them? 'Coop'? 'Hen house'? It's a small shed with chickens. Although they've all left. I can see them outside, looking in at me through the chicken wire. Is everything in their world named after them? *Chicken* wire, *hen* house, *egg* box. Anyway, they look confused. Is that confusion? No, it's not. It's . . . opprobrium. They're judging me. Chickens! Dumb chickens. Dumb, thick chickens. Judging me. Cocking their heads on one side. Tutting. Glaring at me with their beady, little, black eyes. It's reproach. They think I'm a disgrace. The really big one, the one with the buff-coloured feathers all puffed up behind her, she could be my mum. That's the look my mum gives me.

It stinks in here, but it doesn't stink of animal shit. You'd think it would, but no, it's ammonia. That's what I can smell. That's what chicken shit smells like. It's the asphyxiating stuff the chemistry master sprays around the classroom at the end of every lesson. He's a dick. He needs someone to punch his lights out and I might be that person. If I ever go back. Which I won't. How does he get off on that? Spraying it around. It must catch his throat like it does ours. Must make his eyes water. Make him gasp for breath. Like chemical warfare. What a dick.

I can smell fire too. Old fire. Old smoke. Smoky clothes. From when Wilf and I set fire to that embankment. That was a laugh. Didn't even mean to do it. Just lying in the grass on the embankment. Wilf's Swiss army knife with the magnifying-glass attachment. A few tufts of dry, dead grass. Bit of smoke. Bit of flame. Hard to see it in the bright sunshine. Is it hot? Yes, it's just burnt my hand. Then, woof! Like it had petrol on it. It spread so fast. Dried-up, wilted bracken and brambles. Dead leaves. Burning so hard. Tried to put it out at first but quickly gave up and just laughed at it. Had to move back. Whole embankment up in flames. Massive clouds of smoke billowing up around us. And a train coming! A train! But it went straight through. It was all right. Through the smoke. Worried faces at the windows. Wilf and me pissing ourselves laughing. Better run anyway. So we ran. We could hear the sirens in the distance. Police or Fire? Could have been both. We didn't stop to find out. Ran down the bridle path. Stinking of smoke. Wilf went home.

I tell you what I like in here. It's the straw. Straw or hay? I don't know. I don't know the difference. But I like it, whatever it is. It must have been fresh when I came in. It's springy. A bit spiky, but really comforting. Smells like newly mown grass. So probably hay.

It was a choice to come in here last night. There were options.

I could have gone to Wilf's house. But I'd have had to deal with his dad. His dad with the tattoos. The tattoos he's tried to cut out of his own arm with a razor. Big scarred arms. He doesn't like them. 'Never get tattoos.' That's about the only thing he's ever said to me. Merchant navy. Has he been to New York? Buenos Aires? Up the Congo? I bet he knows how to kill a man. Or a boy.

The buses had stopped but I could have walked back to school. Could I? Ten miles? Got to be ten miles. Maybe fifteen. At that time of night? Could have hitched. At that time of night? Dangerous. Seventeen-year-old boy. Lot of Jimmy Saviles about. Hitching. Late at night. Could have been that pervy canoeist.

We've all heard things. Hitchhikers getting murdered on the news. What type of person would open their car door at that time of night? To a teenager smelling of booze and smoke.

Besides which . . . I've been gone for two nights. Why give up now? I need to get further away. Not go back. Going back is giving up. Going back is losing. No one cares about me anyway. I should get to Scarborough. There's work on building sites there. I've seen stories in the papers. 'Super Hod'. He's just a bloke that carries bricks. That's all he does. The papers are full of stories about him – a builder's labourer who can deliver bricks in his hod faster than anyone else. He's earning twenty grand a year. More than Ted Heath, the prime minister. He's got gold taps in his bathroom and a Rolls-Royce with the number plate 'HOD 1'.

I can carry bricks.

It's Nichola's dad's chicken coop. Nichola could have been more obliging. She's not my girlfriend, I know that, but I'm a man on the run – she could have found that appealing. We've snogged before. I waited in the phone box on the village green. Very cold. Smelled of piss. The phone box, not me. But maybe me as well. Kept ringing her. Eventually she came out to see me – she wouldn't take me back to the house. We snogged, but not for long. 'You stink of smoke,' she said. She went back home and I followed and stood near the gate, she could see me and kept shooing me away silently through the window. She came out and spoke to me. 'Dad'll call the police if he sees you.' No snog this time. Quite brusque. Quite rude. Quite right.

But I'm stuck. I'm properly stuck. I've got nowhere to go and nothing to get there with. It's starting to rain. I look for somewhere to sleep. I find the chicken coop. Hen house. Whatever it is. Nice new straw. Or hay. Very tired. Fitful sleep. Stinks of ammonia. It's like sleeping with the chemistry master.

• • •

Dawn breaks and a plan forms. I spend the last of my money on the first bus back towards Pocklington. *Towards!* I haven't given up yet.

There's a boy called Andy, a day boy, he's got his hair to stand up like Andy Mackay's from Roxy Music, he lives in a village not far from the school. It's not New York, it's not Buenos Aires, it's not the Congo, it's Bishop Burton. But I happen to know that his parents are away for the week, because he was planning a party . . . you can possibly see where this is heading. And yes, it does go that way.

To be fair, Andy is slightly reluctant, it's not like we're best friends or anything – we know each other, but only as classmates. But I stink of ammonia and smoke and possibly look slightly unhinged, possibly volatile, possibly berserk, and I eventually persuade him to let me stay in his house, on my own, while he toddles off to school. This is the closest I ever get to being Malcolm McDowell in *if . . .*

I settle down with a cup of tea and a packet of his mum's ginger nuts and switch on the TV – *Watch with Mother*, *Pebble Mill at One*, *Crown Court* – it's not the most exciting TV schedule but it's made more delicious by knowing that I should be at school. I drift in and out of sleep. Andy interrupts an episode of *Time Tunnel* when he comes home. He's a bit flustered. Apparently they've got the police out looking for me. The police!

'Is it about the fire?'

'What fire?' he asks, looking round anxiously at the house.

'So it's just about running away?'

'It's about you going missing,' he says. 'They don't know where you are.'

I think Andy wants to help me, he's a nice bloke, but he doesn't want to get into proper trouble. He doesn't know me well enough for that. Fair enough.

Money can't buy you love, but with no money at all, you're

Hilary, Dad, me and Mum sporting the four hairstyles available in Bradford in 1958.

Me, Dad and Mum in Nicosia, 1958. Dad very pleased with his gun. Is that lanyard supposed to hang there? Is it safe?

Wolseley Barracks, Cyprus, 1959. The house that became known as 'the Cockroach House'.

And, lo, the angel of the Lord came upon them . . .

Giving the girl's name thing a good testing. Dad is in the background washing his beloved car – the boot catch of which will become his nemesis.

Onward, Christian soldiers! Me out front, naturally, then (*left to right*) Grandma Ed, Mum, Hilary and Grandad Ed. Bolton Abbey, 1961.

Dad and me ready for Matthew's christening, channelling Flanders and Swann.

On the roof of the flat in Bahrain, 1965.
Gun, sword and hat – all the tools.

A young berserker in training.

Off to Hutton Junior High, 1968. With these shorts, these glasses and this hairdo, no one will dare say I've got a girl's name.

Pocklington. This young groover is keen to break into the hard/cool set, and is prepared to stand in a hedge until it happens.

Me and Grandma Sturgeon. Looks like she's just won at canasta. Again.

Tsavo National Park, Kenya, 1972. Six of us packed into a Renault 4. Lions in the long grass wondering if they need one of those special keys you get with a tin of corned beef.

With Hilary in Uganda, 1972. I'm thinking about the *Goon Show* scripts I have in my suitcase.

Me (*far right*) at school, playing The Logician in *Rhinoceros* and doing a fairly reasonable impression of Jacques Tati.

Pocklington, 1975. *Left to right:* the homemade bass cab, Iain, then me playing the old egg slicer. I'm not singing – I'm crying out in pain.

Peace of Thorn being majestic. Ian on drums, Iain's hand to the right, me front and centre, in my *Melody Maker* clothes and national health specs, hoping my fingers won't bleed too much. I know it's a bit blurred but, frankly, so were we.

Pocklington School Smoking XI 1974/75.

Dave, who took over on bass (*middle row, first from left*).
Andy, whose house I stayed in when I ran away (*back row, first from left*).
Me (*middle row, third from left*).
Iain, guitar hero and the boy who said 'Nah' (*front row, second from left*).
Bike shed on the right.

stuffed. I ring Bradford, reversing the charges; I ring my parents, and confess.

A couple of hours later I'm in the car with Dad on the way back to Bradford. He's absolutely furious. So furious he can't speak. He's literally quivering with rage – I can feel the vibrations through the cheap metalwork of the modest family saloon we're travelling in. My dad was never good at heart-to-hearts, and in this instance I'm glad of it, because for the first thirty minutes he doesn't say a word. And I offer nothing in return.

Finally, as we negotiate the interminable roadworks on the still incomplete York bypass, he breaks the silence. He's had the journey over to consider his tactics, but his opening gambit, delivered with an air of heartbreaking desperation, is:

'Adrian, what are you going to *do* with your life?'

I think for a while before I answer. It occurs to me that I'm in such trouble already that I might as well go for broke.

'I want to be an actor,' I say.

This is true. It's all I've ever thought of being since I first played Angel Gabriel in the school nativity. Besides 'rock star'. But actor seems more likely at this stage. After all I'm halfway through rehearsals for the school production of *Hamlet* – and I'm playing Hamlet!

The Nativity is where it started. Oh yes, I owe it all to our Lord Jesus Christ. But not the angry one from the Mission – the nice middle-class one from the Church of England. Thora Hird's one. The one without the fire and brimstone. The one with the jolly story about the innkeeper and the donkey, and Mary and Joseph going to pay their taxes, in the school assembly hall.

In the early sixties, thanks to Dad's constant flitting about, I go to four different primary schools in successive years. At each of these, because of the white hair of my early childhood, I'm chosen to play the Angel Gabriel in the Nativity.

It's a wonder schools do the Nativity every year because it's not particularly kid friendly, acting wise. Mary and Joseph are on a hiding to nothing – kids don't understand conception yet, let alone the immaculate kind. The wise men have too many props. The shepherds have to divvy their lines up amongst the three of them, though I've seen a production with fourteen. So the only real meat is in the inn keeper, or, if you're particularly adept at physical comedy, the donkey. The Angel Gabriel is usually reserved for the shy child who stands on a stool at the back and is gently guided through it by the 'kind' teacher.

But the white hair gets me the job. I'm the one that looks different, other-worldly – I look like an angel. And after doing it at two schools in a row I start to get my tongue round the King James dialogue, which is the standard text at the time: '*Hail, thou that art highly favoured, the Lord is with thee: blessed art thou among women. Fear not, Mary: for thou hast found favour with God.*'

I've no idea what it all means, even now, but I can make it sound like I do – which is what acting is really about. It's all a con trick.

Between the second and third schools my mum, taking a punt, holds onto the wings during the move and slips them under the rug to keep them flat. She feels a bit guilty about not making new wings and adds some extra bits of tinsel to make up for it – so they grow incrementally into something pretty spectacular.

And by the end of my fourth outing in the role, what with the RuPaul wings, the diction, and the crystal-clear faking of the text: most of the audience are talking only about the Angel Gabriel – his stage presence, how confident he is, and how they're glad to see him feature in the annunciation to the shepherds, a scene normally reserved for a lesser, second angel – because 'they just want to see him again'. 'It's as if a professional actor had come on.'

Ah, the smell of the crowd, the roar of the greasepaint. That's when I get the acting bug. Except it's more of a disease than a bug, and there's no known cure.

Of course my parents want me to be a lawyer, or a doctor, or at the very least an accountant. Something respectable. Something middle-class. Something that might get me into some august institution like the Rotary Club. And when your parents have such 'high' hopes for you, the line of least friction is to mumble along with their narrative, but secretly do something completely different.

One virtue of being packed off to boarding school is that our lives separate when I'm twelve, and from that point on they don't have the slightest clue as to what's really going on in my life. Not only am I in every school production: Brecht's *The Caucasian Chalk Circle*, Ionesco's *Rhinoceros*, Shakespeare's *The Taming of the Shrew* and *Hamlet*, Ted Hughes's *The Tiger's Bones*, but I'm also a stalwart of the annual House Arts Festivals, when each house offers up a play. I become producer, director and star; I put on productions of Alfred Jarry's *Ubu Roi*, Boris Vian's *The General's Tea Party*, R. C. Sherriff's *Journey's End*, and endless short pieces by Harold Pinter, N. F. Simpson, Tom Stoppard and Samuel Beckett. My friend Rob and I do a two-man version of *Waiting for Godot* on the banks of the Chellow Dene Reservoir in Bradford.

The programme from the production of *Journey's End* features my name many more times than modesty allows: I produce, direct, and star, I paint the scenery, record the sound effects, and I even write an excruciatingly pompous introduction. Plays are definitely my thing. I mean, come on – I'm playing Hamlet!

Although, hang on, I've been suspended, I'm not playing Hamlet any more, am I?

Oh, no, oh, that's a bit of a blow. Wonder what they'll do? They can't recast at such a late stage, can they? There's only a couple of weeks to go . . .

I haven't been paying attention to my dad's response, but become aware that he's pulling off into a lay-by. He stops the car, switches off the engine, and puts his head in his hands. After an eternity of slowly rocking backwards and forwards he raises his head and speaks into the car roof.

'Adrian, you'll never get a mortgage!'

I don't really blame Dad for being how he was. He was ten when the war started, so he'd spent all his formative years, up to the age of twenty-five, on rationing. Money was never easy when he was young. People were careful. Finances were precarious. And strangely, being in hock to some bank for twenty-five to thirty years had become the accepted 'safe' way to do things. A badge of prudence and respectability. 'They must be good people – they owe thousands of pounds to the bank.'

The school suspension doesn't last long. I'm not the only one to notice that doing *Hamlet* without Hamlet is going to be difficult. I'm invited back a few days later. In a bizarre meeting with Guybrows and my dad I'm made to promise that I will join the army when I finish school, because this will make a man of me. The army will be able to channel my 'high spirits' into an efficient fighting machine.

I don't join the army, I become an actor, and a fairly successful one too – at least financially. You can't argue with that, critics. By my late twenties I have a large and refreshingly expensive mortgage – interest rates peak at 16 per cent at one point. But I have spare cash too. Enough to give my parents a sizeable chunk to help them buy a bungalow for their retirement.

We never mention the moment in the car. But to be fair we never mention *anything*.

Part 4

International rock god

A musical background

This could have been my autobiography, the one about me as a rock star.

I did have one number one hit in 1984 – 'Living Doll' with Cliff Richard and The Young Ones. And in 1988 my own composition 'Cashing in on Christmas' with Bad News – the spoof metal band I create as a strand for *The Comic Strip Presents . . .* – stalled just outside the official top forty.

If . . .

There are many forks in the road and sometimes I feel I've blithely turned left when I could just as easily have turned right. And sometimes I feel like I crashed into the signpost.

The first instrument I'm ever given to play, at the age of seven, is a big bass drum at Swain House Junior School in Bradford. It sits rather precariously on a fold-up stool and I stand beside it and bang out the first beat in every bar.

The rest of the class are playing recorders, a little group of three are playing new-fangled melodicas, there's someone on triangle, and one child is gamely blowing into a harmonica. Although he's not always blowing, I can see his sheet music – under each note he has written either *suck* or *blow*.

Our repertoire is not large. We play the theme from *Z-Cars*, 'The Blaydon Races' and 'Onward Christian Soldiers'.

It's an inauspicious start to my musical career. To be frank it stalls completely after our first end of year concert – because Dad drags us all off to Bahrain and some other kid gets the big drum.

It doesn't resume until I return from Bahrain a couple of years later and spend a year at Hutton Junior High in Bradford where they have a brass band (this is Yorkshire). The school has a brilliant scheme to encourage potential new members of the band: they own all the instruments and will happily lend them to anyone who's interested. I'm allowed to choose one and learn how to play it. I can even take it home.

I don't know why I choose the euphonium. Maybe it was chosen for me. Maybe there's a euphonium pusher at the school? Taking its name from the Greek *euphōnos* 'having a pleasing sound,' it seems someone made a mistake, unless they find the sound of raspberries being blown down a long fat tunnel pleasing. It's also enormous, it weighs a ton, and as I live just inside the 1.5-mile limit before a free bus pass kicks in, I have to lug it the 1.4 miles to school and back on foot. After a week I swap it for a cornet, the smallest instrument in the band.

Being smaller doesn't make it any easier to play. I can only dream of joining the rest of the school band to play 'Land of Hope and Glory', 'Jerusalem' and 'The British Grenadiers'. I get stuck on book one, page one. I can't read music, I can't make my mouth into the right shape, and the sounds come out like high-pitched farts. It's all very unsatisfying. If occasionally amusing.

To make things harder, Dad banishes me to the garage because he can't stand the 'noise'. I tell him it's music, but even I don't believe me. It's the middle of winter, the garage is unheated, my fingers are too cold to operate the valves, and I give up.

It's odd that my dad doesn't encourage me more. I'd have thought he'd want me to play an instrument. Perhaps he regards brass bands as inferior.

Sir Thomas Beecham, the renowned conductor, once said; 'Brass bands are all very well in their place – outdoors and several miles away.' So apart from conducting four of the leading orchestras of the day he was also a pompous oaf. But perhaps my dad agrees with him. Perhaps Dad is a pompous oaf too.

Rumour has it that Mum could play the piano, but we don't have one, so I never hear her play.

No, that's not quite true, I do hear her play once, but only for precisely thirty seconds. She's visiting my house in the 1990s. My house by then is full of musical instruments: several guitars, ukuleles, penny whistles, recorders, an autoharp, harmonicas, a full drum kit, and . . . a piano. She again makes the boast that she can play the piano.

'Go on then,' I say.

'Oh no,' she replies.

'Then I simply don't believe you,' I say, rather pointedly.

She looks me in the eye then suddenly sits at the piano and starts pumping out something like 'Roll out the Barrel'. She could be one of those characters in a war film, cheering up the pilots in a good old-fashioned pub before they fly out the next day on an obvious suicide mission. Her left hand is brilliant, jumping up and down the keyboard thumping out a bass line, and her right hand bashes out the tune mixed with the occasional passing chord. It could be Winifred Atwell, or Russ Conway – I'm trying to decide which when she abruptly stops playing, and stands up.

'That's enough of that,' she says, closing the lid.

And I never hear her play again.

Thirty seconds. That's all I ever got from her. She won't even talk about it. Who taught her? Where and when did she play? For how long? Why did she stop? The brief snippet sounds like she enjoyed a really good knees up, but I never see that in her, I've never seen her dance.

I'm beginning to wonder if I dance like a lunatic because I'm making up for all the dancing my parents never did.

And why didn't *she* encourage me to play an instrument? Why didn't either of them encourage me to play an instrument. I'm not bragging but I have what's called a 'good ear' for music, I'm self-taught on every instrument I play, but think how good I might have been if I'd ever had lessons! If someone had taught me to read music!

And it's not that they don't like music, it's just that Dad sees classical music as a mark of civilization, a mark of class, as something more or less unattainable – this is Bradford, we know our place – and he makes music into an intellectual chore. As a child I'm forced to endure an hour of 'high culture' every Sunday morning. Dad believes exposure to this sort of thing will increase my IQ. Dad is very keen on IQ.

The seatbelts in our car are peculiarly complicated and when someone new gets into the passenger seat he counts back from 160 slowly in tens – once the newbie has managed to fasten the belt Dad stops counting and is fairly confident that the number he has reached is that person's IQ.

Our house is full of popular IQ test books. I am forever deciding whether a box with a triangle, a circle and a parallelogram in it is the mirror image of another box with a parallelogram, a circle and a triangle in it. These tests measure cognitive ability; they have more to do with the way people learn and solve problems than with actual knowledge. They don't measure creativity, or imagination, or emotional intelligence. Or thinking outside the box.

To improve my ability to recognize what comes next in a sequence of geometric shapes, every Sunday we have to sit and play chess whilst listening to classical music for at least an hour. Some of which is probably conducted by the musical snob Sir Thomas Beecham.

Dad's classical record collection is fairly small, about fifteen records: we have a few Beethoven symphonies, some Mozart, Vivaldi's *Four Seasons*, Mendelssohn's *Fingal's Cave*, Handel's *Arrival of the Queen of Sheba*, and, slightly out of step with the rest of the collection, Bizet's *Carmen*.

The indoctrination works at first. In 1964, aged seven, I'm in the back of the car as Uncle Douglas takes me, Hilary and my cousins, Janet and Liz, on a trip to see the lights get switched on in Blackpool. Janet and Liz are in their early teens and are as cool as fuck.

Janet and Liz start banging on about The Beatles. They are obsessed and know the words to every song. They ask Hilary who she likes. Hilary is a couple of years younger and a little out of step in the coolness stakes because we've been in Cyprus for the last six years – not only are we the country mice, we are mice from a different country altogether – but she professes to like Nana Mouskouri, the Greek chanteuse who was a hit in the recent Eurovision Song Contest. And she gets away with it.

Janet and Liz then turn to me and ask me who I like. Perhaps they're expecting me to say some child-friendly act like Dave Dee, Dozy, Beaky, Mick & Tich, or The Seekers, or Freddie & The Dreamers, but I say:

'Beethoven.'

They laugh hysterically for the rest of the journey there.

They laugh hysterically for the whole journey back. Even Uncle Douglas is laughing – the big wheezy laugh of a sixty-a-day man. He has tears rolling down his cheeks.

Janet and Liz bring it up ever after, and indeed they will *still* bring it up at any opportunity. It is one of the great family jokes.

• • •

One of my favourite episodes of *Bottom* is 'Bottom Culture', the one where Richie and Eddie are without a telly and decide to make a virtue of the situation by having an evening of 'culture'. It is based directly on those Sunday mornings with Dad.

Richie and Eddie sit down to play chess, though they only have five regular pieces and make up the rest with various stand-ins, including a bottle of brown sauce, a small cactus with a paper crown on it, and sixteen frozen prawns. And just as they are about to start playing Richie pipes up:

> *Richie*: Wait! I know what we need! Music! Of course! What shall we have? Ohhh, James Last, Burt Bacharatch (*mispronounced on purpose*). No – Molière! Molière! He could bash out a tune or two! (*He hums the main theme from Vivaldi's 'Spring'.*) Tum tum tiddly tum tum tum tum, tum (*he forgets the repeated refrain*) . . . And the other twiddly bits. He was Scottish, you know.
> *Eddie*: Who? Vivaldi?
> *Richie*: I'm talking about composers! It's football, football, football with you!

It gets big laughs as people recognize someone desperately trying to seem cultured whilst obviously not having a clue.

I'm sure Dad isn't clueless, but his view of classical composers is that they're all gentlemen of tried and tested virtue. Paragons. They are the living embodiment of those little busts that people have on their mantelpieces – upright, noble, brim-full of integrity, and always staring into the middle distance in an important sort of way. Despite all having long hair, Dad believes they are people who would have loathed electric guitars and the long-haired degenerates he's caught glimpses of on *Top of the Pops*.

I wonder if Dad knew that Vivaldi, aged forty-eight, took up with a seventeen-year-old soprano. That Jimi Hendrix lived in the same apartment that Handel once occupied on Brook Street, in London. That Mozart's music was so revolutionary at the time that it upset people exactly like him. And I'm not sure how good Dad's French is or whether the orchestral instrumentation papers over the subject matter, and makes him think that it's all very wholesome and intellectual as we hum along to *Carmen*, but does he know it's about cigarettes, smuggling, sex and violence? I doubt it.

On a day trip to Haworth, Dad refuses an ice cream from the Mr Whippy van because the bloke behind the counter has nicotine stains on his fingers. It must be hard being right all the time.

To love and be loved in return

Dad's record collection is tempered by what I realize now are some of my mum's choices. They're very different to my dad's. We spend so long on army bases in foreign countries that I wonder if Mum thought of herself as an 'army wife' or an 'officer's wife', with its connotations of duty and subservience – someone who suppresses their own desires in order not to rock the boat. Did she do what she was told? Did he ask her to stop playing 'Roll Out the Barrel' on the piano?

Many years later, after Dad has died, I pick her up from King's Cross station and she says: 'Have you noticed anything different?'

I think she's suggesting she's had her hair done and fumble for a compliment.

'No,' she says. 'I'm wearing trousers. Your dad didn't like me to wear trousers.'

So maybe this slim collection of pop records is her small rebellion. They're all singles, and I've always thought of singles as more ephemeral and throwaway, which makes them a bit more dangerous than albums.

There's 'Stranger on the Shore' by Acker Bilk. I've only just learned that Acker's tune 'Jenny' was originally written as a love letter to his newborn daughter but was renamed 'Stranger on the Shore' when it was used as the theme tune for a TV programme of the same name. It was subsequently released as a single under this new name and reached number two in the charts. I loved it then but I love it even more now; it sounds very different knowing that it was written out of love for a daughter rather than sadness, which the title 'Stranger on the Shore' suggests.

'Downtown' by Petula Clark. An absolute banger of a song. Still as alive today as it was in 1964. I have no idea where this mythical downtown is – this throbbing citadel of lights and excitement – it certainly isn't in Bradford, or Limassol in Cyprus, or Manama in Bahrain, or Jinja in Uganda, or Pocklington. The song has such a yearning quality to it, even Petula sounds like she's never actually been there, and I wonder if my mum ever hankered for a little more excitement in her life. That's certainly the meaning it has when Rik, Robbie Coltrane and I sing it in *Kevin Turvey: The Man Behind the Green Door.*

If Dad had ever learned that Jimmy Page was one of the session players on Petula's recording I wonder if he might have banned it. On the one occasion I play *Led Zep IV* on the family record player whilst they're out for the evening, I forget to tidy it away and come down the next morning to find Dad has left a note on the album: 'Yes Adrian, but what does it all *MEAN*?'

'Sucu Sucu' by Nina & Frederik. Long before the UK joins the Common Market, and despite having European accents and being obvious foreigners, Nina & Frederik have their own show on British telly in the early sixties. 'Sucu Sucu' is one of their most popular singles – a song written by a Bolivian, performed by a Dutch/Danish singing combo, to a vaguely calypso rhythm, with Frederik affecting a faintly Caribbean accent. This is 'easy listening' back in the early sixties. Today's cancel culture would have a field day and it would probably be reclassified as 'hard listening'.

'Distant Drums' by Jim Reeves. This is number one in the charts for five weeks in 1966, beating off competition from Small Faces, The Who, The Beatles and The Rolling Stones, so I'm now wondering if Dad has a hand in buying it. Though its lyrics – about a man wanting to get married before going off to fight in a distant war – are often interpreted as being about Vietnam, so perhaps not. On another note, I love that as Jim sings, 'I hear the sound of bugles blow' we then hear a bugle blow – as a child I wait for that moment and mime playing the bugle – and the cheesiness of it still makes me laugh today.

'Mary's Boy Child' by Harry Belafonte. Christmas isn't Christmas until Harry sings.

Then there's an EP with a selection of Nat King Cole songs: 'Mona Lisa', 'Unforgettable' and 'Nature Boy'. I've just listened to them all again and they're simply spellbinding. This may be partly nostalgia – what other art form can transport you to another time and place so effortlessly? But listening as objectively as I can it seems to me they are masterpieces. What a voice – rich, effortless, full of expression.

The biggest surprise is the emotional heft of these songs, which seems at odds with my parents' diffidence on that front. There's a line in 'Nature Boy' that goes, '*The greatest thing you'll ever learn, is just to love, and be loved in return.*' And I wonder what my parents ever thought about that. Did it connect? Did this mean something in particular to Mum? Or did it just wash over them – a series of sounds that simply rhymed?

My Dad was unapproachable on this front.

At the age of sixteen he catches me as I'm leaving the house. He obviously wants to talk to me about something, and he doesn't want Mum or the rest of the family to hear him.

'I need to have a word with you,' he says. And then says nothing. We stand awkwardly outside the back door.

'What about?' I ask.

His mouth tries to form some words but they won't come. A minute passes. I catch a glimpse of Mum looking anxiously out of the kitchen window and then disappearing rather quickly, and then I twig: he's obviously been sent out to give me the birds and bees talk. A bit late. I mean, I'm still a virgin but it's not for *want of trying*. Another aeon goes by.

'Adrian,' he ventures at last. 'Adrian . . .' His face contorts with the effort and the embarrassment of it all. '. . . when I was a young lad of your age . . .'

'Yes?'

'. . . when I was a young lad of your age . . . I think I spent too much time on my bicycle,' he says, then abruptly gives up and dives back into the house.

Perhaps if we'd sat down on Sunday mornings and listened to 'Nature Boy' whilst playing chess he might have been able to allude casually to the lyrics whilst keeping his eyes fixed firmly on my Sicilian Defence, and start a conversation that way.

Researching 'Nature Boy', I discover it was written by eden ahbez, an early Californian hippy with a beard and sandals and white robes, who hated capital letters but incongruously lived rough under one of the capital 'L's of the Hollywood sign in LA. What if Dad had known that? It doesn't seem to matter how clean something is on the surface; there's always something else underneath. Perhaps the same is true of my parents?

A single in the collection that is definitely Dad's is 'If I Was a Rich Man' from *Fiddler on the Roof*, sung by Topol. Topol was a name Rik and I discussed when we came up with Eddie Monsoon, not as a potential name, we just thought it was brilliant to have a single short name – think how easy signing autographs would be.

Dad sings along with Topol on 'If I Was a Rich Man'. He knows every word, and joins in with such conviction on the last couplet: '*Would it spoil some vast eternal plan, if I were a wealthy man?*' It seems extraordinary to me that Dad should be so attracted to this song full of Yiddish expressions, and the cadences and ornamentation of klezmer music. It's at such odds with his rather Teutonic classical collection.

I think what grabs him is the subject matter. He relates completely to Tevye's desire to lift himself out of the struggle of his daily life into one of idleness and luxury.

It's fair to say that once his adventures to foreign postings come to an end Dad becomes completely disillusioned with teaching. He struggles to find a job when he comes back from Uganda. Perhaps newer candidates have better qualifications – degrees compared to Dad's simple Certificate in Education. He never seems happy at any of the schools where he teaches, some boy even throws a knife at him from the back of the classroom at Belle Vue, and he eventually ends up at Drummond Middle School, which becomes mired in controversy when the headmaster Ray Honeyford writes articles in the *Times Educational Supplement* about how difficult it is to assimilate children who don't speak English.

The anti-immigration lobby take it up as a cause célèbre, the tabloid press get involved, and all nuance goes out of the window. There are protests outside the school, Honeyford gets sacked by the Mayor of Bradford then reinstated by the High Court, and Dad gets an ulcer. And even more pissed off. Blood and stomach pills! Quite literally.

For the last few years of his working life my abiding memory of Dad is of him spreading his paperwork out on the dining room table every evening. This isn't marking homework or doing lesson plans, or anything to do with school, he's trying to work out how early he can retire.

He's worked for so many institutions that he has various bits of pension entitlement from many different sources, and little bits of money squirrelled away, some of it in a bank in Jersey, which sounds dodgy. Some of it is obviously tied to interest rates, and in these days before computer spreadsheets, each evening he looks up the indices in the newspaper, adjusts various predictions, factors in inflation, dreams up possible variables, considers future interest rates, looks at his bank balance, tots it all up, and comes up with an *exact date*. Every day.

He does eventually succeed in retiring a few years shy of his sixty-fifth birthday, but I'd say he'd already put in the extra shifts by working on his pension schemes every night throughout his fifties. It's swings and roundabouts.

While he's working on his pensions he can hear Mum listening to 'Eye Level' by the Simon Park Orchestra – the theme music to *Van der Valk*, a TV detective show with Barry Foster as yet another cynical if brilliantly intuitive detective. I bet the lovely Barry Foster doesn't spend every night working out his pension.

Val Doonican – comic nexus

Another record we have, an album, is *The World of Val Doonican* by Val Doonican. World? It's two top ten hits, three comedy numbers and some fillers, but looking into it I find it's been a major influence on my life.

And what is it with my parents buying music from people who have TV shows? Val kicks off on the telly in the early sixties and is a fixture of Saturday nights for twenty years, with audiences that peak at 19 million. Given that Ant & Dec's *Saturday Night Takeaway* only gets a peak of 8 million, and bearing in mind that the population was 20 per cent smaller in the sixties, you can see how staggeringly popular he was.

The World of Val Doonican features his hits: 'Walk Tall' and 'Elusive Butterfly', and various other middle-of-the-road tunes that meant very little to me back then and mean even less to me now, but it also contains three comedy songs that I still sing to myself to this day: 'Delaney's Donkey', 'O'Rafferty's Motor Car' and 'Paddy McGinty's Goat'. Two of which mention dynamite, and one in which he sings light-heartedly about suicide.

Digging further into these songs, I discover that they have a deeper resonance with me than simply enjoying them at the time.

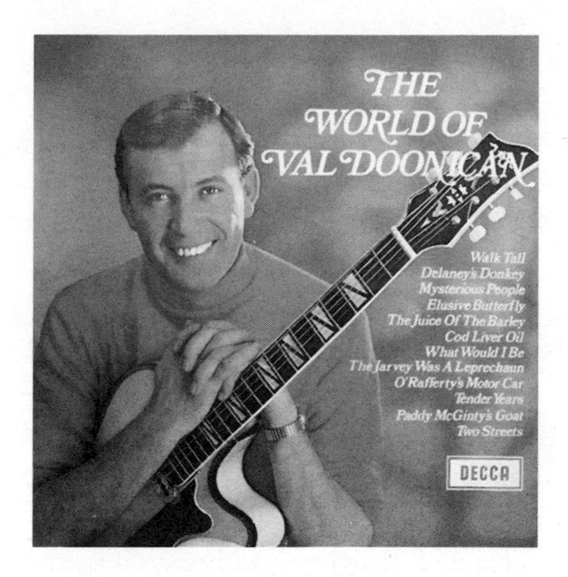

'Delaney's Donkey' is an old-fashioned comedy song written by William Hargreaves in 1916. Hargreaves wrote a lot of music hall songs. Bizarrely, he was married to a woman who was a male impersonator, for whom he wrote 'Burlington Bertie from Bow' – a song I sing regularly to my grandson Bertie. I'm also married to an occasional male impersonator – one of the two fat sexist men in *French & Saunders*, and Liam Neeson in their *Star Wars* spoof 'The Phantom Millennium'.

'O'Rafferty's Motor Car' was written by Tommie Connor, who also wrote 'Mickey's Son and Daughter', a song covered by the Bonzo Dog Doo-Dah Band, one of the tracks on their seminal album – the album that brought Rik and me together – *Gorilla*.

'Paddy McGinty's Goat' is another music hall number. A 'paddy' song – based on the premise that Irish men are thick – written, of course, by two Englishmen, R. P. Weston and Bert Lee. They wrote more than 300 songs in around twenty years, including 'Good-bye-ee', the song associated with people leaving for the trenches in the First World War, which must have been an influence on the Peter Cook and Dudley Moore song of the same name. They both wrote words and music, alternating between the two, but according to Bert: 'Bob has the brains. I put the laughs in.' I think this is generally the way Rik and I operate in the writing room, with me at the keyboard thinking more structurally and Rik pacing up and down behind, firing off absurdities. I recognize the dynamic. They also wrote 'Knees up Mother Brown', and I wonder if Mum ever played it on the piano.

Uncle Douglas is always good for a ten-bob note at Christmas. 'But that's for your birthday as well, mind,' he always says – ah, the curse of a January birthday.

Ten bob in the mid-sixties would buy you roughly seventeen pints of milk, today it wouldn't buy one. But I don't spend it on milk, instead I go into Boots on The Broadway in the middle of Bradford, clutching my brown bit of folding money – the fact that it's a note makes it feel so much more valuable.

Upstairs they have a fairly limited selection of records but I know they've got the one I want because I saw it there on the rack before Christmas. It's an EP by Val Doonican called

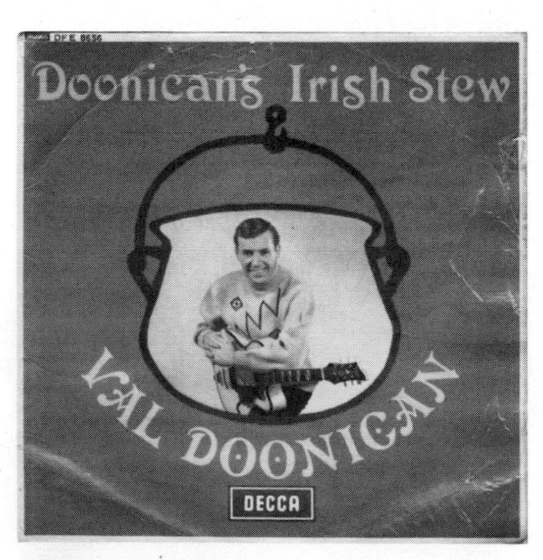

Doonican's Irish Stew. It's got a picture of Val Doonican holding his guitar but the photo is *inside* a graphic of a stewing pot – one of those big ones you hang by its handle over an open fire – this is how I can tell it's funny. It's got 'O'Rafferty's Motor Car' on it, which we already have on the album, but I haven't heard of the other three tracks, and judging by the cover they must be *hilarious*. I spend my Christmas money, get it home and . . . it's a huge disappointment. The other three tracks are mushy middle-of-the-road songs. I've been robbed. I can't take it back because you're not allowed to take records back just because you think they're a bit shit. I've wasted ten bob – the biggest monetary haul of the year.

Are you ready to rock?

As first experiences go in buying records it's not the best, and sadly the pattern is repeated when I reach secondary school and buy my first LP. I go into the newsagents in Market Place in Pocklington. Upstairs they have a fairly comprehensive selection of today's poptastic releases.

It's 1971, I'm fourteen, and it's time I bought my own proper record. I need a rock record, not a novelty one – I've left Val Doonican at home – not only because the other boys are a bit pissed off with me listening to their records on the common room record player, but because I have to make a statement about the kind of person I am. That's what albums are about, surely? Your album collection defines who you are.

There are four boarding houses at the school and they each have their own house style: Gruggen are into west coast, country rock stuff – The Eagles and Buffalo Springfield; Hutton are into psychedelic rock – Jefferson Airplane and Tangerine Dream; Dolman are prog – Emerson, Lake & Palmer and King Crimson; and Wilberforce, my house, are doggedly into 4/4 rock – Free and The Who. Tellingly, each of the four houses claims David Bowie as one of their own.

But my task is to find an album that shows I'm a) a loyal member of my tribe, and b) a tasteful individual.

I find a Rolling Stones album I haven't seen before: *Gimme Shelter*. One that hasn't been seen before? That's going to be really good for my street cred, isn't it? Imagine turning up with a *new* Rolling Stones album.

Hang on, it's got songs on it I already know: 'Jumpin' Jack Flash', 'Honky Tonk Women', '(I Can't Get No) Satisfaction'. This makes me slightly suspicious, so I ask the guy behind the counter to put it on the shop record player to make sure there's nothing wrong with it. Maybe it's one of those *Top of the Pops* albums from the Hallmark series where all the tracks have been covered by some sound-a-like session musicians? He puts on side one – it sounds like The Rolling Stones, it *is* The Rolling Stones, it sounds great.

I read the back of the album cover – it tells me that these are some of the tracks featured in their *Gimme Shelter* film, and that side two captures the Stones in concert at London's Royal Albert Hall. The Royal Albert Hall? Royal? You can't get any better than royal, can you? At the bottom of the blurb it says: ***You're holding an LP by the greatest Rock 'n' Roll Group in the World! Why aren't you playing it?***

Fair enough.

'I'll take it!' I shout.

I rush back to school and the common room and put it on. Everyone is impressed – I think I may have defined myself – though one of the real aficionados points out that all the songs on side one have already been released as singles, or on previous albums like *Beggars Banquet* and *Let It Bleed*. He says it's a bit like a greatest hits album which is a bit naff. But he also says side two is a more unusual collection of songs. So I turn the record over. It begins to play . . .

It's an absolute disaster.

I knew it was live – it was recorded at the Royal Albert Hall for Christ's sake – but it appears to have been recorded in front of thousands of adoring female fans, and they scream through the whole bloody thing. They don't even scream at moments of high emotion, like Mick wiggling his hips, or points of musical significance, or the ends of songs, they just scream constantly at the same pitch for the full twenty minutes. The aficionado pipes up: 'You might as well go and suck Marc Bolan's knickers.'

Even though I secretly like Marc Bolan I realize this is a damning verdict and that I may never be cool.

It's the rule that you can't take records back to the shop just because you don't like them because they're afraid you might have scratched them, or gouged out the grooves with a stylus that's too heavy. And if they've played it to you in the shop you can't complain that it was scratched. So I'm stuck with it. And in fact I'm still stuck with it. It is still in my record collection. I have roughly five hundred vinyl albums and it's still there. The first one. I've just played side two again for the first time since 1971. It's as mind-numbingly awful as I remember. This is why The Beatles stopped touring – crappy PAs and so much screaming you can't hear the music. But I still have it because, as I said, your albums define who you are, and this mistake is part of who I am. I will not throw it out, but having owned up to it I feel some catharsis.

Our school house is called Wilberforce House – it's named after a previous pupil, William Wilberforce, the bloke who helped to stop slavery. Unfortunately his teachings haven't reached the house named after him, because at Wilberforce fagging is still in operation.

I'm a fag for one of the prefects. I clean his shoes. I make his bed. I make him toast whenever he decrees. I fetch and carry, and deliver messages. I go to the newsagent and buy his porn mags for him. It's not quite slavery because at the end of every term he gives me a 'tip'.

And at the end of his final term at the school he *sells* me his guitar. I have a guitar. This is progress!

Dad has such disdain for this instrument of the people, this instrument of pop and of protest, that he disparagingly calls my guitar a 'banjo' – the banjo being the lowest of the low in his opinion. Years later when I buy an actual banjo he doesn't know how to refer to it.

At the end of one term when Dad's briefly in the country he picks me up from school, and as I try to put my guitar in the back of the car he says: 'I'm not sure we've got enough room for your banjo.'

At home he makes such a display of watching me fumble about as I try to make chord shapes – tutting and rolling his eyes – that I never take it home again. I leave it at the school, or send it home with another boy if he'll have it.

What is this guitar?

It's very cheap. For a reason. It has the action – the distance between the strings and the fretboard – of one of those egg slicers advertised on the telly in the early seventies. As I try to push the strings down to make chords it tries to cut my fingers into sandwich-friendly slices. And it probably sounds like someone strumming an egg slicer as well. But it is mine, all mine.

Strings are prohibitively expensive. A new set of strings will set me back more than I've paid for the guitar. I can't afford that, so the cuts in my fingertips get filled with rust. But after a month I can play 'Banks of the Ohio' – a current top ten hit for Olivia Newton-John – without crying out in pain too often. It's not only a fine murder ballad sung by a girl who's the subject of many an idle daydream, it's also a three-chord wonder: A, E and D.

The three easiest chords.

With these three chords I can play – to varying degrees of similitude – 'Whole Lotta Love' and 'Rock and Roll' by Led Zep, 'Not Fade Away' by The Stones, 'Johnny B. Goode' by Chuck Berry, 'Wild Thing' by The Troggs (and Hendrix), 'I Can't Explain' by The Who, and 'All Right Now' by Free.

Five or six years later a guy called Tony Moon will draw three chord shapes on a piece of paper and put them in his fanzine *Sideburns*. Beside each shape he will write: *This is a chord. This is another. This is a third*. And underneath he will write *NOW FORM A BAND*. This is supposedly one of the seminal moments of the punk movement, but I would humbly suggest we were already aware of this back in 1971.

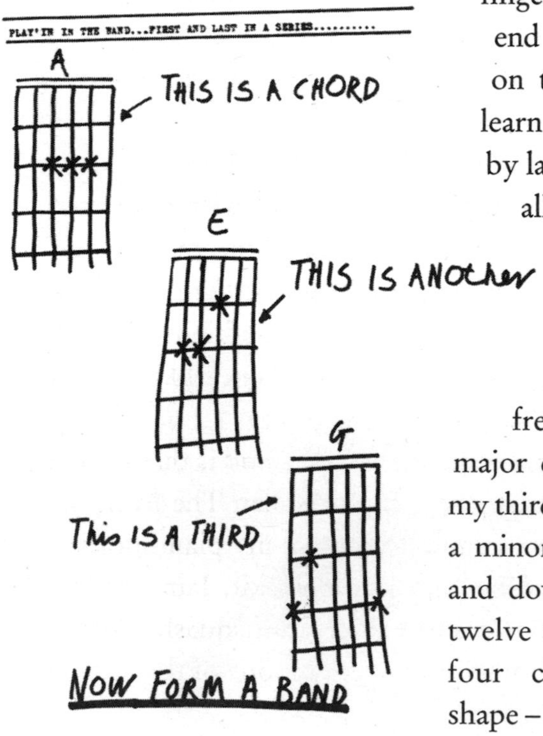

Also, the three chords Tony Moon drew were A, E and G. And G is a shape I won't master for another year – I have to stretch my third finger so far back from my first and second fingers that any slip-up and I'll end up guillotining my hand on the old egg slicer. I then learn how to form a barre chord by laying my first finger across all the strings and bending the other fingers into an E chord in front of this 'barre'. I can slide this shape up and down the fretboard and play all twelve major chords with it. By lifting my third finger, the shape becomes a minor chord and sliding it up and down again I now have all twelve minor chords. Twenty-four chords with one basic shape – I now have access to more or less every song I've ever heard. This is like finding the Rosetta Stone. I can play anything I want, and I want to play 'Paranoid' by Black Sabbath, and 'Smoke on the Water' by Deep Purple.

Ritchie Blackmore, the guitarist from Deep Purple, is particularly obliging for wannabe players like me – he uses barre chords on nearly every song. I reckon that if I could get a guitar with a lower action – one on which I could fret the chords properly instead of sounding like a plinky-plunky washboard – an electric one, with an amplifier, and if I could get a drummer, and a bassist, and a singer, and if I could write some really good songs . . . I could easily have a band like Deep Purple. I could be an international rock god.

Luckily for me there's already a band in Wilberforce House – well, the beginnings of a band – but the guitarist role is already taken by a boy called Iain. *He's* got an electric guitar, a Gibson Les Paul like Paul Kossoff plays in Free, and he's roughly a hundred per cent better at playing it than me. He can play the intro to Led Zep's 'Stairway to Heaven', and get this – he can almost play without looking at his fingers!

Another boy with the same name but different spelling, Ian, is on the drums. I heartily applaud any parent with the generosity of spirit to give their child a drum kit. Pop music would be nowhere without them. Drumming is something you need to start early. Thankfully Ian's parents are these kind of people and he's already been playing for years. He sounds like the real thing.

The only negative thing about this nascent band is that they're both a bit shy. The guitarist/singer in particular. The first time I'm allowed to watch them I squash into the tiny piano practice room: it contains a piano, Ian and his drum kit, Iain with his guitar and amplifier, and as many boys as can squash into the available space; five or six of us crammed into one of the corners and sitting on top of the piano.

They play 'All Right Now' which has a very distinctive drum pattern and guitar sound. It sounds like the actual record! However, Iain the guitarist is facing the wall. This isn't because there's no room, it's because he's nervous in front of people. And when the point arrives for the vocal to come in . . . nothing much happens. Iain is also the vocalist, but he doesn't let rip like Paul Rodgers, he just mumbles into the wall. He has a PA of sorts – a mic plugged into the spare socket on his guitar amp – but even with that we can't really hear him.

I come away from this three-minute 'gig' with a plan: *I'm going to be in this band.* And I've worked out a way of doing it – I'm going to get a bass guitar. Surely anyone can play bass, it's just one note at a time, how hard can it be? If you listen to a lot of sixties and seventies rock you'll find that quite a lot of people had this idea; for every inventive bassist there are ten others who do nothing more than play the root note of each chord. I think it's the accepted 'easy' way into a band.

So how do I get a bass guitar? I'll buy one, obviously – but where do I get the money?

Money

The concept of money is a mystery to most children. I remember teaching my middle daughter how to buy something in a shop: 'Unless you have exactly the right money, you give more than is needed, and they give you some change.' I send her into a shop on her own with a £20 note and she comes back with a copy of *The Beano* and no change – she's simply handed over the note, turned on her heel and walked out, happily reading about Dennis and Gnasher. Her elder sister is better at maths, but has a skewed notion of the supply chain. She hits upon a bright idea to make a quick fortune – she'll put a table up outside the front door and sell the contents of our house.

'And what happens when the house is empty?' I ask.

'You'll get some more things, won't you?'

We're not all little Jacob Rees-Moggs – very few of us learn spreadsheets, investments and the ins and outs of offshore banking in the nursery – as kids we mostly subscribe to the Boom and Bust economic model, we spend whatever we're given on 'pocket money day' on the day, and live on nothing for the rest of the week.

Being sent to boarding school throws this model into sharper relief because there's no food cupboard to steal a square of jelly from in the lean period. In the early years money is deposited with the housemaster and withdrawals are carefully managed to stop us squandering the entire term's allowance on frozen Mars Bars in the first week.

As we get older we're encouraged to open a Post Office Savings account – very useful for depositing Grandma Sturgeon's 2/6d birthday postal order – though something tells me Grandma Sturgeon doesn't know much about money either, because I've checked and 2/6d in 1970 is worth £1.98 in today's money. Happy bloody birthday, don't spend it all at once!

And finally . . . we progress to a *bank account*. This is the early seventies and the bank account comes with a cheque book and a free biro. Presumably they give you the biro to encourage you to write cheques, and this is exactly what I do: I write a cheque to *cash* for twenty pounds. This is the amount I need for the bass guitar I've seen in a musical instrument shop in York.

There is some consternation in the bank when I present this cheque. The clerk checks a couple of ledgers and takes my cheque to some higher authority who looks at it in alarm. From the dark recesses of the bank he looks at the cheque, at the ledger, and at me, then scrapes his chair back and strides forward. This is the moment when I begin to twig that you can't write a cheque for more than you have in your account. My mind is whirring, trying to think of possible excuses as the assistant manager reaches the counter.

'Mr Edmondson . . .' he begins. How sweet of him, I'm only fifteen. 'There's a discrepancy between the amount being withdrawn and funds in the account,' he continues, as if it's *his* fault! He's so generous of spirit, it seems impossible to him that I would try to defraud the bank on purpose. 'There has obviously been some mistake.'

This plays straight into my hands and prompts an immediate and outright lie: 'Yes, my mother says she deposited twenty-five pounds in my account last week.'

This throws the assistant manager into a paroxysm of shame and regret. He instantly cashes my cheque, hands over the readies, and promises to write to 'Mother' and apologize, and to find the missing deposit.

I leave the bank with a fistful of illicit dosh and an enormous problem – what's going to happen when my mum gets that letter? Of course, in normal times, when Mum is in Uganda, the vagaries of the postal service would make this less of a foregone conclusion, but unfortunately this happens on one of the few occasions when my parents are 'on leave' in Bradford.

The easiest and best approach would be to confess straight away, apologize profusely, and hope they might not blackball me from the banking system for the rest of my life. But I don't take the easiest and best approach. It's late Thursday, the next postal collection in our tiny town is Friday, which means the letter will be delivered on Saturday.

So on Saturday morning I skip school and get the bus to York. I stand in the toilet on the train from York to Leeds to avoid paying the fare, but I have to pay for the train between Leeds and Bradford because there's no toilet. It would have been better for me if this plan hadn't worked, but it does – I turn into our street just as the postie walks away from our house. I let myself in, see the bank letter on the mat, pocket it, and then greet my parents, who are surprised to see me but stupidly swallow my next lie that we have all been granted the day off because of . . . disease? Plague? Death-watch beetle? I can't remember the excuse, but whatever it is they accept it, and I spend the day with the letter burning a hole in my pocket before returning to school in the evening.

My absence from school has been noticed and two weeks

later I receive six of the best for truancy, which leave my arse looking like the railway tracks at Clapham Junction.

All this for twenty quid – is it worth it?

Why am I even bothering with school? I should just leave and get a hod.

But I don't. I write a letter *from my mum to the bank* forging her signature, explaining how she posted the cheque to the bank and is rather annoyed that they have lost it.

Things spiral out of control from this point: it's noted that my mum's letter has a postmark from Pocklington not Bradford; the bank write to her again, without my knowledge or any chance to intercept; all is uncovered. I have to give the money back, I have to apologize to the bank, to my mum and to the school. As punishment my parents cut my allowance. I am poorer, I have no bass guitar, I am not in the band, I am full of shame at my own stupidity, and I have a hurty bottom. I resolve never to get into debt ever again.

My first attempt to buy a bass having come to nothing, the following holiday I try to earn the money.

Although they've now returned to Uganda, Mum and Dad have bought a new home in England – a bungalow just outside Scarborough. And for a couple of school holidays, as I am now considered to be of the appropriate age to look after myself – sixteen – instead of being farmed out to the family tree, I'm allowed to stay in this bungalow on my own.

I work like a dog. I work a few days in a supermarket then find a job in a holiday camp in Cayton Bay – changing the gas bottles on the caravans during the day and changing people's money in the penny arcade at night. It pays 20p an hour. But I find a better rate of pay down on Scarborough seafront: 25p an hour! Again I'm working in a penny arcade, but it's much bigger and more crowded.

I work with an old guy called Alan whose job it is to fix the machines when they go wrong. I learn a bit of physics they never taught me at school: if you touch a live wire that is AC it will throw you off, if you touch a live wire that is DC you cannot let go. Most of the one-armed bandits are DC internally. I have to listen out for Alan's shouts when he touches a DC wire, then find him and switch the machine off at the mains. He gets electrocuted about three times a day, generally for about a minute each time.

He is a somewhat frazzled individual, and perhaps the constant shocks have altered the wiring in his brain, because every day he tells me the same joke. I say joke. He thinks it's a joke. It's just a crude rhyme: 'Blacker's Knacker Lacquer – adds that lustre to your cluster.' He says this apropos of nothing. You just need to catch his eye and he'll say it. If you're sucking down 240 volts I believe it gets funnier. There's an idea for a comedy club.

After a few weeks my independent spirit gets noticed by the manager, who owns another arcade further along the seafront. I'm moved to this other establishment where he gets me to call the bingo. This is fun. It's not the big bingo you get in a converted cinema, it's the small bingo inside an arcade with about thirty fixed cards attached to a wrap-around console with plastic sliders to cover the numbers. It's a much smaller card than in proper bingo too. The prizes are pretty worthless so the idea is to get people to play as many games as possible and swiftly move them along.

My job is to make it sound like fun and entice people to play, but the script is already written for each number: Kelly's Eye, number 1; Ted Heath's Den, number 10; Beans Means Heinz, 57.

I make up a few of my own: Days a Week, 8 according to The Beatles; Hours from Tulsa, 24; and my personal favourite, another Beatles reference – Revolution, number 9.

It's only when I get really bored after a couple of weeks that I start messing with them properly: Legs Eleven, 69; Two Fat Ladies, 2; Unlucky for Some, 76 trombones.

There are groans, complaints and some laughs. The manager thinks I'm getting more people to play but that I'm slowing down the game. He can't work out if he's losing money or not. I get a warning, but the holiday's nearly over and I manage to scrape together the money I need for a cheap copy of a Fender Precision Bass with a sunburst finish, so I don't care.

That'll be the day

That same summer, at the impressionable age of sixteen, I see the film *That'll Be the Day*, in which David Essex plays Jim MacLaine, a disillusioned schoolboy. There's a brilliant scene where Jim's in his school uniform on a bridge and he throws his schoolbooks and his satchel into the river shouting: 'Sod the Congress of Vienna, and bloody Napoleon, and the War of Jenkins's bloody Ear,' and rides off on his bicycle to live another kind of life.

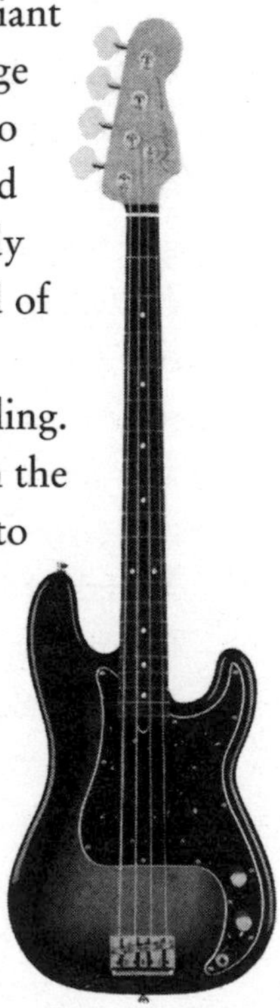

Buying the bass guitar fills me with the same feeling. This could be my ticket to the fantasy world I see in the pages of *Melody Maker*. But first I've got to get into the band.

Returning to school I present myself to Ian and Iain, show them my new pride and joy, and ask if they'd like to have me in the band.

'Can you play it?' they ask.

'Yes,' I say . . .

I put myself through a crash course: luckily our common room has recently acquired a new-fangled 'stereo' record player – I stick my head next to whichever speaker has got most bass in the mix, and painstakingly work out bass lines to the songs I've heard them playing. The action on this new guitar is quite low, and the strings are so thick there's no danger of them cutting into my fingers like the egg slicer, but after a few days I have blisters the size of ping-pong balls. My hand looks like an alien's.

Nothing a little popping, salt and Elastoplast won't sort out – if I'm going to be the bass player in the best rock 'n' roll band in the world I've got to pay my dues. By the time the weekend and the first proper rehearsal comes around I'm feeling pretty confident.

Every budding rock star wants a Marshall stack – a black Marshall amp sitting proudly atop a black Marshall speaker. Years later when I go on tour with Bad News the stage set is simply a twenty-foot-high wall of Marshall stacks, and I play through my very own – one I've still got sitting in the cellar.

I can't afford a Marshall stack as a schoolboy. I pick up a cheap amp with the bass but the budget is so tight that all I've got for a speaker is a loose one bought from the pages of *Exchange & Mart* – the eBay of the seventies. I nab a chipboard box from the prop store beneath the assembly hall – nobody'll miss it, it's just a battered old wooden box – I cut a hole in it, and screw in my speaker. I paint eyes, a nose and a moustache on it so that the speaker itself looks like a wide-open mouth. Ta dah! I look bloody great, and I sound bloody great. Well, I look, and I *sound*. And that's something. If it wasn't for the blood leaking from the plasters on my fingertips I'd say I was as close as it gets to being a sixteen-year-old rock god. I've even got loons and a tie-dyed singlet. Unfortunately I have to wear my National Health spectacles or I can't see where I'm putting my fingers – but look out, world, here I come.

Two years later, in my final week at the school, I'm presented with a bill for the chipboard box. It's not a joke presentation, they want actual money, and quite a lot of it. I might as well have bought a Marshall stack on the never-never.

We call our band Peace of Thorn, and someone a bit arty does an Aubrey Beardsley-type illustration on Ian's bass drum. This is considered quite cool in the early seventies. At least by us. I'm doing history and the Peace of Thorn was a peace treaty signed in the city of Thorn in 1411 between the Poles, the Lithuanians and the Teutonic Knights. To be honest, we simply chose the name out of the index of my history book because we liked the sound of it. It's Peace, OK? But it's a bit 'thorny'? There's like a problem? Isn't peace always a bit problematic? Isn't there always tension? Yeah, deep. Though we could also have been called The Concordat of Worms or The Polish-Bohemian Alliance.

It's a good name for a prog rock band, which we are not, even though we co-opt future playwright Martin Crimp to play keyboard on our version of Deep Purple's 'Flight of the Rat' – on a keyboard he's made himself.

Iain relinquishes the singing duties and I take over because I'm more of a show-off, but I have trouble singing and playing at the same time so I persuade our friend Dave into playing my bass while I go full Freddie Mercury at the front.

See how I do that? I inveigle my way into the back line of the band with little discernible talent and within a few weeks I'm front and centre. This is a disease.

Dave is almost as good as me on bass, i.e. not very good. I am not as good as Freddie Mercury either, though I'm not aware of this at the time. But I do give it some welly: throwing the mic stand around like Freddie; doing the Mick Jagger 'electrocuted chicken' dance; throwing in some of the sensational Alex Harvey's frightening stares; some of Ozzy Osbourne's stupidity; some David Johansen preening and gay abandon. Nobody in the band is trying harder than me, though they're probably achieving more.

I haven't seen any of these people live on stage because Pocklington is in the back of beyond. I'm getting nearly all my references from appearances on *Top of the Pops* and *The Old Grey Whistle Test*.

In the early seventies bands make their money from record sales. They only tour as a promotional event to support new albums. In the UK this tour is generally twelve dates long and never comes anywhere near Pocklington. De Montfort Hall in Leicester is the nearest and most prestigious, it's played by every major band on every tour but it's over a hundred miles away. Sheffield City Hall is half the distance but still hard to get to, and not everyone plays it. York is closer still, but they never have anyone good on.

I see Procol Harum in York and wish I hadn't. They play only the new stuff, which is boring, and I have to wait for the third encore to get 'Whiter Shade of Pale'. It's a horrible trick to pull – forcing people to shout for you to come back three times. We know they have to play it, it's their only hit, so we keep on shouting, but by the third time it's more of a snarl than a cheer.

I see Lou Reed at Sheffield City Hall on the *Rock 'n' Roll Animal* tour, but make the mistake of buying my merchandise *before* the gig. And it's a poster. I roll it up tight and manage to fight my way to somewhere near the front. He occasionally bends down to anoint us with his sweat or touch hands. I'm three or four people back and I can't reach him so I use the rolled-up poster as an extension of my arm, stretching it out in the hope that he'll touch it, whence it will become a holy relic. He's doing the song 'Heroin' and he's singing to us kids right at the front. *'I'm going to try to nullify my life'*, he sings. Does he look me in the eye? Does he look straight at me? He's reaching forward, he takes hold of my poster . . . and he wrenches it from my grasp and throws it into the crowd.

I hate him.

And no one plays Hull.

Except, on 29 October 1971, The Who play it. The Who. In Hull.

I don't know why I'm surprised, I've always been under the impression that The Who are a Leeds-based band, so it's not very far to go. I think they live in Leeds because their 1970 album is called *The Who Live at Leeds*. If only I'd got to grips with grammar sooner I'd have understood the difference between *live* as an adjective and *live* as a verb, and the difference between the prepositions *at* and *in*.

I don't get a ticket for The Who gig because in 1971 I'm not in with the in crowd enough to be included. But I feel like I was there because Iain went and he never stops bloody talking about it until we leave school in 1975. Perhaps he goes on talking about it after that, but I'm not there to hear it. I know the set list; they start off with 'I Can't Explain', 'Substitute' and 'Summertime Blues' – a triple whammy; I know the stage set-up; I know what everyone was wearing; I know that Pete Townshend didn't smash a guitar that night but 'looked like he might'; and I know that they played 'My Generation' as the first encore – something Rik, Nigel Planer and I do when we tour together in 1983.

As time progresses our tastes stray more towards Bad Company and Lynyrd Skynyrd, and we change our name to The Rancid Polecats. Which sounds like a really good punk name.

We play almost entirely at school arts festivals but manage to get one proper paid gig during our two-year existence – at the Pocklington Town Rugby Football Club. It's the end of the season and the burly savages of old Pocklington Town are in a drinky and boisterous mood. In typical berserker fashion I get steaming drunk to ramp myself up for the gig and through my provocative stage performance somehow turn these muscle-bound mouth-breathers against us. Ian gets badly beaten up in the toilets. That's the trouble with being a drummer – it's so hard to make a quick getaway.

We do make one single. It's a 7" Flexi Disc of Humble Pie's 'Four Day Creep'. It's not quite the same recording process Glyn Johns would use. We take one of those small oblong cassette recorders into the rehearsal room, we press *play* and *record* at the same time, and we express ourselves. We then get on the bus to York and go to the railway station where they have a Flexi Disc machine. It's little more than a novelty – you can record a message on it and post it to your loved one, that kind of thing. We put in our money, press *play* on the cassette recorder and hold it up to the mic. Three minutes later a Flexi Disc falls out of the machine. A Flexi Disc looks like a regular 7" single but is made of ultra-thin plastic which is very floppy. We just get the one copy. We get back on the bus to Pocklington, run to the common room and bung it on the stereo. It's a decidedly lo-fi experience, but through the crackle of the thin plastic you can just hear me screaming the repeated refrain at the top of my voice: *'I want you to lo-ve me!'*

Nothing much has changed in the fifty years since.

Bizarrely, despite not been cool enough to see The Who in Hull with the cool gang in 1971, about twenty-five years later I go on stage with The Who, in Hyde Park, in front of a quarter of a million people.

What? Do you?

Yes, I do, Iain.

How does that happen, Ted?

Well it happens a bit like this: For a little while in the early eighties, Pete Townshend stops making music and becomes an acquisitions editor at the book publishers Faber & Faber. It's at a time when the *Comic Strip* group is in its pomp. We're considered 'groovy' and we're brimming over with ideas, and Pete Townshend comes to see if we have any groovy ideas for books. The talk moves to the pub. We all have a jolly good time, and at the end of the evening we part, slightly inebriated, without an idea for a groovy book, but sort of 'chummy'. It was a convivial evening and we enjoyed each other's company. Who wouldn't? It's Pete ruddy Townshend!

When I did even worse than expected in my O-levels I stuck the official record of my results onto my bedroom wall and affixed a cut-out of Pete Townshend, from a photo in *Melody Maker*, smashing them to pieces with his guitar. That'll teach the forces that be, I thought.

Though it didn't.

Some years later his youngest kid ends up going to the same nursery school as my youngest. So Pete and I occasionally meet when we're picking up our children. And he still knows who I am, because, like a lot of old rockers, he's fond of the *Comic Strip* episode 'Bad News Tour' which follows the ignominious career of a young rock band on the road, and whilst it was meant as a scurrilous piss-take, he, like many others, sees it for the love letter it really is.

One day, at the school gate, Pete tells me that The Who are going to perform *Quadrophenia* in Hyde Park as a fundraiser for a charity that helps disadvantaged young people. Having heard me as the lead singer of Bad News he wonders if I might like to play the part of Ace Face/Bellboy. Ace Face is the leader of the mods though he works as a lowly bellboy for a big hotel to earn his crust. The bits I'm given to sing were sung by Pete Townshend and Keith Moon on the original record and the part was played by Sting in the film version. I'm not sure I have the required looks or indeed vocal cords but my initials are A.C.E. (Adrian Charles Edmondson), so I feel some kind of weird synchronicity.

He tells me that the actor Phil Daniels is going to reprise his role as the narrator/hero of the piece, that Gary Glitter (pre court case and jail obviously) will be playing the king of the rockers, and that Stephen Fry will be giving his hotel manager. It all sounds rather jolly and of course I agree.

I go to a rehearsal on a soundstage at Shepperton where I discover why the three surviving members of the band are so profoundly deaf – they play far too loud. I happen to walk in front of John Entwistle's bass rig during my big number and the sound waves have such a physical presence that I become unbalanced and almost fall off the stage. It's like moving through a vortex. I have a drink with John in the Shepperton bar afterwards and have the most surreal conversation I've had in my life. He cannot hear a single word I say, nor can he be bothered to lip read, but he avoids any kind of social awkwardness by simply presuming everything I've said. Half an hour of complete non-sequiturs ensues before he leaves with an attractive young woman.

There's another rehearsal on stage in Hyde Park scheduled for the morning before the show itself. I turn up and I'm directed to a backstage area. And this is where things change. I thought we were all here for a good time. I mean it's a charity gig, we're all there to raise money, obviously, but we're also there for the fun of it, so let's all have a jolly good time together.

But no – the three remaining members of the band have walled themselves off from the rest of the performers, and a burly security guard mans the tiny entrance to this inner sanctum. A bouncer *inside* the backstage area. I'm in another portacabin with Phil, Gary and Stephen. It's probably exactly the same as the band's portacabin but it doesn't have a wall round it or armed guards.

All right, I'm exaggerating, they're not armed.

Backing singers and the other musicians needed for the show – the horn section etc. – mill around, and the atmosphere outside the inner sanctum is very jovial, very positive. But to my mind this seclusion, this division, comes as a big surprise. It feels like a definite 'Know your place.' I could be back in Bradford.

The plan is to run the show in the morning before they let in the crowds in the afternoon. We take our positions as asked and are graciously joined by their majesties Pete, Roger and John. Things get underway and it's all sounding quite good actually. I make a decent stab at my bits as they crop up.

Gary's got one of those old-fashioned mic stands – one with a tripod of long legs attached to the base – and he's swinging it round for all it's worth, really enjoying himself, when at a point of particularly high excitement, he swings one of the aforesaid tripod legs straight into Roger Daltrey's eye.

It's a big moment. Roger drops to the floor like a sack of spuds. The band stops playing. And everything goes quiet, and very still.

And I'm thinking, 'I should go and help him and make sure he's all right,' but I'm *also* thinking, 'But I can't – because I'm not in his social set! I should leave this to his friends and close companions of the last thirty-odd years.'

I look at his friends and close companions of the last thirty-odd years – neither of them seems about to move forward and tend to their stricken comrade. And it strikes me that everyone else on stage is paralysed by the same social divide that the band so effortlessly put in place earlier in the day.

It feels like a week goes by before anyone moves, and that person is the old St John's Ambulance man who's been appointed the official first aider for the rehearsal. He clambers up onto the stage, he must be roughly 117. He reminds me of Private Godfrey in *Dad's Army*.

St John's Ambulance use a handy mnemonic when dealing with any situation – DR ABC; Danger, Response, Airway, Breathing, Circulation. Private Godfrey assesses the danger and moves swiftly on to part two: 'As you approach them, introduce yourself and ask them questions to see if you can get a response,' it says in their handbook.

'Hello,' he says to Roger, who's lying inert on the stage. 'I'm Private Godfrey. Do you know who you are?'

Roger's body suddenly snaps round and he barks at the man, 'Of course I know who I am, I'm Roger fucking Daltrey!'

Of course we all make our own social divides.

Roughly thirty years after we leave school Ian, Iain and I meet up, to 'get the band back together again'. It's an odd reunion, prompted by the lure of Friends Reunited – the older you get the stronger the pull of the past becomes (some people even write books about it). In between murdering 'All Right Now' by Free and the Peter Frampton version of 'Jumpin' Jack Flash' we talk about what happened after school and why nobody kept in touch. Iain says something quite telling. He says he packed his stuff into his dad's car on the last day at school and was getting into the passenger seat when his dad stopped him.

'Aren't you going to say goodbye to all your mates?' his dad asked.

And apparently Iain looked back at the boarding house we'd all shared for the most formative years of our lives and just said 'Nah.'

'I thought about the seven years I'd been cooped up there with all those other boys, and just said "Nah", and got in the car.'

It turns out we each have a similar tale to tell. There was no swapping of addresses, no vowing to be friends forever, there was nothing. It just ended. After midnight on the last night of school myself and a guy called Hamlet (his surname) got a pair of stencils and painted some monster footprints all the way along the short road from the main school building to our boarding house. The footsteps disappeared into a shrubbery. And we did pretty much the same thing.

I feel I left my family when I joined the school, and when I left the school I did so entirely alone, again. Not unhappily, just without emotion. Those relationships I'd fought so hard to create turned out to be ephemeral. A mirage? There's no doubt they happened, and that we thought they were real at the time, but it turns out they had no substance, that they were unimportant. It was about survival. Like prison. For a long time I thought it was only me that had ducked out in this way, but it's strangely heartening to find that Ian and Iain had done the same. It makes me oddly normal. 'Strangely Strange But Oddly Normal' as Dr Strangely Strange would sing.

Unless it's just the three of us that are fucked up?

Part 5

Manchester (before it was cool)

A fork in the road

At the end of school I'm faced with the problem of 'how to become a professional actor or international rock god'. There are no signposts at all – not even one to crash into.

There isn't a desk for either at the sixth form careers fair. Potential engineers, doctors, lawyers and vets are very well served; the armed forces each have a stand; and I think briefly about becoming a spy in the Diplomatic Service (a form of acting); but there's nothing for aspiring stars of stage and screen or rock gods.

The careers master is decidedly unhelpful, I ask him about drama schools and he tells me that the Rowntree's factory in York has a very good amateur dramatics society. I tell him that I want to be a professional actor, I've just played Hamlet, for Christ's sake, and my plan is to work at the Royal Shakespeare Company. He gives me the look that says, 'You're a time waster.'

He's right in one way – it takes me forty-two years to get to the RSC.

In the days before the internet, finding out about anything is limited to what's in the school library. From scant reference material, some of it dating back to between the wars, I learn that there are no rock god schools and that drama schools hold frightening *auditions* that practically nobody gets through. The funding isn't clear cut either, so I apply to do drama at university instead. Manchester will let me in with relatively easy grades.

I get shockingly bad grades – but they let me in anyway. Rik gets in through clearing – his grades are even worse than mine. 1975 must have been a thin year.

Gap years are not a thing in 1975 so I don't go around the world getting off with girls, getting pissed on moon-kissed beaches, swimming with dolphins, and making friends for life. Typically Tropical are top of the charts with 'Barbados' but I'm not going there either, I'm going to work the summer in an iron foundry in Bradford with a guy who keeps threatening to wrestle me to the ground. He's the under-eighteen wrestling champion of West Yorkshire or some such, and I'm glad when a splash of molten iron lands on his crotch and he disappears for a while. I build up some cash and arrive at university with dirty hands and a clean slate: unattached and unfettered – ready to make new friends.

Trouble is, half the people in my department are girls. I've grown up at an all-boys school and I don't really know how to talk to girls, so that cuts out half the department at a stroke. Though I have been in a band – perhaps that will count as some way of starting a conversation?

Accompanying yourself on electric bass is not much fun so I trade it in and use some of my iron foundry cash to buy a fairly decent new six string. There is good news – I'm virtually the only guitarist in my year, which makes me the best guitarist in my year by default.

I'm hoping that girls might be impressed by someone who can sing songs and play guitar, so I set about being that someone.

Learning songs in 1975 is difficult because you have to do it all by ear. TAB or tablature – the bluffer's way to read music in which the six guitar strings are drawn like a music stave and numbers tell you where to put your fingers – hasn't become mainstream yet. There are books of song transcriptions in some music shops but bizarrely they're mostly written for 'Organ and Vocals'.

Who's playing the organ?

Exactly! There must be a massive secret society of organ players sitting at home with their Bontempi organs rocking along to Bob Dylan or Fleetwood Mac with a bossanova accompaniment. In these 'Organ and Vocals' books all the songs seem to be written in Bb – a difficult key for guitarists. And, it turns out, quite a difficult key for organ players. But cornet players must be having a field day – if only I'd stuck with it!

The new guitar is brilliant. The action is good, I can fret the chords properly and I start to sound like the real thing. It's not quite the babe magnet I was hoping for but the songs I play start to give *me* pleasure. After some serious application I learn to play the intro to 'Stairway to Heaven'. Unfortunately I accomplish this feat at exactly the same moment punk arrives and my local guitar shop puts up a sign in the try-out area saying *NO Stairway to Heaven! NO Smoke on the Water!*

My two best numbers . . .

In the Student Union building there are a couple of piano practice rooms. I think you're supposed to book them, but there's never anyone in them, so I just go in, close the door, and start figuring out chords.

And this begins the pattern of my life. Autodidact sounds rather grand, but self-taught sounds slightly pejorative. Whichever, over the next forty years I become relatively competent at banging out chords and tunes on the piano, the guitar, the bass, the tenor guitar and the mandolin, with a less-practised but OK-ish ability on the drums, the trumpet, the banjo, the ukulele, the banjolele, the autoharp and various recorders. With a fair wind I can scrape a tune out of a fiddle, and squeeze an accompaniment out of a melodeon. And I can play the coconuts and the triangle. I've played all these things on stage when people have been paying to listen.

But I still can't read music. If I take an inordinate amount of time I can pick things out from written music, but it's not fluent. Why? It would take no less application than learning 'Stairway to Heaven' or teaching myself the shape of chords on a piano from scratch. I think it's a mental antipathy to the kind of authority written music represents. All right, let's be honest, an antipathy to my dad, the man who wanted classical music to remain lofty and unattainable, a symbol of his class and intellect.

It's as if I'm shouting at him (even though he's dead): *'Look at me! Look at how I'm playing all these things! AND I DIDN'T DO IT YOUR WAY!'*

Like the line in the Neil Innes song 'How Sweet to Be an Idiot' when he sings: *'But Mother I play so beautifully, listen. Ha ha!'*

Creativity

At Manchester University Drama Department creativity is a completely different proposition to anything I've previously encountered. The structured course itself is rather slight, it's like English, but with play texts, and the commitment is not too onerous: you *have* to attend two lectures and a tutorial each week, and . . . that's about it.

But they also have the Stephen Joseph Studio – an old German chapel converted into a shabby performance space and a few rehearsal rooms. And it is *ours*. We are allowed, nay encouraged, to do anything we bloody like in it. This is not part of the curriculum, there's no right or wrong, nothing will get marked or *count towards* anything. It's just a place to create stuff *for the sake of creating it*. Every Monday is Studio Night when the whole department (about a hundred people) will gather to watch each other's creations.

It is bliss. There is no maths, no French, no Latin, no games, no cadet force, no bulled boots, no cane – we just make theatre all the time, and when we're not making it some very clever people are telling us about it. I will never know freedom like this ever again.

Years later my daughter Beattie comes to the same university to study the same course, we even share a tutor, but the studio is no more. The Stephen Joseph has been divided into a series of drab seminar rooms for another faculty. The drama students now have more lectures, they have to 'book' rehearsal rooms, and 'rent' theatre space. I suppose there's no metric for measuring how valuable the old Stevie Joe was, and, as is the way these days, if it can't be measured, it's deemed a waste of money.

And yet, there is something wrong with all this bliss and I think it's . . . me.

I spend my first term doing a lot of acting. There's a mature student in our year, Peter Fieldson, who's already written a lot of plays. Not only has he written them, he's had them produced on BBC Radio 4. He has already *made money* out of drama. This makes him incredibly glamorous. He seems impossibly old to me, but he's probably only about twenty-three. I'm very impressed during freshers' week when he asks me to help him buy a writing chair.

When he says 'help him buy' he really means 'carry it home for him'.

He's in university accommodation and says the chairs are rubbish and he can't sit and write all day without proper lumbar support. He buys what is basically a posh office chair, which is on wheels, and I trundle it back to his shared flat and hoick it up the stairs. Peter rewrites all his radio plays for the stage, and perhaps because I'm in awe of him and hang on his every word, or perhaps because I carried his chair, he casts me in *all* of them, and I get a reputation as an 'actor'.

The department is quite small, thirty people in each year, but it quickly becomes very cliquey. Trouble is, I don't get into a clique. I stumble along in Peter's virtual repertory company, but I'm not really in his social group. I think he likes me more as a raw performer than as a friend.

By raw I don't mean skilled, I mean unafraid to be embarrassed. I'll throw myself out there, I'll over-emote. You can give me notes and bring me back, but generally if you give me a character to hide behind I'll give it 150 per cent while most people are only on about 35 per cent. It's the berserker approach to acting.

If you're a playwright with concerns about your work not having enough 'vitality', and you want someone to give your words some energy and attack, I'm your man.

But I'm a bit of a lonely berserker. I'm emotionally feral – which isn't an attractive character trait. I wonder if the actual Viking berserkers had trouble making friends? They probably did when you think about it. Off their heads, biting their shields – how do you start a conversation?

I don't manage to get into a hall of residence – an easy place to develop friendships – and a lot of the boys in our year, Rik included, end up at Owens Park, where they form a strong group of their own.

I find myself out on a limb in a bedsit in Chorlton-cum-Hardy. 'Chorlton-cum-Hardy,' I hear you cry. 'That sounds very posh.' Well my bit of it isn't. No matter how much money I pump into the meter I can only get two inches of lukewarm water into the filthy bath. I share a dingy mouse-infested kitchen with two PhD students; one is studying the chemistry of soap but doesn't appear to use any, and I don't know what the other is studying because he never says a single word to me. Perhaps he's got issues of his own. At length I discover that our landlady is stealing things from my room. I haven't got much to steal, but any spare change, the odd cigarette, even a new tube of toothpaste goes missing.

I think I'm mostly lonely. I feel I don't really fit in. By the second term I feel so unattached that I tell my tutor I'm going to leave and try to get a job at the Alhambra Theatre in Bradford. I say I don't think university is for me, that I want to move straight into proper work, and that I'm happy to start at the bottom, just sweeping the stage, anything. I'm not exactly Mickey Rooney in *Babes in Arms* – 'Let's do the show right here in the barn' – but I have a romantic and possibly overly dramatic view of myself and my 'arc'.

It turns out these are signs of a rather fragile mind, but my tutor probes a bit – this is the kind of pastoral care that was never evident at school – and suggests it might just be the bedsit that's making me unhappy. Some questions are asked around the department, and one of the girls in my year, Caroline Cooke, says there's a space in the large student house she's living in.

Tyntesfield House is more than a large house, it's an actual mansion set in its own grounds. It was built by a rich Victorian banker but now belongs to the university. It's gently decaying and has been badly divided into twenty high-ceilinged, if rather shabby, bedrooms with an enormous communal kitchen. It gets knocked down a few years later.

I share a room on the top floor with Markus, a Norwegian student. I ask him if he knows any of the Edmondsons over in Norway. He says he doesn't. I immediately doubt whether he actually *is* Norwegian. Though he has some supporting evidence in the form of his Norwegian Army dog tags. They still have conscription over there and he says he's just come out of the army. This could be true, he's very well built – he looks like Action Man – and he's financially very well-off, especially in student terms. But he's more playboy than berserker. He owns a Triumph TR4, talks about 'dolly birds' in the accent of the Swedish chef on *The Muppet Show*, and is rarely home. So I get the room to myself mostly.

There's a reason why they still have some accommodation available – it's in Timperley.

Is that part of Manchester?

No, it isn't. It's in Timperley, midway between Sale and Altrincham. It's a full seven miles from the university, an hour's bus journey away.

I like Caroline and discover she's about as fucked-up as me, only her fucked-upness is rooted in bog-standard Catholic guilt. She's also London Irish which means if I give her the money I can get my pint of mild without waiting for everyone else to get served first.

What?

Let me explain.

The pub out behind the Drama Department is called the Ducie Arms, but is known more simply as 'The Ducie'. It's an old Victorian pub marooned in the middle of a car park; 1970s Manchester has been subject to a lot of slum clearance and the land behind the university has been more or less wiped clean of its previous use except for The Ducie and another pub half a mile away standing on its own in the middle of nowhere, obviously preserved as a 'community asset', though at this time it has no surrounding community.

I'm not the only thing waiting to be developed.

The Ducie has a built-in community because it's an Irish pub. It's a traditional boozer, cramped and convivial. The main room is long and thin with a bench seat going all the way down both sides and across one end. There's no piped music and it smells of tobacco, beer and mutton stew, even though no food is served. They collect for the blind, but only in 2p pieces – there's a stack of interleaved 2p coins standing like a medieval turret on the bar. This bar is guarded by Marion, the publican, a short woman with tight curly hair and a drinker's complexion, who is so brusque and offhand that people come from far and wide to see the legendary misanthrope in action. No matter what time of day it is, Marion's husband Michael is always completely pissed, and it is he who eventually knocks over the stack of 2p coins.

There's an air of Republican sympathy to the place, indeed many think the collection for 'the blind' is actually for the IRA, and English accents are viewed with suspicion. It's one of the 'session' pubs where traditional musicians are welcome. Out of nowhere, fiddles, whistles and a bodhrán will appear and play a set of Irish jigs and reels. It's my first exposure to this kind of music and I find it intoxicating; it sounds like the feeling of running pell-mell downhill – in the way you feel exhilarated but simultaneously out of control. It has the same energy and vitality as the punk music that is developing all around us. Little do I know it but one of the underage fiddlers who turns up occasionally is Andy Dinan, who will join my band The Bad Shepherds about thirty years later.

The Ducie is possibly considered the general hang-out of the Drama Department not just because it's the closest pub, but because we have such a large Irish contingent on our course. The English among us can stand at the bar for twenty minutes waiting to be served, but if Marion spies one of the Irish set come in the door behind us she'll shout over the throng: 'What'll you have, Síobhra?' or 'What'll you have, Paul?' Or indeed 'What'll you have, Caroline?' Result.

Caroline and I share the bus to and from uni and become proper friends. We look out for each other when it's getting close to *last bus home* time. It's a platonic friendship, there's no hanky-panky involved. She's my first proper female friend. My hanky-panky interest is focused on her room-mate, a psychology student.

I keep getting asked to perform in people's shows: Peter Fieldson's plays, Louise Jeffrey's production of *The Dark Tower* by Louis MacNeice, fellow student Ian Christensen's take on Everyman called *Everybod*, and the department production of Ben Jonson's *Bartholomew Fair*.

The move to Tyntesfield is a success in that I no longer want to leave. But something's still not quite right in the state of Denmark . . .

A bit nuts

Leaving school at sixteen, my mum trained as a hairdresser. It's something I find hard to believe because she cut our hair when we were children, and was forever snipping our ears with the scissors. She stopped hairdressing when she married my dad and became a full-time mum.

But when the family finally return to Bradford, and my two younger brothers finally start secondary school, she gets a job at the Occupational Therapy Unit of the Bradford Royal Infirmary. She has no training, she's there as a general helper. Our house fills with ornaments covered in plaster of Paris with seashells stuck into it: lamps, trays, fruit bowls.

The patients mostly have mental health problems, but Mum refers to them as 'the nutters'. She takes them in the department minibus on a day trip to Scarborough and complains of losing one of the 'nutters' on the beach. She buys a painting from a rather gifted 'nutter' but takes it back and asks him to paint over one of the clouds because she thinks it looks like the devil.

It's hard to tell who's really nuts.

Isn't it?

In 1976, aged nineteen, I find myself in a room in the

psychology department at Manchester University. Electrodes have been attached to my head and chest which run to a complicated-looking machine with lots of dials. We're in the darkly gothic building in the middle of the campus and I feel like I'm in a 1950s B movie.

Caroline's room-mate, the psychology student, is now my girlfriend, and she's using her friends as guinea pigs. She and her dad, both keen canoeists, are planning to kayak around the top of Baffin Island in the Arctic Circle. She has read that the local Inuit have the ability to slow their heart rate at will in order to conserve energy, and is testing to see if this is possible.

A lot of her chums have been roped in, and some can do it and some can't. I'm the last guinea pig of the day, but the readings from my brain go a bit berserk. She fiddles with the dials but . . . it's the end of the day, and she says she'll sort it later, and I can join the second bunch of subjects the next day.

I turn up again, and this time I'm in the middle of the queue. The people before me give regular readings, but my brain feed goes weird again. She can't understand it. As a test she wires up the next person and it works perfectly well again. So it appears it's *me* that is the problem. She's only been studying for a year, so can't explain it, and I am put down as a 'statistical outlier' . . .

But that's not when I realize that I am 'nuts'.

She and I get married. We are both nineteen. Nineteen! This is very odd, even for the seventies. No one else at uni is getting married. Eyebrows are raised. The night before the ceremony I look in the mirror and see that even my own eyebrows are raised. In the car, with my best man Dave at the wheel, I get the jitters, and at a T-junction we discuss whether to turn left towards the registry office, or right towards . . . I dunno . . . Mansfield?

I don't know her reasoning for getting married rather than

just 'shacking up' like everyone else, and I only know mine in hindsight: I want someone to prove that they love me. I want to love and be loved. I'm not sure I've ever experienced love. Of any kind. I don't know what it is.

Dave says that running away now or afterwards is basically the same thing, the only difference being a piece of paper, he says that divorce is easy, and more importantly that he's hungry, and that there's free food, so we turn left and the deed is done.

Dave's right. It doesn't last long. Eighteen months later she throws her wedding ring under the wheels of the passing traffic as we argue on the kerbside. I'm the instigator, but I can't think straight, and in my confusion and unhappiness I become jealous of the ring being crushed into the tarmac.

Later that night I slacken the brake cables on my motorbike so that they're basically useless, and go for a ride. At a crossroads in the wasteland between Whalley Range and the university I can see traffic going to and fro across the main road and I approach at speed and cannot stop. The other drivers swerve, skid about, blow their horns . . . and miraculously avoid me. I spin out at the other side and gradually slow to a halt a few hundred yards further on.

I'm not entirely well. I see the uni doctor and I don't understand what's happening to me. He puts me on tranquillizers, and I sit in a catatonic state in our flat staring at the slugs climbing up the wall – it's a terrible flat, the paraffin heaters chuck out so much moisture that it's basically become a wetland reserve. I'm expecting a pair of great-crested grebes to take up residence sometime soon.

The doctor speaks to my tutor and I'm offered a bye for the finals – I don't have to sit my exams.

But that's not when I realize that I am 'nuts' either.

No one mentions the phrase 'mental health'. I'm imagining it's some kind of virus? No one talks about *anything* – *No one* about *anything*. My parents grew up in the trauma of the Second World War; my Uncle Douglas's face sags on one side, a kind of palsy brought on by watching his friends die under a tank as it slowly sank into soft ground with them sleeping underneath. But nobody talks. And that attitude still persists in the seventies. I don't know I've got a mental health issue.

I don't like the tranquillizers. I don't like not being able to think, even if the thoughts are somewhat gloomy. I stop taking them, I start going back to lectures; like Uncle Douglas I pretend nothing has happened. I sit my finals, get a 2.1, thank you very much, and head up with the rest of the gang to do the Edinburgh Fringe again. The force of repression has always been strong with me. And I'm quite good at drinking. And biting my shield. And letting things get worse.

The Bonzo Dog Doo-Dah Band are the soundtrack to my life, and the intro to 'Sport (the Odd Boy)' goes *'Let's go back to your childhood . . . childhood . . . childhood . . .'* into an infinite echo.

And of course childhood is everything. As Aristotle said; 'Give me a child until he is seven and I will show you the man.'

On my seventh birthday I go to kiss my dad goodnight, as usual, but he stops me, and says now that I am seven we should stop hugging and kissing like girls and shake hands. We shake hands and I go to bed. This is hardly emotional torture, and it seems novel and interesting at the time, but years later it's a moment that replays in my head like a dream sequence in a Fellini film.

He's still affectionate with my elder sister, and I never see him 'shake hands' with my two younger brothers. And if it weren't for the obvious family resemblance in our facial features, I might suspect that I'm a cuckoo in the nest, and that this is causing the antipathy. Nothing I do is ever good enough for him, even when I'm to all intents and purposes 'quite successful', and eventually I come to accept that maybe he doesn't actually *like* me.

The mind is an odd thing. Abstract notions of liking and loving are still inexplicable except as a series of chemical reactions within the brain. I'm in my late thirties when I realize this, and it's about the same time that I become an insomniac.

Then, while I'm rehearsing an episode of *Bottom* at the BBC, I suddenly get savage chest pains. Rehearsals stop and I see a doctor who wires me up in almost the same way I was wired up twenty years before. Turns out I'm not about to have a heart attack, I'm hyperventilating. I learn to breathe into a paper bag when feeling particularly stressed and carry on with my life.

At a dinner party I sit next to another psychologist – I describe a few scant details and ask if I should see someone about it. Her advice is that unless my daily life is being unduly interrupted, unless I can't get out of bed, can't get to the shops, I probably needn't go.

So now I have a professional (albeit casual drunken dinner party) opinion that I am not nuts.

Or am I?

I think suicidal thoughts are normal. I've lived with them all my life. I've looked at the tube trains rushing into the stations, it just seems so easy. I've looked out of windows, over cliffs, I've read up on the contents of the medical cabinet. I know how to do it.

In 2007 I'm writing a sitcom with my new friend Nigel Smith called *Teenage Kicks*. Nigel has had an unusual experience.

In his late thirties his tongue suddenly felt fizzy. He rang a doctor friend who told him to go straight to hospital and twenty-four hours later he was in a coma which lasted several months. His own immune system had attacked him. When he came out of it he found he couldn't walk properly any more, and he'd lost the ability to swallow and had to feed himself through a tube.

These problems don't go away. He walks with a stick and still feeds himself through a tube.

When we go for a drink he takes a mouthful of beer to savour the taste then spits it into his tube. We call getting pissed 'getting tubed'. He's *remarkably* cheerful. One day I ask him how he manages it, and with the benefit of the writing room intimacy – in which you can talk about things you might not in regular social environments – I tell him that I'd've probably topped myself if I was him. He nods, and says he's noticed that I am very much a 'glass half empty' kind of person. He is very much 'glass half full'. In fact half a pint is almost a pint as far as he's concerned. He says that suicidal thoughts are *not* normal.

This is a shock, and it's when I start to get an inkling that I *might* be nuts.

I finally tell Jennifer, my wife since 1985, about my history of suicidal thoughts. It's not the sort of thing that comes up when you're dating, and I've never found the right moment to tell her that I'm nuts.

There, I've said it, perhaps I've secretly known all along. Obviously she's been aware of the insomnia, the hyperventilation, the emotional difficulty with my dad, and my short-trigger temper – but suicide is news. She's shocked – I am a *very* good actor – she's sad, and worried, and sympathetic and tells me that I really need to see someone about it. I agree and . . . prevaricate. I suppose I'm afraid of tranquillizers and catatonia. The condition, not the band.

In 2010 a close friend blows his brains out with a shotgun sitting on a rock on Dartmoor. He works in marketing, he's in horrendous debt, has unrequited love, and thinks he's being heroic.

A year later an even closer friend hangs himself. He doesn't think he's being heroic, he's completely lost his place in the world, he just can't think; he hasn't slept for weeks, his brain is scrambled, and he wants the pain to stop.

I learn how equally aggressive these acts are towards everyone that is left. They devastate so many people and I resolve never to cause that amount of pain.

Deciding suicide is not an option is a game changer. I finally go to see a nut doctor. He's refreshingly expensive but doesn't say much. He's roughly ten quid a word. He asks questions but doesn't give any answers. He puts me on antidepressants and I worry they will alter me and take away my creativity. Is being nuts part of the spark? Will the pills take away the berserker inside me? Obviously I want to be altered, I want to feel happier, but I still want to be me. Who am I? Oh God, here come the Bonzos again.

'OOOh, you done my brain in, right in.'

I read a review in the newspapers for a book called *Philosophy for Life: And Other Dangerous Situations* by Jules Evans. I'm intrigued, I buy the book, and . . . it changes my life. Not often you can say that.

It's based on the philosophy of the Greek slave Epictetus, one of the Stoics, with the fundamental notion that we don't feel pain because of what's happened, we feel it because of what we *think* about what's happened. It's not possible to change what's happened, but it is possible to change how we *think* about it. This is basically 2,000-year-old Cognitive Behavioural Therapy. The book asks me to take my mind to a virtual gymnasium, I have to train it, I have to think carefully, and often, about what I can and cannot control. I cannot control any external events or what people think about me, I can control my own thoughts and actions. I have to practise my first responses to things: my dad, road rage, malfunctioning machines.

I get quite good at it. My wife and children will testify that I become a much easier person to live with. Calmer, more biddable. My temper, in particular, is almost completely erased. It's very different to the stiff upper lip 'Stoicism' of my parents and Uncle Douglas – it's not about repression, it's about accepting, and having a different response.

I can't say I am normal. But then I don't think *anyone* is. Certainly all the people I know well have . . . idiosyncrasies.

A grebo on the bus

On my first day at university I'm puffing away on a fag on the top deck of a bus heading down the Oxford Road in Manchester when I see a young bloke sitting in the seat in front of me. He's wearing a dirty denim jacket and has greasy shoulder-length hair, and he's constantly flicking his head to get this hair out of his eyes – like he's trying to be The Fonz in *Happy Days* but has forgotten his comb. His hair's so greasy it falls back over his spotty forehead almost as soon as he's swept it back.

Art Garfunkel's 'I Only Have Eyes for You' is creeping up towards the number one spot, and whilst I don't exactly fancy this grebo there's something about him that demands attention.

His every move is considered, as if to say, 'Look at me, look how great I am.' He pulls a cigarette from a packet of No.6 and ostentatiously taps both ends against the box – it's something you only need to do with the unfiltered end, the whole purpose being to crimp the paper around any loose tobacco to stop it falling out. This is how I know this bloke is an idiot. He lights it, inhales deeply, and blows six perfect smoke rings – thick circles of rippling, tightly configured smoke, all perfectly equidistant from each other. This doesn't endear him to me either, because I've never been able to do that, so I'm jealous.

He gets off at the same stop as me, and he's not following me, because he's in front – well, he is to begin with, but we swap places several times as we negotiate crowds of new students and numerous fire doors – but in single file we both make our way to the Drama Department and I discover that his name is Rik Mayall.

I don't see much of him during the first year, which is odd because it's a small department. Of course I'm aware of him – we have lectures together, and do movement classes together, and do the department production of *Bartholomew Fair* together – but we're in different social groups. Well, he's in a group, I'm the sad wanker who's struggling to find his place.

He's only seventeen when he arrives, the youngest in the year, and he's a bit over excited: it's his first time away from home, he's living in halls with lots of similarly hyperactive new chums, there's cheap booze in the Student Union, he can smoke without having to suck a polo mint on the way home so his parents don't find out, and he can stay out all night if he wants to.

Having been to boarding school I've already experienced communal living, not giving a fuck, and no longer being under parental control, but for Rik, who comes from a very loving but responsible home life, it must be quite a thrill.

He does a lot of shagging by all accounts. Though this is nothing new if his tales of schoolboy conquests are to be believed. And who wouldn't believe them – he's a shockingly handsome boy, and he carries himself with such easy confidence. He manages to be amiably available to everyone without ever coming across as unpleasantly pushy, or arrogant.

I don't know what it is that makes him so beautiful. Is it something to do with the width of his forehead? His cheekbones? The angular nature of his jaw? His smile? The way his hair almost stands up at the front?

The older I get the more I realize that beauty mostly comes from within, and with Rik, especially in the early student days, he's just remarkably *uncomplicated*, and I think that's what people find attractive. You get what you see – a fun-loving charmer, someone who's easy to be around, someone who wants to laugh and to make other people laugh, a bit of a show-off but someone who just wants the night to go well.

A few years later when we're doing the Edinburgh Fringe Festival I watch a girl fall in love with him, right in front of me. We're at the Fringe Club, a performers-only bar, like a student union, where the drinks are cheap, and there's a small stage where people can show off or try out new stuff. It's very much an amateur/student festival at the time, not the showcase for established comics it is today.

Our fringe show is a lunchtime event in a church hall around the corner, so we're often to be found in the Fringe Club in the afternoon and evening. One night we're doing a new sketch about two Yorkshiremen on deckchairs trying to explain why American cars are so big and Japanese cars are so small (something to do with perspective and the earth's rotation), and as we blunder through it a girl walks by close to the front of the stage. Nothing unusual in that, it's a casual performance space, people are free to move about – it's a bar with a stage in it. But, when she sees Rik she just stops in her tracks right in front of the stage, and stares at him. She never looks at me, only at him, but I'm there and I've got a ringside seat. She's only about three feet away from me. It's quite an illuminating experience for me. I watch her fall for him, from very close quarters. Watch her gape in wonder. I see her smile grow into a beam. I see her eyes transfixed. It's like she's been injected with a wonder drug that makes her glow from within. This is his power.

We finish our little sketch, clear away our deckchairs, and the compère announces the next act: it is the girl. She sings 'My

Heart Belongs to Daddy' – a teasing, sexually charged song made famous by Marilyn Monroe in the musical *Let's Make Love*. She sings it directly at Rik. There are an awful lot of signals in it and he responds to every single one. As I said, he's very uncomplicated. I don't see him again until we do our show the following lunchtime. He's quite tired.

He's a performer in more ways than one.

I'm not sure how many students come to the university wanting to be actors when they leave, but those of us that do are terrified of one thing: Equity cards. Or more specifically, the lack of one.

There are only three recognized routes into the union: getting offered a job with a repertory company (these jobs generally go to people from proper drama schools), T.I.E. (Theatre in Education – a slog round the schools doing scenes from *Macbeth* in matching T-shirts to children that look on you with a mixture of pity and loathing), or Variety contracts. Variety contracts are a loophole – they can be handed out by clubs to any acts that perform there, and if you provide Equity with enough of them, they will apparently give you a card.

As we start the second year, two of Rik's friends from his school in Worcester – Mike Redfearn and Mark Dewison – enter the first year. The three of them were close at school, the bond is still strong, and they've hit upon a plan to get Equity cards.

There's a jazz club on Swan Street in Manchester called The Band on the Wall. It's now a swanky arts centre but at the time it's a magnificent Victorian pub, the kind George Orwell would have liked – dark wood, long bar, nooks and crannies, lots of mirrors, a nicotine-coloured ceiling. It has glorious stained-glass windows that alter the light so much you lose track of time. The licensing laws in the seventies mean we get chucked out at three in the afternoon, and when we are, the sunlight – what am I saying, this is Manchester – the 'bright drizzle' catches us by surprise, blinding us, and reminding us, especially if we are feeling a little unsteady, that we've been naughty. It's a delicious feeling and the thing I miss most about the old opening hours.

The proprietor is a bit of a jazzer with an artistic temperament. In the evenings the place is packed with people listening to jazz bands, but at lunchtime trade is a bit thin, so he comes up with the idea of 'Lunchtime Theatre' to act as a draw. He can't afford to pay anyone and thinks students will do it for free and the promise of some rather dubious Variety contracts.

He's right.

The idea Rik, Mike and Mark have is to do improvised shows, partly because this is a novel and daring artistic form, but mostly because they haven't got time to learn loads of lines every fortnight. Then it occurs to them that doing an hour's improvisation with three people is quite a big ask, especially as they haven't done it before, and they decide to enlarge the group to five. Rik asks me to join the group, possibly because I've been in a lot of productions during the first year; he also asks Lloyd Peters, possibly because he has a car.

We are drama students so we know all about the pub theatre movement that was born in the 1960s in London, and we imagine this lends the project an air of intellectual respectability. There will be no sets, no lights, no tech of any sort, just a bare stage, and we will get changed in the toilets – we interpret this not as a lack of resources, but as a positive aesthetic decision. We offer to do a three-day run every fortnight: Thursday, Friday and Saturday lunchtimes.

A new way of thinking

This leap into the dark coincides with a great lesson I receive from my tutor Nick Roddick.

At school we were taught to venerate our teachers and, above all, textbooks. My appreciation of, for example, Shakespeare, was learned through the prism of Shakespearean scholars like William Hazlitt, A. C. Bradley, Dover Wilson, or at the very least CliffsNotes. The teachers expected my essays to be littered with references to these experts – to prove the validity of my arguments. Their names are etched in my memory.

In my second year at university Nick gets me in for a chat and says my essays are strewn with other people's ideas. I think I'm being accused of plagiarism, and I show him the footnotes where everything is dutifully attributed. I'm actually quite narked.

Nick's very kind – a man of the 1960s. He's not an actual hippy, but I think he may have dabbled. He wears a waistcoat that he might have bought in India or Afghanistan and has a slightly unkempt horseshoe moustache.

My favourite novel is *The History Man* by Malcom Bradbury, it's the one I've reread more than any other. The main character is Howard Kirk – a permissive and radical sociology lecturer who loves stirring things up, mostly just for the fun of it.

Nick reminds me of Howard – they're both such gentle and humorous revolutionaries. He points at my essays with their references to well-known scholars and says, with a broad grin peeking out from beneath his moustache, 'But I don't want to know what *they* think, I know what *they* think, I've read their books, I wanna know what *you* think.'

It's a mental revolution.

It 'blows my mind', as Nick might say.

Nearly everything they taught me at school was wrong, thank God my parents weren't paying for it.

Let that be a lesson to you!

The idea that *my* opinion is worth something – *without a supporting argument from an acknowledged source* – unblocks a dam inside my head. Up until now I've only been an interpreter of *other* people's work, now I start to create my own. I write the department pantomime – the script and the songs (rock god); I create a one-man show and take it to the National Student Drama Festival; another group of us create a play about the Baader Meinhof group; we take new offerings to the Edinburgh Festival, new plays, two-man shows, something called a 'review'.

But this whirlwind of creativity begins with Rik, Mike, Mark and Lloyd.

The group of five finds a name – 20th Century Coyote, a

weak pun on 20th Century Fox. I'm not sure how many people get the reference, even though we play the 20th Century Fox theme tune at the start of every performance. Are we trying to suggest that we're more wild and dangerous than the mainstream? Is a coyote more wild and dangerous than a fox? Who would win in a fight? Or is it an allusion to Wile E. Coyote in the *Road Runner* cartoons?

Whichever, the name sticks, perhaps because it's so vague it doesn't pin us down. And group names are only ever as good as the work they produce: The Beatles and The Rolling Stones are pretty poor names objectively, but carry weight because of the work associated with them.

20th Century Coyote is a happy group. Every fortnight we pile into Lloyd's car and drive to The Band on the Wall pretending to be in a James Bond film. We sing the theme tune at the top of our voices – that tune that has the quiet bits (dum, dum, dum dum), followed by the loud horny bits – (da-da de-daah, de da-dah, daddle-de-dah, de da daaah) and Lloyd, a man who should never have been given a licence, swerves out into the traffic obligingly as we fire imaginary pistols out of the windows.

We do shows with titles like *The Church Bizarre – a Fête Worse than Death* and *The Typig Error*. In my memory they are murder mysteries? Cowboy spoofs? Is there one about a dragon? I'm sure I remember a guest performance from Paul Bradley – a fellow student who goes on to be a regular in *EastEnders* and *Holby City* – sucking deep on a fag, blowing out smoke, and pretending to be a Welsh dragon even though he's Irish. There's no recorded evidence to remind me of the quality of these productions, no scripts, and no photographs. So you have to rely on me to tell you what they were like.

What were they like, Ade or Adrian?

They were brilliant. God, you should have been there.

Who knows? We amuse ourselves immensely, and play mostly to fellow students from the Drama Department who come along to give us support.

I hand the hat round at the end of every performance – our only chance to make any money – and on one occasion I approach a couple of women sitting near the back who look like they've just popped in for half a shandy whilst waiting for a bus. One woman reaches into her purse for a couple of coins but her friend puts out a hand to stop her.

'No, don't,' she says. 'They're only strolling players.'

Her friend puts a few pence in the hat anyway, but I barely notice because I can't wait to tell the boys. I rush back to the toilets where they're changing amongst the puddles of piss and johnny machines.

'Strolling players!' I shout. 'A woman just said we're strolling players!'

We are cock-a-hoop. Strolling players. This is the validation we've been seeking. This is tantamount to being called professional artistes. Who needs an Equity card when someone is already calling us strolling players.

Turns out we do. The proprietor of The Band on the Wall doesn't see enough of an increase in his lunchtime trade and the dodgy Variety contracts do not materialize. We stop doing the gig after a few months.

Our last outing as a group of five is to the Edinburgh Fringe in 1977. Though Lloyd Peters has been replaced by Chris Ellis, who you might remember from *The Young Ones* as one of the sixteen-year-olds on 'Nozin' Aroun'' complaining that he can join the army and kill people but can't go into pubs. Mark Dewison also turns up a few times in *The Young Ones* as Neil's hippy friend who dresses exactly like Neil, has long hair like Neil, and is also called Neil.

The Edinburgh experience in the seventies is very different to the glitzy one you hear about today. It's amateurs and students. Brotherhood of Man are top of the charts with 'Angelo' and people are driving around in beige-coloured Austin Allegros – and that's pretty much how it feels.

We go up as part of Manchester Umbrella. As the name suggests it's an umbrella organization for lots of different shows, all from Manchester University. And a joke about how much it rains in Manchester. It does rain a lot. We are perpetually damp.

We hire the Zetland Hall in Leith. It looks like a large semi-detached house from the front but behind it expands into a spacious hall that is used for ceilidhs by the Shetland Society, who own the place.

Manchester Umbrella is a massive outfit – we are like a mini festival in one venue, we put on several plays, a revue, poetry readings and even a dance event, and there are perhaps forty of us in the company.

We all sleep . . . in the hall. Yes, we sleep in and amongst the scenery and the chairs, simply crawling into sleeping bags and lying on the bare wooden floor. The night-time lullaby is the sound of people trying to have sex without making a noise. One girl picks up the wrong glass of water and drinks someone else's contact lenses. Could have been worse.

Every morning we have to get up early and start queuing for one of the two bathrooms, because the doors open at 9.00 and the first show starts at 10.00. Many of us never make it to the front of the queue. I imagine the hall stinks of unwashed students and leftover spud-u-like (not a euphemism), which is probably one of the reasons our shows are so ill-attended. That and the fact that we're so far away from the main drag in Edinburgh.

There's a company rule that we won't go through with a performance if the cast outnumber the audience but we have to forgo the rule pretty sharpish or we'll end up doing no shows at all. Apart from the japes and the constant boozing it's a pretty dispiriting experience.

Our show in 1977 is called *My Lungs Don't Work* – I can't recall anything about it, and wonder if there isn't much to remember. Ever since we stopped the shows at The Band on the Wall the group has fallen into some kind of limbo.

It feels like the world changes in the summer of 1977. It's when Elvis Presley, Groucho Marx and Grandma Ed all die; when Ron Greenwood becomes the England manager, when the National Front are rebuffed at the Battle of Lewisham, when Virginia Wade wins Wimbledon, and when The Sex Pistols get to number six with 'Pretty Vacant'. I don't know which, if any, of these is a possible catalyst, but the time is ripe for change, and when we return to Manchester 20th Century Coyote is just a two-man outfit – Rik and me.

A double act

It's often said that a double act is 'like a marriage' – it's an effort to explain the closeness of the partnership; the abiding love and affection; the living in each other's pockets; the telepathic anticipation of what the other might be thinking. But it also acknowledges that, like in many marriages, the love and affection can be taken for granted; that people can feel suffocated; and that they can sometimes yearn for divorce.

After Oliver Hardy died in 1957, Stan Laurel lived on for a further eight years, but refused to perform in any other films because he thought it would be a betrayal of their relationship.

The 1975 film *The Sunshine Boys*, written by Neil Simon, has George Burns and Walter Matthau play a vaudevillian double act asked out of retirement to resurrect their famous 'Doctor Sketch' for a TV special. They haven't seen each other for eleven years, the resentment that caused their break-up festers like an open wound, they bicker and fight, and the Walter Matthau character ends up having a heart attack.

The double act Rik and I share for thirty odd years lies somewhere between these two stools. To carry the marriage analogy further – our courting days are really good fun.

You can't really make comedy as a double act without learning a lot about each other, because creating together is more or less a sharing of everything you know, and the more you share already, the easier it is.

Rik and I learn the following: our mothers sent us to university with exactly the same dressing gown – a paisley-patterned job from C&A; we both own a treasured copy of *Gorilla* by The Bonzo Dog Doo-Dah Band and think Vivian Stanshall is the funniest human alive – he's anarchic and unpredictable, and has a dangerously cavalier attitude to his art which we want to emulate. I spent my last two years at school doing a more-or-less permanent impression of Viv, which is why I talk the way I do whilst the rest of my family have broad Yorkshire accents. It's also the reason Vyvyan in *The Young Ones* is called Vyvyan.

We love Spike Milligan's novel *Puckoon*, and are both obsessed with Samuel Beckett's *Waiting for Godot*. We are the only people we know who think it is an out-and-out comedy. We find the bleakness hysterical. We've both been in productions of it with Rik playing Vladimir and me playing Estragon, and we can recite whole chunks of it at will.

We think the *Road Runner* cartoons are better than Shakespeare.

We realize that we held very similar positions at our separate schools; that we were the ones who did *all* the plays; that we both had a healthy disregard for authority; that neither of us made prefect; that we both failed to get the A-level grades predicted for us because we were too cocky to work hard; and that we both have a similar idea of what happiness looks like – playing pool in the backroom of a cosy boozer, with a good seventies jukebox, a packet of fags, and a pint of lager.

We share a love of other playwrights too: Eugène Ionesco, Alfred Jarry and Harold Pinter. We've watched and enjoyed Bob Monkhouse's programmes on silent comedies; ~~Rolf Harris's~~

Cartoon Time; *Morecambe & Wise*; *Tommy Cooper*; *The Goodies*; *It Ain't Half Hot Mum*; *Some Mothers Do 'Ave 'Em*; *Monty Python*; Max Wall; even Freddy 'Parrot Face' Davies.

Whilst we're at university we gobble up the new comedies that emerge: *Fawlty Towers*; *Ripping Yarns*; Spike Milligan, again, being occasionally brilliant, often appallingly bad in the *Q* series; *What the Papers Say*; Peter Cook's short-lived *Revolver*; and *The Muppet Show*. God, we love *The Muppet Show* – we will ask to stop rehearsals early in order to get back in time to see the Muppets, often to the bewilderment of our fellow students.

We are always desperate to laugh. Desperate in the proper sense of the word. Frantic, despairing, distracted. It's like a disease. Constantly hunting for amusement, though 'amusement' is too weak a word. We want it hard, we want to mainline it, we want to laugh our bollocks off – we want to go berserk.

Rik and I become a fixture at the weekly Studio Night. There's a nominal budget of ten quid per show to help 'realize' your ideas. One week we spend the cash on two pink duvet covers from Brentford Nylons – our idea is to get into them, suspend ourselves from the ceiling, and pretend to be God's testicles (which will talk, obviously). In the technical rehearsal we find that the nylon – famous mostly for causing a sweaty night's sleep and excessive static – won't hold the weight of a grown student. I get a bruised arse, but our creativity is undimmed, and with the remaining, unshredded duvet cover, we instantly create another short piece entitled 'How to get a man out of a bag'. We have no fear.

We find that improv isn't really about trying to make an audience laugh, it's about trying to make each other laugh, and Rik and I make each other laugh. We have a shared set of references, as wide and disparate as *Tingha & Tucker*, the Boer War, and where Monsieur and Madame Dupont went on their holidays in early French lessons (*à la plage*, as some of you probably know). These give us a shorthand way of knowing where the other might be going in any improvisation.

This simpatico relationship develops into us hanging out together. We go to lots of gigs. We like a particular kind of gig: it's not about a particular style of music, we just like bands that aren't particularly popular so that it's easy to get to the bar. And we like the stage to be within sight of the bar. We like watching a blues band called Gags who have a residency in the upstairs room at the Cavalcade pub in Didsbury.

The Bonzos have a photo in one of their album inner sleeves which features one of them looking suitably wacky with a speech bubble that reads 'Wow, he's really expressing himself!' Our last two years at Manchester see the spread of punk and we watch a lot of people trying to 'really express' themselves, and not just the bands, the punters too. In fact the punters are often funnier.

There's a venue belonging to the Student Union on Devas Street called The Squat. This is where the people dressed in bin bags like to hang out, and we like to go and watch them. The Squat is a ramshackle building, more church hall than historic rock venue, but it features future stars like The Fall and The Buzzcocks in its time.

On one occasion Lloyd Peters is acting as the DJ before a performance by Alberto y Los Trios Paranoias. They're a comedy rock band – closer to The Barron Knights than The Bonzo Dog Doo-Dah Band, but their song about drinking too much Windolene is one of our favourites.

We get there pretty early to watch Lloyd's antics and the place is quite empty as he puts on 'New Rose' by The Damned. It's a fast song. In fact it's 173 beats per minute, which is going some when the average bpm of stuff in the charts at the time is around 120. It's the kind of speed that defies disco dancing and is why pogo dancing is born: just jumping up and down as fast as you can.

The handful of us that are there at this point are leaning against the walls, dutifully nodding our heads in time to the music, when in walks someone who looks exactly like Neil from *The Young Ones* (who we are yet to meet). He has the trademark long hair, sad face, and flared trousers, but is also wearing a thick tweed jacket with leather buttons that he must have got from his dad. He walks into the centre of the room, studies the people around the edge, thinks for a moment, and then begins to pogo.

He gives it a really good go. In fact he goes berserk. He jumps up and down as fast and as high as he can go. As he does so things start to fall out of his pockets: pens, pencils, a protractor, his wallet, a hanky, loose coins, a spare leather button, lentils. Mercifully punk songs are fairly short, and two minutes later his exertions come to an abrupt stop. He's very sweaty, and his possessions are scattered all around him, like in a satanic ritual from some Dennis Wheatley book. He looks thoughtful for a moment, perhaps processing the experience, then nods as if to say 'the experiment is complete'. He picks up his things and stuffs them back into his pockets, and walks straight back out again. It is the best part of the evening.

We laugh a lot. We drink a lot. We drive around together on my motorbike a lot. By the time we leave university we are proper best friends.

Part 6

The accidental comedian

The accidental comedian

The OED defines 'accidental' as: *happening by chance, unintentionally, or unexpectedly.*

I don't have any more accidents than the average man – I've still got all my fingers and toes – though there have been some good ones: as a child I'm pedalling my bike along a path in an army camp in Cyprus, when a wasp flies into my eye, panics, and stings me – it's exceedingly painful but leaves a very pleasing star shape in the middle of my iris that lasts for more than a week (very David Bowie); playing mountaineers in a tree on the same base, for reasons unknown I 'belay' the safety rope around a high branch, secure it around my neck, and promptly fall out of the tree – only the swift action of the soldier who lives next door saves me from certain death (hanging is abolished the following year and there are no further incidents of this kind); driving my BMW R65 motorbike with its distinctive cylinders that stick out on either side I misjudge an overtaking manoeuvre and get trapped between two cars moving fast in opposite directions – I lose both cylinder heads but come out of it unscathed (cf. the opening motorbike sequence in *Guest House Paradiso*).

But most of my career happens by chance, unintentionally

or unexpectedly. Accidental defines much of my life, and most definitely describes the way I become a comedian.

Many ambitious young actors I meet these days seem to have their lives planned out. They've got a good agent from their final year show at drama school, and now they're going to do theatre for two years – the National or Royal Court, not the 'ghastly' commercial stuff – then get a good supporting role in a drama series, and go off to LA for the pilot season . . .

I've never planned my life further than a few weeks or months ahead. Even now, when a job is coming to an end and people ask 'what are you doing next?' I generally answer, 'I'm currently unemployed for the rest of my life.' I say it as a joke, but it's disappointingly true. At the moment of writing it's happening again next week.

Certainly, fresh out of uni, the general state of play is to wake up in the morning and see what happens that day.

Of course I have preposterous dreams: I will play Hamlet at the RSC; I'll be the new Malcolm McDowell or John Hurt; I'll be in the next Nic Roeg or Mike Leigh film. But these things are out of reach because I don't even have an agent. No one in the world of theatre, television and film knows that I exist.

No one, that is, except Rik.

If you'd asked both of us what we intended to be when we arrived at Manchester we'd have both said 'actor'. I tell a lie, Rik would have said 'sex god', but he'd have wanted to become a sex god through being an actor – like James Dean or Steve McQueen.

There's a Wikipedia rumour that we used to go around in our final year shouting, 'We're going to be stars! We're going to be stars!' But this is another of those dreadful Chinese whispers, and is in truth a story about Paul Bradley.

Another of the London-Irish set, Paul's witty and jokey. He

likes drinking, rugby, larking about, and . . . doing impressions of what he imagines Ian McKellen and Derek Jacobi are like in their everyday lives.

It's a time when people still sell the communist newspaper the *Morning Star* on the steps of the Student Union building every day.

'Morning Star!' the news vendor will shout as we climb the steps.

'Morning love!' Paul will reply, doffing his imaginary trilby. 'No time for autographs today, I'm afraid.'

It's a particularly stupid gag that amuses me every time. And if I spot Paul in the vicinity I will wait at the bottom of the steps and go up with him just to hear it again. Perhaps I like it so much because, although it's a joke, it epitomizes the kind of 'comical luvvie world' I seek to enter. It feels like such a joyful world.

Rik, Paul and I all think we're heading towards a life in the theatre. We joke that the last term should really be focused on how to order a gin and tonic at a crowded bar on a first night, and the three of us invent a kind of music hall patter song which we sing to the tune of 'The Laughing Policeman':

Theatre, theatre, theatre, theatre, theatre, Peter Hall
Theatre, theatre, theatre, theatre, Lauren Bacall
Theatre, theatre, theatre, theatre, Tommy Court-e-nay
Theatre, theatre, theatre, theatre, Laurence Ol-iv-ier

You will have spotted that there are no jokes in the lyrics – well done – no, the fun comes in performing it with knowing winks and nods which imply that all these people are our closest theatrical chums.

But we find ourselves being steered towards comedy, firstly by chasing the Variety contracts at The Band on the Wall, and perhaps secondly by the way we're perceived by our fellow students. Every group finds its natural comedians, and while others explore more serious means of self-expression – I particularly remember a nude version of Marlowe's *Edward II* set in a cage – we will happily take the piss.

We also have very few options: we don't have Equity cards and these bloody Variety contracts seem to be our only route in. But even they are proving elusive – how can we get them? Well, by being 'comedians'.

I've said that Rik and I were always desperate for a laugh, but gagging for a laugh doesn't necessarily mean you want to be a comedian. Every single member of The Beatles was a very funny guy, but they never wanted to take up comedy as a career. Judi Dench, one of our greatest tragedians, is by all accounts one of the funniest people on the planet, who laughs all day long even when she's making rather bleak films like *Philomena* or *Belfast*, but she's never professed herself to be a comedian. My youngest brother Alastair was always thought of as the joker in our family but he ended up driving big trucks in Australia.

Yet Rik and I leave university more as comedians than as actors.

We're not thinking in terms of 'career choice' – indeed the idea of a 'career' seems frankly laughable at the time (and still does) – we're just taking the line of least resistance. It's the only line we've got.

The word comedian is going through a strange time in the 1970s.

To some it's a bit of an insult, meaning someone who's not quite all there, who's not taking things seriously enough. Policemen will say, 'Oh, we've got a right comedian here.' In fact they're still saying it in 1981 when I'm arrested in Soho for being drunk (berserker).

I'm many sheets to the wind and I'm taken to the cop shop in Savile Row – though frankly they're no better dressed than policemen elsewhere – and when taking down my particulars they ask for my profession and I say: 'Comedian.'

'Oh, we've got a right comedian here,' they say, rolling their eyes.

'Yes, that's what *I* said,' I say.

The trouble with playing to an audience of policemen *in* a police station is that they have the ultimate heckle – they lock me in a cell for the night.

To others the word comedian means the TV show *The Comedians* on which a series of club comics, mostly wearing dinner jackets and bow ties, tell jokes. These jokes are along the lines of 'three men went into a pub . . .' or 'a fella goes in to see a psychiatrist . . .' It's frankly unexciting stuff, any of the jokes could be told by any of the comedians, and there's an unhealthy whiff of racism and misogyny to it.

The stereotypical live comedian when we leave university in 1978 is a fat, white man in a DJ who tells jokes about his mother-in-law, Irish people, and people with a darker skin tone than his. He finds Pakistanis particularly hilarious, and homosexuals are a scream. It's not really comedy at all, it's more sharing insecurities about things with people who are similarly affrighted.

This isn't in any way what we're about, and we don't see how we can enter this world of live comedy, which at the time is centred around the working men's clubs, and places like the Batley Variety Club. We ring a couple of variety agents but I don't think they like our middle-class accents.

Another route is the folk club circuit where Billy Connolly and Mike Harding both cut their teeth before moving on to bigger things.

And the third route is to go to Cambridge University and get into Cambridge Footlights, who seem to have a direct line to the BBC Comedy Department, but neither of us is brainy enough.

There had been a fourth route. It's amazing how many post-war comedians started off as conscripts performing in little concert parties for groups like ENSA (Entertainments National Service Association): Benny Hill, Kenneth Williams, Spike Milligan, Stanley Baxter, Terry-Thomas, Harry Secombe, Peter Sellers, Frankie Howerd, Denis Norden, Eric Sykes, Tony Hancock, Harry Worth, Tommy Cooper and Jimmy Perry, the creator of *Dad's Army*.

We aren't working class enough, folky enough, or brainy enough. And we haven't been to war.

Manchester University is one of the so-called 'red-brick' universities – one of the nine universities founded in the nineteenth century in industrial cities like Liverpool, Leeds and Birmingham. They're called red-brick because they're not made out of honey-coloured limestone like the buildings at Oxford University, nor are they endowed with the stained-glass windows and fan-vaulted ceilings of Cambridge University – they are more simply fashioned out of bog-standard red bricks. It's the cheaper and less prestigious alternative, perfect for people like us.

We are red-brick comedians. And there aren't many of us around in 1978. Precisely none, as we see it at the time. And as when leaving school and trying to find a way to become an actor, there isn't the faintest hint of a career path. Which means we have to invent our own.

So I sit in my study – by which I mean I sit in the cupboard in the hall of the flat I'm now renting in Tamworth, just outside Birmingham. It's no wider than the door frame, but I've managed to cram in a desk and a chair. I write to every single arts centre and student union in Britain, and when I say write I mean I physically type every single letter. There are no computers and home printers yet, and I don't have a Roneo machine (a Rotary Neostyle duplicator, beloved by schoolteachers, which don't so much 'duplicate' as produce a smudgy, purple 'impression').

Our time at uni coincides with the birth of punk, and that DIY spirit is coursing through our veins – who cares about conventional theatre? We will play anywhere, anytime. And in our first year out we play . . . four gigs.

Out of the 400+ institutions I write to only a dozen or so reply, and none of them offer us a gig. We play one date back at Manchester University where the Stephen Joseph Studio charitably invites us to perform, we do another at Bromsgrove College of Further Education where Rik's dad is a drama lecturer (nepotism), and we do the National Student Drama Festival in Southampton as mature (!) students, where we manage to get another offer of a gig from Hatfield Polytechnic.

'Here's three chords, now form a band' is the famous mantra of the punk movement. We know the equivalent of more than three chords, in terms of comedy I think we know at least four, and one of them might be augmented (almost jazz), and we've got a 'band', but we don't know how to make people listen to us (also like jazz).

Gloria Gaynor is top of the charts with 'I Will Survive' and that's basically all we're doing, surviving. We're doing dead-end jobs to earn money – Rik's back living with his parents and working in a meat-packing plant in Droitwich, I'm living in a council flat in Tamworth and working in the Exhaust Pipe Warehouse in Birmingham – and this rather hampers our creativity. We're living either side of Birmingham, forty miles apart, and have to make do with weekends getting pissed and improvising into a cassette recorder.

He comes over to mine every Saturday. We go to the pub, drink lager with whisky chasers, play pool, and put 'Revolution

No. 9' by The Beatles on the jukebox several times in a row. After chucking-out time we go back to my flat and the chip pan will swing into action. We press *play* and *record* and make each other laugh and laugh and laugh. The next morning we listen back – it's mostly unfunny gibberish with the sound of kitchen accidents in the background. It's a painful way to make comedy. It's not the hilarious profanity of Peter Cook and Dudley Moore's *Derek and Clive (Live)* that we were aiming for: it's just profanity. We decide we need to be more professional.

So the following year we move to London and book ourselves a ten-date tour of church halls around the capital. It's a sketch show called *The Wart!* that includes an early version of the Dangerous Brothers – two psychopaths who think they are light entertainers.

We're promoting ourselves, hiring the venues, doing our own publicity, sending things to anyone and everyone; there's a lot of cutting and pasting going on – actual cutting and pasting, not the computerized kind – we try everything we can think of to drum up an audience. The blurb on the handbill reads: 'Soon the world will be divided into those who missed *The Wart!* And those who didn't bother to go at all.' This ends up being more or less accurate as the average audience is about six people, but one of them happens to be a reviewer from *The Guardian*. I don't know what seduces him to come and see it. I've written to every single reviewer but he's the only one that comes. Maybe it's the handbill which features the 1623 Droeshout portrait of Shakespeare . . . with a huge hairy wart stuck on the end of his nose. Critics love Shakespeare.

He gives us a small but positive review, remarking on Rik's 'rubbery-faced intensity' and describing me as 'the eternal little man'. Though remembering those phrases again, I'm not sure if it is a positive review . . . but we think it is at the time, and look on it as validation that we are 'professionals'.

Another member of the tiny throng at a church hall in Kennington is a large, fiery Welshman who's the manager of a venue called The Tramshed in Woolwich. He's only recently taken over the organization and he's a man on a mission to turn it into a place of daring artistic excellence. He wants to create a new kind of cabaret on Friday and Saturday nights and offers us a residency. We grab it.

Should have gone to Egypt . . .

The Tramshed, it turns out, is as much a community centre as an arts centre, and it's a positive thriving asset to the local area: it's busy all week long with community events and youth theatre projects and on weekends they create their own fun night out – which attracts quite a few squaddies from the local barracks – a jolly sketch show called *Fundation*, led by a guy called Joe Griffith, which features, among others, another comedy double act called Hale & Pace.

But the fiery Welshman has taken against *Fundation* – he considers it too lowbrow – and wants us to replace it (!). He also wants to revolutionize the artistic output and we get bit parts in his production of *Macbeth* set in Vietnam with soldiers smoking dope through shotguns.

'I want it to be really relevant, really punk you know – like . . . GREEN HAIR' becomes a phrase of his that we remember forever. We use it whenever we want to describe something that is catastrophically misguided.

So every weekend he puts on a kind of variety show and we come on in between the jazz band Greenwich Meantune and the speciality act of the week. It's not our milieu – we're doing our Sam Beckett piss-takes and the locals and the squaddies want Cannon and Ball. We end up doing the few sketches from *The Wart!* that work in that environment. We do them over and over again, separating the wheat from the chaff, until we're basically just doing the Dangerous Brothers.

The Dangerous Brothers are like this: Rik plays Richard Dangerous who looks as demented as Ron Mael, the mad keyboard player from the band Sparks, but on amphetamines. Like Ron he appears to have a hidden agenda but he's wired, anxious and hyperactive. I play Sir Adrian Dangerous who is fundamentally a berserker – he is furiously violent and out of control. He's the obvious foot soldier in the relationship, but is too stupid to understand his position. There's always a suspicion that they are being watched by a higher power – Mr Cooper – and that if they fuck up they will suffer serious consequences, so there's a frenzied urgency to get everything right. They're more like hitmen than comedians, but it becomes evident they've been sent to deliver a bog-standard cracker joke:

'What's green and hairy and goes up and down? A gooseberry in a lift.'

But they never get to tell it in this simple form.

Rik springs onto the stage and shouts: 'We are the Dangerous Brothers! I am Richard Dangerous! And this . . .' he says as I rush on after him '. . . is Sir Adrian Dangerous!'

At which point I run forward and headbutt the microphone. It not only makes a brilliant sound, but usually bursts from the mic stand and lands in the audience.

They argue and bicker and fight. They're never stationary. They have enormous problems with logic. The joke they've been given isn't as simple as it seems – how did the gooseberry get in the lift? How did it press the buttons? Why would it want to go anywhere? It's a fucking gooseberry! It's basically a sketch about not being able to tell a joke, delivered with terrifying conviction and a lot of violence and nipple tweaking.

The Tramshed isn't a well-paid gig, it's basically beer money, and we still don't get our Variety contracts. We're still doing 9-to-5 day jobs to keep ourselves afloat. Rik's working in an employment agency, I'm a motorcycle messenger. It's fair to say that the abysmal *Macbeth* is an absolute turkey, and the weekend show isn't doing much better. The fiery Welshman is basically killing the venue.

We perform to a steadily dwindling audience that are getting harder and harder to please. But to be honest, it's probably the best thing for us at the time, because it makes us focus on making the good bits work really well. We learn to hone our craft. What works, and what works really well are two very different things. We model, shape and sharpen the act until it is the shiniest diamond anyone has ever seen. Even the squaddies are laughing.

In late 1979 – when The Police are top of the charts with 'Message in a Bottle' – we see a message, an advert, in the back of the actors' weekly newspaper *The Stage*. We read the small ads every week in the vain hope of seeing some offer of non-unionized work that we might be able to apply for. Unfortunately neither Lindsay Anderson nor Peter Brook ever slip in ads for 'completely inexperienced and non-unionized actors who have absolutely nothing to show for themselves', but this week it does have an advert for a new club that's opening in Soho called the Comedy Store. It says:

> Are you trapped in a boring 9 to 5 job when you are a very funny person who wants to become a comedy star . . . If your answer is 'yes' to that question, then contact us – The Comedy Store in Soho and become part of our Comedy Revolution. If you have the talent, we will help you to become a Comedy Star.

It's asking for us. It's asking directly for us.

The funniest thing I ever saw

The Comedy Store is in Meard Street, a rickety little alley in Soho that looks like a set from a Dickens film. The club is a tiny fire hazard of a room, accessed by an equally rickety old lift that only holds four people at a time, and one of these is the even more rickety lift operator. It's the Nell Gywnne Club the rest of the week – a strip joint – but late on Saturday nights, when the men in raincoats go home to their wives and families, 'Darling, I'm home!', it hosts the Comedy Store, an idea stolen from America.

It's a gong show – there's a gong hung to one side of the stage, and if the audience don't like the act they're watching they shout 'Gong!' 'GONG!' If enough of them shout, the compère strides on, bangs the gong, and the act in question has to leave the stage. Tail between legs. So, it's basically bullying. A real bear-pit atmosphere. All the comics are understandably concerned about the potential humiliation. Well, not so much concerned, as cacking their pants. But it makes the club what it is.

We meet other people like us: Alexei Sayle, a Chelsea Arts School graduate who's been doing a fringe theatre show about

Bertolt Brecht and is involved in a Saturday night show at The Elgin pub in Ladbroke Grove called *Alternative Cabaret*. He wears a porkpie hat, is rather gruff and looks like a bouncer. There's Peter Richardson and Nigel Planer, who have a double act called The Outer Limits. They've been doing some kind of festival show in more or less empty fields in the West Country that features music and sketches, they now do things like 'Are You being Severed' – a version of the trad sitcom *Are You Being Served* reimagined with contract killers, and Nige does a solo spot as Neil the Hippy.

There's a stream of acts each night. There has to be, in case the gong gets gonged so often they run out.

However, whilst we're all fearful of the 'gong', there's one act that revels in the idea. It's an act that is the funniest thing I've ever seen.

The terrible thing is, here I am, telling you about the funniest thing I ever saw, a moment of great importance to me, and . . . I can't remember his name. It might be Day, or Davy Day, or Davy Dave – I've googled it and I can't find him. I'm sure someone out there knows, but please don't write in, because I've discovered I don't really *want* to find it. I want this act to remain pristine in my memory. I want it to be *my* memory of it, not somebody else's. I don't want it clouded by photos, or video, or even worse – the truth.

We all remember things differently. Remember the Numskulls.

To me it's a work of sublime stupidity, and I don't think there's enough stupidity in comedy these days. Comedy's broadly changed in Britain from people being stupid, and making fun of themselves, to people being clever and making cruel observations about other people. I prefer the former. So I want to keep this golden nugget of stupidity safe in my brain.

I feel morally obliged to try and describe the act for you,

even though I know I can't do it justice. So, we're all going to be disappointed, but here goes: a man comes onto the stage with a music stand and a violin, but never gets round to playing it.

That's it. That's the act. He never says anything. There're no words. There aren't even any 'jokes'.

What is a joke? I keep coming back to this and can never find the answer but I think if someone else can tell your joke, like a joke from a joke book, then it's probably not really funny. It might be witty, but it won't be *funny*. Real comedy has something to do with hysteria. The writing's just a code for something to be doing while you try to pump up the hysteria.

But back to the act . . .

Is it a mime?

Nice try. It's a sort of mime – but a mime with the things he's miming. Sometimes there're moments that echo that Carlsberg advert when Norman Wisdom tries unsuccessfully to erect a deckchair, but Dave Davy Dave's act is never the same twice. That's not what he's going for. And music stands have a fiendish life of their own anyway. He isn't trying to get a laugh off doing things badly. I think he's trying to get a laugh by playing with people's expectations of what he's about to do.

Most people come on with some kind of attention-grabbing joke (I headbutt the microphone off the stand into the crowd – I've still got the scar tissue on my forehead to prove it), but David Davy Dave David appears with only a slight smirk in the corner of his mouth. He's got a kind of grace – he looks a bit like Kenny Dalglish in his prime, he has a mullet hairdo and wears a light grey suit, the kind footballers wear when they walk out onto the pitch before the FA Cup final.

I hate it when people try and explain comedy. So I'm going to hate myself now. But the act lives – oh I sound like such a wanker, 'the act lives' – it lives in the tension between himself and the crowd. He knows they'll eventually shout 'Gong!' He *wants* them to want to shout it. He's daring them to shout it. I don't think he actually has an end to his act in mind. So if they don't, he'll be stuck there for ever.

And why is this funny? It's about riding the audience reaction. He surfs them. And the more he surfs them, the more they shout, but the more they laugh as well. A man arrives on the stage with a music stand and a violin . . . or was it a flute? Or a clarinet? But whatever it is, the sight of a man coming on with a music stand and – a trumpet? – is sufficient to pique people's interest. So the audience get in. But once they're in, once he opens that door, all he does is play them. He works solely off them. They are the material. The laughs are all on his reaction to them, OR his *lack* of reaction to them. But all driven by them.

The whole ethos of the club is that the audience think *they* are controlling *his* destiny, but in fact *he* is controlling *theirs*. (Oh God, I really hate myself now . . .)

But that's the truth as I see it – it's about being stupid, it's about hysteria. It's about going berserk. Because, although people are screaming for blood, they're screaming with laughter at the same time.

Alexei, who's the compère at the club, is bright enough to realize that the act relies on people enjoying shouting 'gong'. And Day David Davy David turns up almost every week, so he and Alexei basically become an unwitting double act as the weeks roll by. So Dave goes on, and doesn't manage to put up the stand, and when he eventually does, doesn't manage to play the oboe, bassoon, euphonium, whatever it is, and the crowd get louder and louder. Really enjoying themselves. And Alexei's head will appear round the curtain near the gong. He won't immediately go for the mallet. He'll play the situation. And now Davy David will be playing the audience *and* Alexei. So that by the time the gong is indeed struck he'll get the loudest cheer of the evening. And everyone will have won.

It's a masterclass in just being stupidly funny.

Christ, I hope he was trying to be funny . . . He was. I'm *sure* he was. Surely he was?? Or maybe he too was an accidental comedian?

The gong element of the club is eventually dispensed with, and his act disappears along with it.

The line between success and failure can be exhilarating. It's where thinking disappears and funny can take over. It's that moment during 'Bottom Gas' that I've previously described where the hitting and punching go on so long that it veers into failure before building a kind of stupidity that is so stupid it's just stupidly funny.

Sturgeon's Law

Double acts work on trust. The trust that if one tries a gag that doesn't work the other will never belittle it, or scoff, or say it's crap, but will just let it pass by and wait for the next one to come along, which by the law of averages will be better.

Your partner is the first audience, the test audience, and the best audience in the world: it will never boo, it will never get restless and start coughing, it will never heckle, or leave.

You have an unspoken agreement that you will not let the other fail. Under any circumstance. This starts in the writing room, or during improvisations. The more you can offer your partner unwavering support, the more daring they will be and the better the act will become. You have to feel safe enough to try.

Like with panning for gold, you simply cheer louder when the nuggets appear. Getting the odd pan with no gold at all is just part of the process. You have to accept it. You can't get gold without occasionally getting no gold.

It's a beautiful feeling. Many's the time I've sat with Rik as we struggle with a scene. We'll have the bare bones of the idea, the set-up, and we'll have some of the dialogue, but then we'll try and develop it. We each offer up potential lines. None of these lines will be *bad* lines, because even the lines we don't use help us find the line we do use. The key thing is not to rubbish each other's suggestions. We'll grin or nod at each suggestion, an acknowledgement that it's a good idea, a potential idea, but perhaps not the best idea. Until eventually one of us will say something that makes the other really laugh, and that line will go in.

That's not to say these moments aren't without tension. We sometimes sit for a whole morning trying to resolve a scene or find the right line. On one of these days when we're really struggling, and starting to feel frustrated, as if we're under siege from our own work, the phone rings, I pick it up and say:

'Mafeking.'

And we both laugh for nearly ten minutes.

For those of you who don't recognize the reference, the Siege of Mafeking was a moment in the Second Boer War in South Africa in 1899–1900. The siege lasted more than seven months and made a hero of Baden-Powell (the founder of the Scouts) for his heroic defence under such continual attack. It's a marker of how Rik and I share such a shorthand of references: did we know about it through *Look & Learn* magazine, or through some story in *The Victor* or *The Hornet* comics? Perhaps our laughter is fuelled by this extra realization of how close we are. It's the same joy people feel when they reminisce about things from their childhood – when they remember dandelion and burdock, or Noggin the Nog, or chopper bikes – and the more obscure it gets, the better it feels.

You can only create in an atmosphere where failure is accepted and doesn't hurt.

I realize that Dad never accepted that failure was a thing. And this is peculiar, because some years after he died Mum tells me that he failed his Higher School Certificate when he was eighteen and didn't get into teacher training college as he'd planned.

He failed!

It was only through the intervention of a friend of a friend in the church that he managed to get an interview at a college in Chalfont St Giles. I've looked it up – Newland Park Training College – and it was described as an 'emergency teacher training college' when it opened in 1946. I imagine the lack of teachers after the war was the emergency, rather than Dad's predicament, but either way they let him in.

DAD! You never told me that you failed. You never told me that you too were vulnerable. That you were as fallible as the next man. That you were as *human* as everyone else. I spent my entire life hiding my failures from you because it seemed you expected perfection in all things.

If I have any talent as a creative writer I owe some of it to those sessions trying to explain my school report to my dad:

> REPORT
> Even Adrian will admit that his term in charge of a dormitory was a minor disaster.
> WHAT ACTUALLY HAPPENED
> Couldn't be arsed imposing the stupid school rules. Let people listen to Radio Luxembourg after lights out. Encouraged midnight feasts as long as they gave me some.
> AS EXPLAINED TO DAD
> I tried to run the dorm as an Athenian Democracy with everyone having a say, but a small group of citizens became unruly and spoiled it for everyone else – listening to the radio when they shouldn't and having illegal midnight feasts.

The crimes are all written in such obscure, obfuscating language. They never talk directly about anything. I am constantly beaten and the report will merely say 'some disciplinary problems this term'. Maybe they don't want to admit how often they hit me with sticks? It's Catch 22 – do I tell Dad how much I get beaten? Or does that mean I have to admit my crimes? And you'd think Dad, as a teacher, would understand the code the teachers are using? Maybe this is why he failed his Higher Educational Certificate.

> REPORT
> He must learn to understand that school rules are there for a reason.
> WHAT ACTUALLY HAPPENED
> I find the school environs stultifyingly dull so I go into town at every opportunity to smoke fags and drink coffee.
> AS EXPLAINED TO DAD
> Well, Dad, you see the thing is they don't serve *enough* food, and certainly not enough *fresh* food, so I was found outside the school grounds during school hours because I needed to buy some fruit – it was either that or get scurvy.

Failure's important. Failure is part of success. They're flip sides of the same coin. Imagining constant success is like spinning a coin one hundred times and it coming down heads every time. Like in *Rosencrantz & Guildenstern Are Dead* by Tom Stoppard. It's impossible. But the modern world of social media only expects heads, only expects continual success, and wants it to appear effortless.

After recognizing Dad's problem with accepting failure I start telling my children every time I don't get a job, so that at moments when they're not feeling particularly successful they might take some comfort in knowing we're all in the same boat. Everybody in the world is in the same boat. Even apparently successful people. I do a lot of auditions, and I fail 90 per cent of them. People might imagine I have a level of notoriety whereby I just sit back and read through offers, casually turning them down until the right one comes along . . . This certainly seems to be the idea most actors try to sell:

'And then this script popped through my letterbox and I just *had* to do it.'

When perhaps they should be saying:

'At last someone offered me a job, I'd have accepted it no matter how crap it was.'

It's normal not to be successful; I am unsuccessful more of the time than I am successful. Writing this book I can spend hours staring at a blank screen being unsuccessful, getting up from my desk, making coffee, looking at my Fantasy Football team, arranging the piles of detritus on my desk into slightly different piles of detritus, fiddling about on my mandolin, looking out of the window, lying down, standing up, rummaging through the kitchen for a snack. Then I write stuff that is unsuccessful, stuff that I will cut later, but that might be the nub of an idea. And then occasionally I might write a sentence I'm almost pleased with.

Maybe you're surprised at that last paragraph getting through the net but that's how low the bar is sometimes. Failure is a part of it. The main part of writing is keeping your bum on the seat.

Rik and I always referred to writing as 'mining'. I still say today: I'm off back down the word mine. Like gold miners identifying a seam of shiny-looking metal, we'd recognize a seam of possible jokes; we'd take something as mundane as a pair of tights and dig out every joke we could about them, chipping away in the metaphorical darkness with metaphorical pickaxes until there was nothing left. We'd then bring these jokes to the metaphorical surface and see if there were any nuggets, probably throwing out 90 per cent of them.

You can see the tights jokes in a finished show; an episode of *Bottom* called 'Bottom Finger'. Richie and Eddie need to hide their identities as they steal a car. Normal villains wear a stocking over their heads, but we only have a pair of tights, so we cram our heads into a leg each and are then hampered by having to go everywhere with our heads tied together. It might look easy, it might look successful, but it's the product of a 90 per cent failure rate.

There's a lot of shit around. There always has been, and always will be.

Theodore Sturgeon – no relation – was a popular American science fiction writer of the 1950s. In a talk to New York University in 1951 he was asked to defend science fiction as a genre, the public perception being that it was all a bit trashy. He admitted that a lot of it was trash, but suggested that the best was as good as the best fiction in any field, and went on to state that 90 per cent of EVERYTHING is crap.

This became known as Sturgeon's Law: 90 per cent of everything is crap – books, TV, film, pop music, hairstyles, breakfast cereals, other people. And this is a subjective exercise, so your 90 per cent might not match my 90 per cent – it is in the eye of the beholder.

George Orwell wrote in 'Confessions of a Book Reviewer': 'In more than nine cases out of ten the only objectively truthful criticism would be "This book is worthless".'

And Rudyard Kipling said something similar in *The Light That Failed*: 'Four-fifths of everybody's work must be bad. But the remnant is worth the trouble for its own sake.' So he's gone for 80 per cent there, the romantic fool!

Failure and your approach to it are fundamental parts of creativity.

Guerrillas of new wave humour

But now it's 1980, and we meet with a little success.

Dexy's Midnight Runners are top of the charts with 'Geno'. I'm in Soho, and I feel like I belong. This is a new feeling. I'm a full-time professional comedian and I have a 'place of work'. *'No, I'm not being flash, it's what I'm built to do.'*

There are articles in groovy magazines that suggest that Rik and I are at the cutting edge of what they're calling 'alternative' or 'new wave' comedy. These are terms that are thrust upon us, we have no hand in making them up. We're not sure how revolutionary we really are, but we're very happy to go along with it: we've spent the last few years doing rubbish temping jobs trying to earn enough money to allow us to perform at the weekends. I've been filling car batteries with acid, working in a pork pie factory, and in the stationery and photocopying department of an international bank. But now we're doing a show every night, in a club that we've set up with some like-minded comedians. It's called the Comic Strip Club.

I blithely write 'we've set up' when actually the prime mover is undoubtedly Pete Richardson. He's the one who thinks we're all different and that we need our own venue, our own showcase.

He's one of us – he's a performer – but he's also the one who's arranged financial backing from theatre impresario Michael White and the Pythons' film producer John Goldstone to set up the club.

The main upshot being that we're being paid to be comedians. Full time. That's the real revolution.

Walker's Court is the liveliest and most brightly lit alley in the area, and also the seediest. A passageway between Berwick Street and Brewer Street, it's at the heart of what's called the Red Light District. It's full of signs: *Peep show*; *Model 1st Floor*; *Non-stop striptease*; *Live Bed Show*; *Nude Encounter*; *Table Dancing*; *Sex Aids* (sadly ironic considering what's coming), and in the evenings it smells of rotting veg from Berwick Street market; the traders leave whatever they can't sell lying in the street. Bruised cabbages become footballs for the pissed-up stag parties looking for Amsterdam on the cheap.

Heavy-looking bouncers lend an air of theatrical menace to the scene. They're dressed anachronistically in sixties suits and hats because they're part of the show. They're not there to stop the wrong sort of people going in. They're there to stop them coming out, or to stop them kicking up a fuss when they're forced to buy small tins of Heineken at extortionate rates during the purposely long wait for whichever form of mild titillation they think they've paid for. This is the scam, this is where the sex joints make their money. But the bouncers know me now, and they smile at me because I'm part of the scene – I'm working at The Comic Strip.

'Evening, Vernon, evening, Ray,' I shout.

'Evening, Nigel,' they shout back.

Well, perhaps they don't know me as well as I think they do, but at least they *think* they know me.

Our club is in the Boulevard Theatre, one of two small theatres inside the Raymond Revuebar which takes up most of the western side of the alley. The other theatre still does strip shows, twice nightly, at 8 and 10. On the wall at the Brewer Street end of the alley there's a huge backlit sign which reads 'The World Centre of Erotic Entertainment', 'Festival of Erotica', and more importantly, 'Fully Airconditioned'. And then, down near the entrance, a much smaller poster in a glass frame proclaims *The Comic Strip Club* with the strap-line: 'Guerrillas of New Wave Humour'. Guerrillas. Not Gorillas. None of us really know what it means, but it's from a review and we interpret it as a sign that we are as hip as Che Guevara, and he's never been out of style during our lifetimes, so that's good enough for us.

The two theatres share the same bar, which makes for a diverse crowd, and the outrageously expensive drinks are served by topless barmaids. For an alternative comedian this is called having your cake and eating it.

At one end of the bar sits Paul Raymond himself, the self-styled 'King of Soho', famous for publishing a string of porn mags – *Men Only, Escort, Club International.* As a sixth former I was one of his chief customers. He looks like Peter Sellers doing an impression of a porn baron: he's wearing fur, he's got long shaggy hair and a moustache, and he's dripping with gold, with so many heavy rings on his fingers you wonder how he's able to lift his drink. But he's friendly and affable, and he always says hello as we walk through the bar to the backstage area. We very rarely order drinks from the topless barmaids because, even though we like breasts, and even though we're working full time, we simply can't afford the prices.

The boys' dressing room stinks; it stinks mostly of the two suits Rik and I have acquired as our stage gear. We bought them from a stall in Peckham. The bloke said they were made of wool, but I know my wool, and this definitely isn't wool, it's some kind of heavy plastic masquerading as wool. The material is about half an inch thick, and as soon as we put them on we start to sweat profusely. They're mostly purple with strange black squiggles and stripes. We want to look 'crap', but as if we've made an effort; we want to look like unsuccessful cabaret artistes – and I think we often succeed in more ways than one.

Beneath the suits we wear bright red shirts, and these are probably the biggest problem: they're cotton and obviously soak up the sweat with ease, so by the time we come off stage they're wringing wet – literally. We just wring them out. We never take them home. We never wash them. We simply wring them out and put them on hangers to 'air dry'. When we arrive each evening they are indeed bone dry, brittle almost, with huge white tidemarks of dried sweat, as if they've been tie-dyed with bleach. It takes some effort and not a little scratchy discomfort to force them on; sometimes we hear a 'crack' as ribbons of salt give way, but within a few minutes of donning the suits the new sweat makes them soft and pliable once more – it's a foolproof system.

The boys' dressing room is like our own private club. And this is a new feeling too. It's fairly small, about ten foot square, with two sinks and a costume rail. But it's ours. It belongs to us. It's the first time we've had a dressing room – before this we've always changed in the toilets or the kitchen. It's another revolution. It's our *professional* home. We're not students or amateurs any more.

We load the sinks with ice from the machine down the corridor and fill them with the beer we bring in. Whilst the punters are paying through the nose, we each bring in a 'four pack' of lager – four cans held together with one of those annoying plastic ring things – which cost about a quid a pack. The 'four can' show is the template: two for the first half, and two for the second, perhaps saving the last for post-show before going on somewhere else. It's deemed a badge of honour to bring in the cheapest four pack, with extra points for the most ridiculous name: Kestrel, Kaltenberg, Charger, Heldenbrau . . . It's 1980 and there's a race to the bottom amongst British lager brewers at the moment, but we're young, full of antibodies, and it gets us to the right level. See? Revolution's easy once you've got yourselves organized.

The regulars in the boys' dressing room are Rik and myself; Pete and Nige; Alexei; and Arnold Brown, a chartered accountant by day who makes great play of being both Scottish and Jewish – 'Two racial stereotypes for the price of one'. Arnold isn't a big drinker so the two sinks basically hold twenty cans of beer. We have occasional guests: the Americans rarely drink, generally preferring less-fattening stimulants; semi-regulars like Ben Elton know to bring their own cans; and the others we don't really mind offering to as long as they're amusing.

I know Ben from the Manchester University Drama Department, though he was a couple of years behind me. He's a prolific gag writer, a hilarious social commentator, and has the wiry enthusiasm of a terrier puppy. Our relationship, and that of our two families, grows over the years into a thing of great depth and wonder, though – as a man who's always keen to win – he's never got over the fact that whilst playing for the final 'cheese' in a game of Trivial Pursuit he once had to ask me, 'Who played Vyvyan in *The Young Ones*?'.

The dressing room next door is where the latest double act to join the group, French & Saunders, share a less drink-based evening with the house band – Simon Brint, Rod Melvin and Rowland Rivron. Pete worried about not having any women on the bill so auditioned some female acts, and their room is called the girls' dressing room even though it's 60 per cent male.

Dawn and Jennifer have a range of sketches from a Dolly Parton parody – a twosome country act called The Fartons – to the Menopazzi Sisters, two wannabe circus daredevils in black leotards with nipple tassels on the back, who are incredibly cowardly and unadventurous – a leap of six inches is treated as a great feat of derring-do. Hired to address the gender balance, they are incredibly funny and by no means a token – and they go on to be the most successful out of the whole group.

Dawn is still a full-time teacher when she starts at the club and she brings a little of the schoolteacher with her – she's organized, likes things to be done properly, and is not averse to telling people off if she thinks they've misbehaved. Jennifer is just the coolest person on the planet.

Simon and Rod are rather effete, they're slightly older than us and have experience of living in the sixties – they have a seductive experimental edge about them. Simon and I invest in an eight-track reel-to-reel tape recorder together, and we keep it in his flat, so I'm always round there. We become very close.

Rowland, the drummer, is hard to know when he first arrives. He's recently been punched in the face by a complete stranger in the street. This broke his jaw, which has been wired together until it heals. He drinks protein shakes through a straw and can't say much. Once the wiring is removed he never stops talking. We spend a large part of the early eighties playing pool together in The Royal Mail in Islington. We become such regulars that we can leave our unfinished drinks on the pool table when the pub closes at three and pick them up again when we come back at five.

The dressing rooms aren't exclusive by any means, people flit between the two, but the boys' room is always a bit rowdier, and the girls' more calm. You can go wherever your mood takes you. Alexei's wife Linda is a permanent fixture in the boys' dressing room, always slightly drunk, and always haranguing us for being too middle class to have an opinion.

Alexei and Linda are very keen on telling everybody, every day, every hour, that *they* are working class. No matter what the conversation is about – politics, art, football, knitting, koalas, a paper-cut – they are both of the opinion that their opinion is the true opinion, because they're working class.

Rik and I often play a game to see which of us can make them say it first. In the same way that if you mention snow someone will say that the Eskimos have fifty different words for it, or if you mention swans someone will be unable to resist telling you that a swan can break a grown man's arm with one flap of its wing, if you adopt any kind of political stance in the presence of Alexei and Linda they will tell you that you're too middle class to have an opinion.

The Comic Strip Club runs for a year and I remember it as a year-long party. The regular acts basically do a ten-minute spot in each half, Alexei compères, and the guest act does whatever it does.

There are lots of guest acts: there's a Peruvian nose-flautist; there's a man who pretends to be a trumpet. There's an act called Furious Pig, I don't know what they're trying to do but there are a lot of them, they have circus skills, and they're furious. Being furious is very much in vogue, the act Rik and I have involves a lot of swearing, shouting and violence; everyone's going berserk. Alexei looks like a psychotic bouncer and likes to frighten people; Keith Allen occasionally shows up and aims to be provocative – he's very angry about something though no one can ever quite tell what (maybe this is making him even angrier) – he's very hit and miss, though always exciting to watch, the failures sometimes more exciting than the successes. There's the brilliant night that Robin Williams turns up late, goes straight on in the second half and does material that Chris Langham has already done in the first – we never find out who the original stuff belongs to.

But my absolute favourite is Hermine.

Hermine Demoriane is a French chanteuse with the artful, vaguely out-of-tune style of Nico from The Velvet Underground.

She sounds like a drugged-up Marlene Dietrich. She's also a performance artist and an occasional tightrope walker. It pays to diversify. She's aloof, and a bit scary, but fascinating to watch, and she only ever sings one of two songs: 'Veiled Women' or 'Torture'.

Her album has a photo on the front of her wearing a cocktail dress and stacking a dishwasher with vinyl singles. It's a photo that amuses me every time I see it. Simon Brint, who played piano and organ on the album (maybe it's Simon that's buying all the 'organ and vocals' books) has the poster for it in his flat and I study it every time I go round. It's an image that sticks with me – a very ordinary situation subverted.

Her performances at the Comic Strip Club usually see her go on stage wearing an enormous cone of newspapers that have been stuck together. As she sings she sprays herself with paint from an aerosol, and then fights her way out as the song comes to a close. There's always some insecurity about the performance, it teeters on that delicious line between success and failure.

The Comic Strip Club gets a lot of attention. A lot of famous types turn up to see us: Jack Nicholson, Dustin Hoffman and Bianca Jagger come on the same night. It's front page news in *The Sun* the next day as BIANCA'S FOUR LETTER NIGHT OUT. It only has 200 seats but the club punches above its weight because it's the only one of its kind.

Is it revolutionary? Are we revolutionary? In one way, yes, because there's nothing else like it at the time. I suppose that's the definition of revolutionary.

We're certainly very different from the dinner jacket and bow tie brigade that still dominate the world of live comedy in the working men's clubs at the time. There hasn't been a club like ours since The Establishment – the club Peter Cook opened round the corner in Greek Street at the height of the satire boom, but that closed in 1964. Nor are we the clever darlings of the Cambridge Footlights. Our red-brickness is the true revolution, the true point of difference.

There's a lefty political edge to all the performers at the Comic Strip, and not just Ben making jokes about 'Thatch', but a generally socialist view of the world.

How do you make the joke about a gooseberry in a lift left wing?

Fair point. It's true we never identify the politics of the gooseberry. But sometimes the politics is in what you don't do rather than what you do do.

'Non-sexist and non-racist' is the overarching battle cry, though Rik and I joke that perhaps it should be 'Non-sexy and non-racy'; in the same way, we often interpret 'Alternative Comedy' as 'Alternative *to* Comedy'.

As you can see, I keep subverting the proposition, and not through some kind of false modesty, or reluctance to be thought revolutionary – who wouldn't want to be revolutionary – but fundamentally because I see our double act as part of a line going back through Pete & Dud, Morecambe & Wise, and Tom & Jerry, all the way to Laurel & Hardy.

Though if you ask me if I've seen an act as berserk as ours before or since, I would have to say I have not.

Perhaps the marker of how revolutionary it is is the number of copycat clubs that spring up after it – after a few years an entire 'circuit' develops – and in that way alone it's at the forefront of a revolution in comedy.

Viva la revolución!

But there's more than one revolution going on in my life, and looking back on it I'm not sure which is the most important. Because the other revolution is – food.

As a young child I'm nicknamed 'The Dustbin' because I polish off everyone else's leftovers. I'm always hungry.

'Ah'm 'ungry!'

My mum makes no claims to be *cordon bleu* – the accepted epitome of gastronomy at the time – though Aunty Margaret *has* done the course and can make a baked Alaska. No, we're eating the staple foods of the sixties: bread and jam, stew and dumplings, egg and chips. Mum has a chip pan full of beef dripping. When not in use it's kept in a cool cupboard where the fat congeals into a hard white block. I love watching the 'iceberg' melt as she heats it up on the stove. Very occasionally we have a roast on Sundays, it's always cooked well done, the beautiful piece of silverside shrinking from a vibrant, bloody thing of wonder to a small block of dense grey meat, like a model of a black hole.

Vegetables are boiled. Boiled. Really boiled. One Christmas morning we go to pick up Grandma Sturgeon to bring her back for Christmas dinner. Her little bungalow stinks of boiling cabbage.

'I thought you were never coming,' she says.

Of course she knew we were coming, she's just playing the martyr to get at my mum – a long-running battle to pay her back for constantly going abroad – and there's nothing else cooking, no turkey, no spuds, just the pan of cabbage angrily boiling away. It's only 10 a.m., and once you look beyond the tragic passive-aggression the implication is that she was going to cook that cabbage for three hours. This is what we think of vegetables in the early sixties. Cabbage must have no bite whatsoever. No butter, no oil. No condiments besides salt and white pepper, no mustard, no horseradish, and packet gravy. I'm not complaining, I love it. I lick everyone's plate clean. And on high days and holidays we have sherry trifle to follow.

School meals really lower the bar: a strange concoction they call 'curry' – mince in a flavourless slurry with sultanas, which expand into tiny footballs as they heat up and burst in your mouth; liver that's mostly tubes and gristle ('boingy schnozzle' my friend Troy calls it), the knives are never sharp enough to do the requisite surgery; and the pièce de résistance – boiled tinned tomatoes on toast. It always looks like a mistake, but it comes round once a fortnight.

The attitude to food at school is epitomized by one of the regular punishments, which is simply called 'toast'. If your name-tagged gym shorts are found outside your personal clothes locker, if the hospital tucks on your bed aren't quite crisp enough, if your tie is considered too loose or your shoes not shiny enough, you will be punished with 'toast'.

Toast involves getting up at least an hour and a half earlier than everyone else and reporting for duty in the kitchen, where Mrs Semple will be congealing some eggs or killing some beans. There's a giant grill which holds ten slices of bread at a time, and your job is to make 240 rounds of toast. Ten slices for each of the twenty-four tables. The grill only does one side at a time so this involves loading the grill forty-eight times.

As we all know, toast sweats, and any toast made an hour and a half ahead of time and piled on a plate is doomed to become a tower of sogginess – this is the plate for the table of your worst enemy, so at least there is some benefit to doing 'toast'. The other benefit is that your table will get the best toast: it will be the last to be made and will be beautifully crisp and dry. The secret to the ultimate toast is to stack it like a house of cards on the vents above the grill.

It's important to provide the top table – the one with the masters and prefects – with good toast too. Because you can be punished with 'toast' for not making sufficiently good enough toast.

University in Manchester doesn't seem much better. Food becomes a game: there's a curry house called the Plaza behind the medical school where if you drink a pint of their 'suicide' sauce you get your whole meal for free – many try, few succeed.

The Danish Food Centre is an all-you-can-eat buffet of cold meats and pickled herring. Of course with my Danish heritage I feel right at home but we have more of a 'Roman' attitude to it – regularly eating a week's worth of food in a single sitting until we're banned.

There's a new-fangled 'vegetarian' cafe called On the Eighth Day on the Oxford Road, serving massive bowlfuls of pulses with rice; it's fairly bland, but very cheap, and fills you up. Then empties you out.

But everything changes when I get to Soho. Many people think of it as the centre of the sex industry, or the film industry, but really, in 1980 it's the centre of Italian food in Britain.

Only about twenty years previously *Panorama* played an April Fool's Day prank on the viewing public by filming 'the spaghetti harvest', which showed them pulling strands of spaghetti from spaghetti trees. I remember watching a repeat of it as a young child and finding no reason to disbelieve them, because as far as I know pasta only comes in two forms – spaghetti hoops or alphabetti spaghetti.

But here are shops – Lina Stores on Brewer Street, Camisa & Son on Old Compton Street – selling all sorts of 'pasta', dry and fresh, some filled with delicious parcels of spinach and ricotta, some infused with truffle oil. Truffle! What's that? Even the jars of pesto are exotic, to say nothing of Parma ham, bresaola, parmesan cheese, tomatoes that taste of something, fresh basil, black pepper. Black! Great chunks of it, not the grey powder I'm used to.

There are vegetables in Berwick Street market I've never seen in the flesh before – aubergine, courgette, artichoke, and *garlic* for heaven's sake – my mum still hasn't cooked with garlic.

And the coffee in Bar Italia – espresso in tiny little cups like ceramic jewels; dark, bitter yet sweet, with that crema of ultra-fine bubbles on top. It seems from a different food source altogether to the instant coffee I've had up until now, which tastes of wet cardboard and smells like dog's breath.

Olives! Salami! I would argue that the revolution from cheese and pineapple on a stick to olives and salami is far greater than the revolution from *The Good Life* to *The Young Ones*.

Rik and I often go to a little Italian restaurant round the corner from the Comic Strip Club, called La Perla. It feels like it's been transported straight from the back streets of Milan – an old-fashioned Italian with the kind of elderly waiters that simply don't exist any more. They wear ties and waistcoats and have aprons round their waists, and they take great pride in their job, treating it as a career, not something to do while waiting for something better to turn up.

The place is actually fairly cheap but it feels expensive: polished wood and heavy white linen tablecloths, with an old-fashioned sweet trolley lurking in the shadows. And the beauty of it is, that because we belong round these parts, we go often enough for the waiters to recognize us, and as we walk through the door they smile and shout to the kitchen, '*Fegato per due!*' because that's what we always have. Calves' liver and onions on mashed potato, with spinach on the side. The perfect hangover cure. Liver that's unrecognizable from the boingy schnozzle of our past – soft, thin and unctuous, with a sauce made from garlic, pancetta, sage and the finest beef stock, a pillow of fluffy creamed potatoes and a side order of mineral-flavoured, al dente, buttery spinach.

Viva la revolución! As Che would say.

My whole way of life is going through a revolution at this point – for instance, I've never been touring before.

Tom Wolfe quotes Ken Kesey saying, 'You're either on the bus or off the bus,' in *The Electric Kool-Aid Acid Test*, a book that documents the birth of the counterculture in sixties America and its experiments with LSD. The phrase has several meanings: it's a metaphor for being 'with it'; it denotes a level of commitment; it can mean you're either in tune with everyone else, or not in tune with everyone else; and, as they're touring America in an actual bus at the time, it's a fair description of their physical reality.

And the physical reality of being on a bus is something I come to know quite well during thirty-five years of regular touring.

My first tour is with this group of comedians from the Comic Strip Club in 1980, and it's a blast. We've been working together at the club for the last year, but here we are out on an adventure. We're going round Britain on a bus. Everything is new.

And this first tour spoils us.

The bus is very swish and has separate areas – tables with bench seats at the front, kitcheny/toilet area in the middle, and a lounge area at the back with swivelling chairs. It's hardly rock 'n' roll – or maybe it is – who are we to know? Though all the stereotypes in films suggest touring is fairly sleazy – a wild smorgasbord of sex and drugs. We drink a lot of cheap lager, but we also enjoy much simpler pleasures. And it's the nicest bus we ever get. If we'd known we were starting at the top . . .

I am the chief inventor of games. I invent a game called 'one leg', in which the contestant, whilst the bus is in motion, has to stand on one leg without holding on to any part of the bus for as long as they can. Sudden braking can lead to instant death, which is the thrill of the thing.

Another is 'boring but true', in which you have to tell a true story that sounds like it's going to be really interesting but ends up being spectacularly dull. I win with a story about motorbiking to Bradford in the snow and my gear lever falling off as I leave the M62; I know that the bike is stuck in a high gear, and that the engine will stall if I let go of the clutch, and that I won't be able to start it again. So, I determine to 'walk' the bike up the hard shoulder, clutch lever squeezed tight, engine revving, all the way up the M606 to the Staithgate roundabout, where a downhill slope will aid me in setting off once more. But, after laboriously pushing it for a mile up the steep hill through a bitter snowstorm, I find that the topography after the roundabout is not as downhill as I'd remembered; if anything it's still vaguely uphill, level at best – there's no way that I can run the bike up to 40mph and jump on, so I simply let the clutch out and let it stall.

See what I mean? Gold medal. Feel free to play this at home.

In another, we colour our faces using Smarties and have to walk around a motorway service station.

All excessively juvenile games but they express our childish delight in what we're doing. It's the days before mobile phones and we have to entertain ourselves and each other. We talk a lot. We laugh a lot. I sit next to Jennifer a lot.

Our tour manager is a large man with an aluminium attaché case. He is not a people person, which you would imagine to be a requirement of the job, no, he is permanently angry and treats us like prisoners on day release. When Alexei doesn't make the bus in time after the gig in Norwich he decides to leave him behind to 'teach him a lesson'. He never lets go of the aluminium case and we decide it must contain either drugs, money, or the body parts of the previous act he was tour managing. Possibly all three. But he can't break our propensity to find fun in everything. And he withdraws into his angry little shell as it dawns on him that he himself has become a figure of fun.

It's the first time I ever stay in a hotel – it's the County Hotel in Sheffield and it's a dump, which I can say without fear of litigation as it no longer exists. The walls are so thin I can hear everything that happens in the room next door. I feel like Paul Simon singing 'Duncan' – they go at it all night long: noises, cries, slaps, occasional whimpering and the sounds of furniture being moved. I try to make out the couple at breakfast the next morning but without success. Perhaps it's the lone businessman?

Simply visiting all the different venues is a thrill first time round. We don't tour our own sound equipment, we use whatever is there. The equipment at Leeds City Varieties is particularly ancient and the microphone has a strange triangular brace around it rather in the shape of an arrow. I don't know this and as Rik shouts, 'And this is Sir Adrian Dangerous!' I rush forward and headbutt the mic but it doesn't fly off the mic stand as usual, it sticks into my forehead, and I look like a Dalek for a short while before I manage to pull it out.

We take this tour to Australia and have the time of our lives. The gigs go well in Adelaide, where we're on as part of a festival. We're in a posh hotel and rubbing shoulders with 'famous' people like jazz pianist Keith Tippett, smooth jazz guitarist George Benson and total icon Joan Armatrading. We're slightly overexcited, and spotting an untouched slice of melon on Keith's tray as he leaves the poolside, I finish it off for him. Yes, I have eaten Keith's melon. Who's sorry now, Mr Careers Master?

We're feeling proud and cocky.

I'm wearing my green and black striped trousers walking down the pavement when a passing police car stops and winds down a window.

'Hey mate, why are you wearing your pyjamas?' asks the copper.

'It's all right,' I say. 'I'm from England, I'm a guerrilla of new wave humour, and I'm allowed to wear what I like.'

Part 7

We're on the telly!

The Comic Strip Presents . . .

The Comic Strip Club reaches its peak just as Channel 4, a new TV broadcaster, is created.

As a new channel they're looking for new talent to make new shows ahead of their launch in late 1982. As 'guerrillas of new wave humour' who have recently offended Bianca Jagger, we fit this brief perfectly. However, at the same time, a producer from the BBC, Paul Jackson, gets wind of the fact that Channel 4 are signing up a lot of this 'new talent' and persuades the BBC to have a look at us as well.

We don't choose between them – we go with both. We get two shows commissioned at the same time: *The Young Ones* on BBC2 and *The Comic Strip Presents* on Channel 4. Bingo.

While *The Young Ones* is two series of six, which take fourteen weeks to shoot, *The Comic Strip Presents* builds up to more than forty episodes, specials and feature films over the following thirty-odd years, and if Pete could get the funding would still be making things today. Pete still rings occasionally to say 'I've got an idea for a film . . .'

The Young Ones is better remembered, it's thought of as more 'iconic' or 'groundbreaking', but *The Comic Strip Presents* is more than just a series of programmes, it's my spiritual home.

It's where I make proper friends: Jennifer, Dawn, Pete, Nige and Robbie Coltrane. These are the people who become like my extended family, the people I go on holiday with, the people I trust, the people I love. Our children grow up together. In fact, just half an hour ago, Robbie's daughter Alice dropped in with a jar of honey from her mother's beehives in Ardnamurchan. (This is both true, and my attempt to get into Pseuds Corner in *Private Eye*.)

Pete Richardson is the de facto leader of the group. He's also the most subversive.

A subversive leader?

Yes, that's what makes it so complicated on occasion. He's frankly incontinent when it comes to budgets. He either wilfully ignores them or sees them as something to be challenged. He always has a nervous laugh tugging at the corners of his mouth when he talks about money, as if he finds it hilarious. As if money itself is too bourgeois. It's very funny to watch but it's a bonkers way to run a business. There's a time in the early nineties when the limited company we're all part of is almost bankrupted by the lease on a photocopying machine. I'm laughing as I write this, both at the thought of a successful comedy group being brought down by a photocopier, and by the thought of Pete laughing about it. Watching Pete laugh is one of life's joys – when he finds something funny he creases up, quite literally, and finds it difficult to speak for minutes on end. And when he finally gets his breath back he'll repeat the first couple of words of whatever it was he found so funny and set himself off again. It's infectious.

It's not like we even do any photocopying. Who's doing all the photocopying?

But Pete's a disrupter – that's his angle, that's where all his comedy springs from, he likes to turn things upside down. He writes with another Pete – Pete Richens.

What?

I know, it's confusing, but there are two of them, Pete Richardson and Pete Richens, a writing team known by all as Pete & Pete. To differentiate them, we sometimes call Pete Richardson 'Mad Pete'. It's an affectionate soubriquet but underlines his style and method.

Like me, Dawn and Jennifer are also 'forces brats' – their dads were both in the RAF. We discover that our three families all did a stint in Cyprus during the early sixties. It's possible we may have met on the swings and roundabouts of a public playground. It's a strange bond, but the three of us know the tedium of camp life; barbed wire fences and armed gates; houses that look like Nissen huts; parade grounds; and the only shop being the NAAFI – the armed forces version of a cut-price Lidl that sold everything from Spam to . . . Spam.

For a special treat Mum will buy a can of Bacon Grill

Dawn is the only one of us who gives up a proper job to risk it all on a six-part comedy series. She's a successful and much-loved teacher when Channel 4 commission us – I still get approached by people who say, 'Dawn was my teacher, she was brilliant.' It's easy in hindsight to think, 'Well, *The Comic Strip Presents* was obviously going to be successful,' but we're living hand-to-mouth at the time and there're no obvious signs of longevity. It's piecework. There's no security. It's a punt. The rest of us are either a) too blinded by the love of our art form, or b) too feckless, to get a real job.

This raises the stakes for Dawn personally, and perhaps because of that she becomes the mother of the group – always keen for things to be properly organized, to make the best of the opportunity. She also becomes the kind of moral conscience of the group. In fact you could say she's sometimes rather serious . . . but this is constantly undercut by her ridiculous clowning ability. She has a clown-like face – I mean this in the most complimentary way – in that her facial expressions always amplify exactly what she's thinking, and it's just FUNNY. Some people are just FUNNY.

When I first meet Jennifer it's hard to know whether she's too in love with her art form, too feckless, or just doesn't care. She's perhaps the most punk amongst us. Like the way Johnny Rotten sings *'and we don't care'* at the end of the chorus in 'Pretty Vacant' – Jennifer appears to not care about anything. Except bands – The Tourists, Robert Palmer, Blondie, Elvis Costello – and gin and tonic, and having a good time, and making Dawn laugh. This appears to be the constant in double acts – the desire to make the other one laugh.

Jennifer lives with her old college friend Jobo and it appears the two of them would quite happily do nothing and live off cat food for the rest of their lives rather than do something that wasn't 'fun'. She has a vicious mimic's skill – she can instantly distil an attitude she's spotted and turn it into a line, a scene, or a character . . . or indeed a series.

Nigel is the one with the biggest acting CV when we start. He's already had a couple of bit parts on the telly and has understudied Che Guevara in *Evita* in the West End – this makes him a big cheese. He's also the only one who's been on a proper acting course at a proper drama school and learned proper 'acting'. This makes him an even bigger cheese. Though as his later hilarious spoof character Nicholas Craig demonstrates in his book *I, An Actor*, he's able to take the piss out of it. Sort of vegetarian cheese.

The double act between Pete and Nige is the least harmonious of the three double acts. I never get to understand the nitty-gritty but during a year at the Comic Strip Club they're always having arguments in the corridor. I think it's probably about levels of performance and what the other is doing on stage. They come from two different styles: Pete would like to be Lee Van Cleef or Clint Eastwood – a kind of close radio-mic type of performer; while Nigel has a great singing range and is more theatrically aware.

The Pete and Nige double act comes to an end once we start making TV programmes. Pete starts writing with Pete. But I end up having a longer working relationship with Nigel than with anyone else in the group. We're still working together now. Over the last few years we've written a couple of plays together. I love sitting in my study with him, chewing the fat, bitching, writing, and laughing.

Robbie is the oldest in the group. He's been to the Glasgow School of Art and he's come to acting in his mid-twenties. He's done theatre shows in Scotland and is biting at the edges of film work when we come across him – who can forget his 'Man at Airfield' in *Flash Gordon* (look harder next time). He's an intimidating giant of a man, hence his future casting as Hagrid, but underneath he's delightfully playful. He has such a beautiful childish face when he finds something funny. His eyes literally twinkle.

I'm following him down to Devon one day to shoot *The Supergrass* – a tale of sex, drugs, cream teas, and murder by the seaside. Robbie's driving one of his beloved Cadillacs, when it starts to rain. I see him switch his wipers on and they promptly fly off and over the back of his car. I can't help but run them over. It sort of sums Robbie up – a big, stylish hulk of a man with an eye for the surprisingly idiotic.

So here we are, a group of inexperienced filmmakers, suddenly making films. *The Comic Strip Presents* is all on film – it's a very different proposition to shouting at an audience in a darkened theatre. Do we feel daunted? NO – we bloody don't. We've all seen a film – how difficult can it be?

Learning on the job

Filming is new. Filming is exciting. We're all learning the craft off each other. It's the days before video playback – the director has to watch from behind the camera and at the end of every take he has to ask the cameraman what he saw in the viewfinder.

That sounds ridiculous.

It is.

The beautiful thing is we get 'rushes' – the day's filming is quickly developed and 'rushed' back to wherever we're based. During the early days, because of Pete's connection with Devon, we film a lot of the episodes in and around the small seaside village of Hope Cove in the South Hams.

We'll all cram into the cottage that's been set up as a makeshift editing suite and watch the rushes every evening. It's a completely joyous experience. And it's where we all learn our basic craft as actors. It's like a party every time. There's beer and wine and gin. We watch each other. We laugh at each other. We hear what works. We see what doesn't. It's an incredibly supportive group, no one's trying to carve out a career solely for themselves – we're all in it together.

And there're so many styles on show – Pete's intensity; Dawn's clowning; Jennifer's distillation of attitude; Nigel's craft; Robbie's sheer presence; me giving it 150 per cent . . . And we're all borrowing bits from each other.

And then we all tumble into the Hope & Anchor, play pool and stick Prince's 'Purple Rain' on the jukebox.

And on top of this we get *paid*.

But we're so wet behind the ears that we mistake the envelope of cash we're given every week for our wages, and can't believe it when we discover these are our *per diems* – our expenses for living away from home. *Free money*.

Weeks later our wages arrive in the form of cheques. None of us have earned this kind of money before. We're earning £1,500 a show. Admittedly we only make six shows a year, but as someone who's never earned more than £100 in a week this is boom time. I splash out and buy Dawn's old Mk2 Cortina from her, mostly so I can listen to the Tom Robinson Band sing 'Grey Cortina' and feel like I'm in with the in crowd. Her Cortina is also grey! Yes! That's just how cool I am! *'Cortina owner, no one meaner, wish that I could be like him.'*

Each episode is different, and in many of the episodes like 'The Strike' or 'War' or 'Gino' we play several parts each. The range of parts is extraordinary: In 'A Fistful of Travellers' Cheques' I play Billy Belfont, 'The Man with No Name' – a sociopath from Bradford who has ended up as an unemployed bullfighter in Spain; in the next I'm Dick, a pompous young prick from The Famous Five; in 'GLC' I play a loopy Prince Charles talking to his plums.

And we play a variety of styles: something like 'Bad News Tour', a spoof documentary, requires a commitment to some form of realism; 'Five Go Mad', in which we are adults playing children, is a more heightened form of parody; *The Supergrass* is pitched somewhere between the two.

It's like a return to the days of the Stephen Joseph Studio at university. Everyone's creating something. Everyone's writing. Everyone's thinking.

When we turn up to film, our costume designer Frances Haggett will emerge from a cloud of her own cigarette smoke. She'll have unloaded her car into whatever space she can find – sometimes a room in whatever building we're using as a location, sometimes a pop-up tent, sometimes simply on the roadside. These are the days before trailers and costume vans – we all hang about the set all day watching each other, making suggestions, egging each other on.

Frances will invite us to pick a costume from the rail. It's the epitome of *playing*. It's dressing up for fun. Frances is brilliant at her job and lays on a curated selection of garments, a kind of palette, and we invent characters at will.

The same is true in the make-up department, where Naomi Donne and Sally Sutton will willingly black your teeth for you, or give you a scar, or make you look like you're on the point of death. Although, depending on the night before, this is sometimes unnecessary.

And I'm not just learning how to write and act, I'm also learning to direct.

Sandy Johnson is a slightly eccentric Scotsman with an enormous handlebar moustache who can whistle more tunefully than anyone I know. He's also a Laurel & Hardy fan, which is always a plus in my book. When I first meet him – he comes backstage at the Comic Strip Club – he's just left the National Film and Television School, and he casts me as the lead in his very first film, a short for TV called *The Magnificent One*: a quirky take on *The Seven Samurai*, set in London, with only one samurai, a young man (my character), who takes it upon himself to stop the Japanese owners of a corner shop being bullied. It's my first paid acting job.

We get on well and I invite him to direct the scripts that I write for *The Comic Strip Presents* and he very magnanimously lets me into the edit room. I go all day, every day, watching how he and his editor, Rob Wright, put things together.

It's the days before computers, everything's shot on 16mm film, and editing is quite physical. We're using a Steenbeck editing table – a massive piece of machinery that looks like it comes from a very early episode of *Doctor Who*. It has four spools that allow you to load a reel of film and a reel of sound at the same time; once you sync the clapperboard to the sound of the clap you can play both together and watch a dimly lit monitor.

Each edit involves: rolling the film back and forth and choosing the edit point; marking the film frame and the sound tape with a chinagraph pencil; taking those film and sound reels off the machine; loading up the film and sound reels of the picture you're cutting to; choosing the edit point; cutting the film (straight cut) and the sound (diagonal cut); then splicing the ends together with what are effectively pieces of Sellotape.

This laborious process means that each edit is chosen very carefully. Re-editing can be fiddly and end up with single frames hanging about which invariably get lost. So every edit is discussed at length, and being party to these discussions is my education. I learn the reasoning, the grammar – I'm learning grammar! – and the aesthetics of film. Whilst editing 'Bad News Tour', 'Dirty Movie' and 'Eddie Monsoon – A Life?' I spend months in the edit suite and learn every day.

I also watch in wonder when Rob the editor gets bored and suddenly disappears up onto the roof of the building to lob water bombs at unsuspecting passers-by outside the YMCA opposite. Rob is a Jekyll and Hyde of a man depending on whether he's had a drink or not, but he also tells me the best limerick I've ever heard (delivered in his inimitable Welsh accent):

Come down to Llanelli my boy
For a fuck that you'll really enjoy
At the height of catharsis
What you'll feel up your arse is
The tongue of a corgi called Roy

When Stephen Frears directs 'Mr Jolly Lives Next Door' – about a seedy escort agency that mistakenly gets a job meant for the contract killer whose office is next door – he has some personal issues to deal with and asks me to direct the action sequences. And when it comes to the editing Rob and I do the bulk of it and Stephen pops in occasionally to see how it's progressing. I love it, and by the time we make 'More Bad News' in 1987 I've taken on the role of director. Sorry, Sandy, you taught yourself out of a job . . .

'More Bad News', about the continuing travails of an unsuccessful and largely untalented heavy metal band, includes a promo video for their first single 'Warriors of Genghis Khan'. It's suitably over-the-top and features a post-apocalyptical future of fires, flags, motorbikes, and a maiden in distress. It also snags the interest of a band called Zodiac Mindwarp & the Love Reaction, and they ask me to make a promo video for their new single 'Prime Mover'. This has a bigger budget, and therefore features a spaceship, a tank crashing into a nunnery, novices that turn into leather-clad groupies, and a mother superior whose head explodes. Come on, it was the eighties.

There's a near fatal accident when the man driving the tank through the polystyrene wall into the nuns' dormitory takes the wrong cue and smashes through too early. Dick Pope, the cinematographer who goes on to shoot all of Mike Leigh's films from 1990 onwards, is on the other side of the wall with his light meter. He is saved only by a large chunk of polystyrene which gets trapped in front of the tank and pushes him along the floor like a snow plough.

I make one for Squeeze's single 'Hourglass' that is full of optical illusions shot on a Dali-esque set – melting guitars, trick perspectives, trompe l'oeil – it gets a lot of airplay on MTV, gets a couple of MTV awards, and helps make it their best-selling single in the US. This kind of success – increased revenue – makes a lot of record companies take notice and I become in demand. Over the next few years I make around thirty videos for the likes of Elvis Costello, 10,000 Maniacs, The Pogues, Sandie Shaw, Fuzzbox and bands whose names I can no longer remember.

This is the art O-level I never did. My 'style' is heavy on visual concepts – a four-poster bed covered in chickens, a sixties nightclub, the inside of a telephone answering machine – and relies on a relationship I develop with the art directors Nick Edwards and Clive Crotty. The beauty of the system is that these things are generally shot in a day and because time is tight the people from the record companies don't get much of a chance to interfere – it's like playing in the biggest art room you can imagine. Every day feels like a play day.

Wish you were here

The line between holidays and work is blurred even further as we shoot episodes of *The Comic Strip Presents* in rural Norfolk for 'Susie', and near Almeria in southern Spain for 'A Fistful of Travellers' Cheques'. But we keep returning to Devon, which is more like a proper British holiday – each day can encompass hours of rain and cold interspersed with five minutes of instant sunstroke. Many of the picnics in 'Five Go Mad in Dorset' are shot in farm gateways and look idyllic – gingham tablecloth, ham sandwiches, cake and lashings of ginger beer – but pull back and you'll see the huge tarpaulin keeping out the driving rain and the enormous lamp standing in for the sun.

Pete was born and bred in Devon and no matter where a film might be set he thinks he can find the equivalent location in Devon. Both his mother and his in-laws live up on Dartmoor and they're such welcoming people – sometimes we stay with Pete's mum, crammed into the makeshift dormitories she used to use for a summer school.

Dawn also has a connection with the area, having been brought up in Saltash just across the Tamar.

We all develop a deep affinity with the place and in time

Jennifer and I relocate to Dartmoor as well. Even Rik, who's more of a part-timer where *The Comic Strip Presents* is concerned, moves in close to where Pete lives in the South Hams.

TRUE HUMILITY

Right Reverend Host: "I'M AFRAID YOU'VE GOT A BAD EGG, MR. JONES!"
The Curate: "OH NO, MY LORD, I ASSURE YOU! PARTS OF IT ARE EXCELLENT!"

But in the end the output of *The Comic Strip Presents* is a bit hit and miss. Sturgeon's Law might be invoked here. The nature of the beast is that they're all stand-alone episodes, albeit with the same repertory of actors, so it's hard to build up a head of steam. One idea can be so different in style and subject to the one that's gone before, that people find it difficult to latch onto it as a series.

This is compounded by the shows never being the same length or in the same place. We start off doing half hours. Then we do some hour-long episodes. Then we switch from Channel 4 to BBC2, and the BBC hour is longer than the Channel 4 hour – because it doesn't have to accommodate commercials. Then we move back to Channel 4. Then to Gold. And in between times we make the odd feature film when Pete can stop laughing long enough to persuade someone to stump up the money. And on top of all this, after the first ten years, the core cast changes as I get busy with *Bottom* and Dawn and Jennifer get busy with *French & Saunders*, *The Vicar of Dibley* and *Absolutely Fabulous*.

It's never entirely cohesive, and it can be a bit confusing, but I'm very proud of the endeavour and I'd say the best TV episodes hold their own in the world of comedy: 'Five Go Mad in Dorset', 'Bad News Tour', 'A Fistful of Travellers' Cheques', 'Mr Jolly Lives Next Door', 'The Strike', 'Gregory: Diary of a Nutcase'. That's six good episodes out of forty-two – roughly 15 per cent. Eighty-five per cent of everything is crap? That's bang in the middle of Orwell and Kipling's predictions.

And yet we get to work with some of our heroes. We can't believe that we get Peter Cook to play Mr Jolly in 'Mr Jolly Lives Next Door'. This man is such an icon, he's the man from *Beyond the Fringe*, from *Not only . . . But also . . .*, from *Derek and Clive (Live)* and here he is saying lines that we have written.

We're in absolute awe. Perhaps in too much awe. We're almost speechless in front of him. At one point, as the contract killer Mr Jolly, Peter is guiding one of his victims down a steep concrete staircase when he slips and falls all the way to the bottom and we briefly think we might have killed him. He gets up swiftly and carries on, and that take is in the finished film, but watching it live as it happened it felt like time had stopped.

Of course he more or less kills himself in the end. A year later in 1989 Robbie and I are doing a sketch together for the Amnesty International fundraiser *The Secret Policeman's Biggest Ball* at the Cambridge Theatre. I get into a lift backstage and who should be in it but Peter Cook and Dudley Moore. They are each holding heavy carrier bags. The ancient lift takes us to the second floor and judders to an abrupt stop. There is the tell-tale sound of bottles clinking in their carrier bags. Peter looks at me and bursts out laughing. At least he enjoyed his drink.

• • •

In a feature film we make called *The Pope Must Die* I get to work with another hero, Herbert Lom – the man from *The Ladykillers*, and the much-put-upon police inspector of the *Pink Panther* films. He's playing Vittorio Corelli, the Mafia boss. I'm playing Father Rookie, the deaf priest who writes down the wrong name when the cardinals are voting for a new pope.

There's a scene where my character is called to the Mafia boss's house, in which Herbert Lom pours a bottle of brandy onto the hat I'm wearing and sets fire to it.

I'm a berserker, I'm very comfortable with stunts and flames, in fact, I don't think it's too boastful to say that I'm actually quite good at this sort of thing. It may be stupidity, it may be a mild death wish, but I've made it into a career of sorts – I'm not afraid of potential danger, especially if I think I might get a good laugh. Berserker.

It's one of those little four-cornered priest's hats, a *biretta*, and under this hat I have a flameproof skull cap. The special effects team smear a good dollop of glue onto the back of the hat. When Herbert sets fire to it with a lighter it instantly ignites into a sizeable flame and I look like a human candle.

The idea is that my character is so stupid he doesn't realize he's been set on fire. He sniffs the air. Is something burning? He looks from side to side – he can't see that anything's on fire.

It's counter-intuitive not to express alarm when your head is on fire – this is where the joke is – but even when you know it's been organized by a special effects team, and that they're standing by just out of shot with fire extinguishers, it takes a modicum of bravery, or premeditated foolhardiness at the least, to act as if it is nothing at all.

I have to blow my own trumpet here and say I do it very well. In the finished film there is a single shot that lasts about twenty seconds of me sitting there with a small inferno atop my head.

At the end of the take Pete calls 'cut' and the SFX team spray me with CO_2 to extinguish the flames. There's a round of applause from everyone in the room, but then, as the room breaks up and the crew move on to organizing the next set-up, Herbert Lom sidles up to me and says, out of the corner of his mouth, 'Very good.'

Herbert Lom!

Herbert Lom is a master of this kind of thing. In the *Pink Panther* films I've seen him fall repeatedly into ponds and off balconies, stand on rakes, chop off his thumb with a cigar cutter, and even shoot himself in the face with a gun that he's mistaken for a novelty cigarette lighter. He knows his onions where physical comedy is concerned. And he says: 'Very good.' It's the best review I ever get.

The Pope Must Die is shot in Yugoslavia in 1990. Timmy Mallet is top of the charts with 'Itsy Bitsy Teeny Weeny Yellow Polka Dot Bikini' – but thankfully this has no impact on the film. Or maybe it does. Maybe that's what the Yugoslavian police are so cross about?

Yugoslavia is standing in for Italy. Some of the architecture is quite similar, and it's a lot cheaper. It's been an independent communist state since the late 1940s and was ruled by General Tito, a strong-arm dictator, until his death in 1980. We shoot the burning hat scene in one of Tito's modernist villas.

In 1990, the cracks between the various republics within the country are beginning to show, people are getting jumpy, and it has a heavily authoritarian feel. The joke amongst the crew is to ask any new arrival: 'What's Yugoslavian for excuse me?'; and when no answer comes, to push them violently out of the way. It seems like everyone over the age of five chain smokes.

I don't know whether it's Herbert Lom's praise or the local plum brandy, šljivovica, that goes to my head, but the evening after the hat scene a group of us have a very jolly time in a restaurant in Zagreb. It's a traditional establishment in a cellar and when we emerge back onto the street we see that something magical has happened – it has snowed.

The Americans amongst us aren't particularly impressed, they're quite used to snow, but we English, particularly the producer Stephen Woolley and I, get over excited.

'Look. It's *sticking*!' we cry.

Memories of childhood winters in Bradford flood my mind. Memories of me and my sister rushing to the window whenever it began to snow.

'Is it *sticking*?' would be the perennial cry.

'No, it's not,' would come the perennial reply, as we'd watch each sad snowflake melt and die as it hit the ground.

Steve, who's the same age as me, was brought up in Islington and has also obviously known the disappointment of snow not surviving long in the British urban environment. But here in Zagreb this foreign snow is doing what it's *supposed* to do – it's *sticking*.

Like giggling children we start scraping it off the roofs of parked cars, making snowballs, and throwing them at each other.

Suddenly two policemen appear.

I say policemen, but they could be soldiers. Or paramilitaries. They bristle with weapons – ammunition belts, pistols, long sticks – and they each hold a stubby machine gun. They shout in Croatian and point their stubby machine guns at us, right into our faces.

Bloody hell. This has escalated quickly.

Steve's wife, Elizabeth, is American. She's lovely, but she *is* American, and to put it politely she has that American sense of entitlement on the world stage that can rub foreigners up the wrong way. As Steve and I are pushed against the wall, hands high, legs spread, and frisked by one of the gun-toting policemen she begins to scream: 'I am an American citizen! You are infringing our human rights! I'll make sure you get fired for this, you stupid bastards! You'll get twenty years in a Siberian gulag!'

Well . . . something like that.

I can't remember her exact words, but I do remember the policemen becoming even more pissed off. No matter what's being said I think that's what they hear. So, whilst I think they might have been about to let us go, now they seem intent on taking us away. We are frogmarched, hands on heads, at gun point, half a mile to a police station. Elizabeth runs along beside us, keeping up a tirade of abuse, and it's not until they slam the door of the police station in her face and lead us down to a bare cell in the basement, that we can no longer hear her.

The Berlin Wall only came down the year before, and though it feels like the Cold War is coming to an end, there is still something chilling about being in a basement prison cell in a communist country, even if it is non-aligned. We've both read Alexander Solzhenitsyn, we know tales of the grim Lubyanka prison run by the KGB in Moscow, and we know that people, dissidents, westerners and troublemakers can disappear.

It's fair to say the šljivovica has worn off by now. Essentially we've been arrested for throwing snowballs, but we can't see the humour in this yet.

After a couple of hours, we're taken to a room where a gruff-looking bloke tries to interview us. He can't speak English and we can't speak Croatian so things don't progress very far and we're taken back to the cell. After another couple of hours this routine is repeated but this time with a policeman who has a small amount of English.

We deduce that our crime is to make a noise under the apartment where the president lives. Apparently we've kept him awake. This seems unlikely: there has only been one 'president' of Yugoslavia, General Tito, and he died in 1980; and it seems weird that any head of state after him should live in a backstreet of Zagreb. Perhaps he means the police chief? Or the police sergeant? Or just a chum who's a bit pissed off? No matter, it seems to be a fairly heinous offence, and some kind of punishment is due, perhaps without trial.

At this point of the proceedings he gets out pen and paper and begins to write down our details. We give him our names. He writes them down. Then he asks for our addresses. We say: 'Hotel Intercontinental'. The pen moves towards the paper, as if he is about to write it down, then stops. He looks up at us.

'Hotel Intercontinental?'

'Yes,' we say.

He looks at the form again, then back at us.

'Hotel Intercontinental?'

'Yes,' we reply. Again.

He lays down the pen, scrapes back his chair, and disappears from the interview room.

Moments later he reappears with two of the other policemen. They are all smiles now, though their smiles seem rather forced, as if they're not used to smiling. One of them tries a chuckle. He shouldn't – it comes out as creepy rather than charming, which I think is what he's going for. The one with the faltering English says: 'Good evening, good evening, good evening,' while motioning for us to rise, and the other two open the door wide and show us the way out. Not just out of the interview room, but out of the police station.

It's 4 a.m. in the morning, the street is dead and thick with snow.

We have to resist the urge to start chucking snowballs about.

We're not sure where we are.

We're pretty sure we've been released, but don't know where to go, or how to get there.

The policemen suddenly seem to understand this. Instructions are shouted to someone inside (I hope they don't wake the president), and moments later a police car swings round to the front and they invite us to get in, and we're driven back to the hotel.

Once Steve has made Elizabeth aware of our safe return we order a couple of šljivovica from the night porter to celebrate our release, and to give us time to process what has just happened. It feels decidedly odd to have two loaded machine guns pointed at you for real, especially when you're not a soldier, just a poncy actor and a poncy producer. We feel quite giddy, though it occurs to us that if we'd been two backpackers instead of two people staying at the Hotel Intercontinental we might never have been seen again.

A year later Yugoslavia erupts into a bloody civil war that lasts several years. I think we were lucky. But ever since then I've always asked to be booked into the most prestigious hotel when travelling to foreign locations. That's my excuse anyway.

Another double act

And much as Elizabeth's shouting may have helped to escalate the situation, it's good to know when someone is whole-heartedly on your side.

Jennifer and I have always been very careful not to talk about each other in public. Partly because our public personas are different from our private ones, so it would be confusing at best, and partly because of the curse of *Hello!* magazine: wherein people who talk about their partners generally end up getting divorced in the next edition.

However, I recognize that she is the most significant person in my life, and I recognize that you might recognize that also, so I will tell you these three things:

1) She is an exceptional snogger. In our early courting days, when she lived with Jobo in a house opposite The Surprise pub in Chelsea, I used to turn up on an almost daily basis. She would open the door and we would snog for ten minutes before saying anything. It's the most ridiculously sensual and loving thing that has ever happened to me.

2) On one occasion she defended me by punching a man's lights out. I was at some charitable awards ceremony when I

was suddenly called upon to 'fill in' during a gap. I'm not a comedian who tells 'jokes' – I work with scripts and character. But some kind of emotional pressure was applied and I found myself at the podium.

Caught in the headlights I told the only 'joke' I know. It's a shaggy-dog story but the bare bones of it are as follows: two women are looking out of the living room window; one of them sees her husband coming home early with a bunch of flowers in his hand. 'Oh no,' she says, 'that means I'll have to lie on my back all afternoon with my legs wide open.' 'Why?' asks the other one. 'Haven't you got a vase?'

I stretched it out to fill the hiatus, and it went down well, but as I left the stage a man who had taken offence at the 'blue' nature of the joke strode forward and punched me in the face. From out of nowhere Jennifer was suddenly at my side and decked the man with a left hook.

That's my girl.

'Jokes' are weird. I can only remember writing one actual 'joke' in my entire life. Rik and I were in Shepperton doing a test commercial for Hoffmeister beer. We had a swell time, and drank lots of actual beer during the filming, but despite our energetic gurning the campaign was eventually given to a Cockney bear. 'Heyyyy – follow the bear.'

But I'm on the set of the Hoffmeister pitch, slightly the worse for wear, when a 'joke' comes to me – the watch gag. It's in the age of wristwatches, before mobile phones, when to know what time it is you have to wear an actual watch on your actual wrist. I hear one of the sparks, a *Cockerney*, say to his mate, in the kind of broad patois they employ to give themselves an air of mystery, 'Have you got the time on yer cock?' And I think – well that's a punchline if ever I heard one, so I invent the first part of the gag: 'What do you say to a man who's got no arms and no legs if your watch is broken?' Quite a lot of people write to me asking about the 'classic' watch gag that Rik refers to several times over the course of five live shows. Well that's it. I hope you're not too disappointed.

3) Try to get round it by veering off the subject.

You already have.

Oh, well done me.

All right, let's have another go:

Why do I do it? I don't know. But, in 1970, at the age of thirteen, I go into the small Co-op at the end of Market Place, pick up a bar of chocolate and place it nervously on the counter.

'And a packet of cigarettes, please,' I say, hoping the cashier won't notice the slight wobble in my voice.

'Which ones?' she asks.

My mind's a blur – I barely have time to get over the shock of getting through the age test – of course, there's a choice. Why didn't I plan a choice before I got to the till? A seasoned smoker would have his regular brand.

'Er, those ones,' I point. 'Park Drive.'

'Tipped or untipped?'

Will this inquisition never end? Er . . . surely only a child would opt for tipped, a proper adult smoker would have to have untipped?

'Untipped,' I reply.

'Ten or twenty?'

Oh God.

Of course, I'm lying when I say I don't know why I do it. I

do it because I want to be hard slash cool and hang out with the bad boys at school. Having joined a year later than most, I'm having trouble fitting in, so I'm making a conscious effort to join the boys who don't care. The great news is that I don't actually care, about anything, because I feel abandoned and I'm practically dead emotionally, so I'm perfect material.

Later, back at school, I realize I've forgotten to buy matches. Then it occurs to me that this might help my cause. I'll have to ask someone for a light, which will prove that I'm a smoker and that I'm hard slash cool, so I ask JB who's on the edge of the hard slash cool set.

A few minutes later we find ourselves in the spinney of trees beyond the sports field and I 'flash the ash' in exchange for a light.

Christ, they're strong!

It's like someone has collected all the smoke from a forest fire and channelled it down my throat in one hit. I cough and splutter and make some excuse about having a cold, and to my relief JB coughs and splutters too and says they're 'not his usual brand'. We have a surreal conversation about all the different brands we've ever tried and soon it's pretty obvious that neither of us has ever smoked a cigarette before.

Nevertheless, at break time, JB and I go along together to the back of the bike shed where the boys who don't care hang out. I give JB another of my fags in exchange for a match – financially this is a ruinous arrangement – and we hang out on the edge of the set. They're actually quite a bonhomous bunch, much less intimidating than I thought, and over time they get over my outsider weirdness and actually laugh at some of the things I say. I watch every TV comedy I can: *Harry Worth*, *Dad's Army*, *Dick Emery*, *Dave Allen*, *Up Pompeii!*, *Robin's Nest*, *Father Dear Father*, and I'm able to bend the shape of the jokes I already know into jokes about teachers and other boys.

There's a particularly rough boy who doesn't trust me. He looks on me like I'm a spy for the teachers – to be fair, I look like a spy for the teachers, a nerd with bad hair and glasses – but luckily the rough boy is even thicker than me and gets asked to leave at the end of the fourth form. Soon afterwards I'm pretty much king of the bike shed. We take a parody photo of 'The Smoking Team' to match the rugby and cricket team photos: three serried ranks, each with a fag on, and who's in the middle at the front? It's me! I'm the captain!

Excuse me, how does this relate to Jennifer?

Please bear with me . . .

The thing about smoking as a schoolboy in the seventies is that the teachers' noses are so full of smoke from the staffroom they can't smell it on you. Anyone told to report to the staffroom during break would turn into the corridor and see smoke literally billowing out of the door. It's as if special effects were in there. I'm surprised they can see. Cheap fags, expensive fags, the art teacher with his cigars, the English teacher with his pipe – the air was blue, thick and cancerous.

So you can smoke all you like, as long as no one *sees* you. We smoke Embassy and Players No.6, the richer boys smoke JPS and Rothmans, and the weirdos smoke 'flaring' Marlboros – is it saltpetre or ammonia? We don't know, and we can't google it for another thirty-five years. And we collect the tokens: I get my first espresso machine courtesy of the fags, one of those aluminium stovetop percolators – it's just a shame I can't get proper espresso coffee for it in this tiny little market town.

This tiny town with its collective tiny mind is so tedious. Perhaps it's the reason we keep on smoking – because there's nothing else to do. We sit in Jasper's Folly, a cafe at the end of Market Place, thinking up new words for ennui and seeing how long we can burn our fingers with a lighter, before we can't stand it any more. Bob is the winner and still has a deformed knuckle. This is twenty-five years before Trent Reznor's song 'Hurt' is released. *'I hurt myself today, to see if I'd still feel.'*

By the time we reach the sixth form one of the window seats of Jasper's Cafe is where everyone wants to be. Which is odd, because the cafe is end-on to the whole of Market Place, so anyone walking down the main thoroughfare can see you, especially if you're in the window. But this is the thrill of it. You brazenly puff away until someone shouts '*Cave!*' (the Latin for 'beware' – it's the only Latin I *really* know), and then you simply hold your cigarette under the table. Whichever teacher is walking by looks in and sees a room full of smoke and a party of faux innocent faces at the window table. I can't believe they don't know. They must know. They probably hope we'll get cancer and die quickly so they won't have to teach us any more.

Even when our intellectual curiosity is piqued – as we start reading Sam Beckett or thinking we might copy George Orwell and piss off to France and wash dishes and have arty adventures amongst prostitutes with hearts of gold who'll love us dearly – the reverie simply becomes an excuse to smoke Gitanes and Gauloise.

Still no Jennifer . . .

Your call is important to us, please hold.

I get to uni and the first lecture is on Greek tragedy. It's a room full of school kids really, mostly keen to be hard slash cool, and all impressed by the fact that we're allowed to smoke in lectures. So impressed we all light up at once. It's a modern lecture room with a low ceiling, and we're all young enough, and enthusiastic enough, to chain smoke. By the time we all light up our third fag, we can't really see the lecturer at all. I think he says something about a goat.

University is a time for experimentation and some of us experiment with small cigars and cigarillos. There's a particular brand called Café Crème – they come in a very pleasing tin which is slim enough to slide into your pocket. With five of us crammed into a tiny tutorial room all sucking away on mini cigars, and the tutor puffing on his pipe, we have to disable the fire alarm in order to continue.

At the beginning of the second year when Rik invites me to join his pub theatre group he writes me a joke 'contract' on the inside of a dismantled fag packet, it says: 'I promise there will never be any money in it, but it might be a bit of a laugh.'

To be honest I could do with the money. My education is paid for by the state, which is brilliant, but my living allowance is means tested and my dad won't pay his share, which means I work every holiday. One summer I work in the John Player's factory in Nottingham. The machinery is phenomenal but when it goes wrong they end up with cigarettes that are ten foot long, and my job is to collect all these mistakes and take them to the 'splitter', where we recover the tobacco. We're allowed to smoke fags from the production line in our breaks, but not the ones that are ten foot long.

We also get a generous weekly allowance of cigarettes to take home and by the time I get to London and the new 'alternative' comedy scene I'm a forty-a-day man. I sometimes reach for a fag as soon as I wake up. In the future people will be fixated by their mobile phones. In the early eighties we're fixated by our fags and all the accoutrements.

I have a lighter made from a First World War bullet casing. It looks pretty hard slash cool but it's a bugger to fill. On one occasion I hold it between my slippered feet while I charge it with lighter fluid, it's a messy job and there's significant spillage. Job done, I strike it up and the whole thing becomes a ball of flame. I drop it, and my slippers, covered in excess fuel, also catch fire. I kick them off and suddenly the curtains are ablaze. Only judicious beating with an atlas nips the inferno in the bud. It's not just cancer that can kill you.

And Jennifer?

Nearly there.

In the mid-eighties, when I'm making *Honest, Decent & True*, a film for the BBC, I get the first inkling that all is not well. I play an anarchic young copywriter and Derrick O'Connor plays the world-weary head of the agency. It's an improvised piece about the advertising industry and at one point my character challenges Derrick's character to a race around Lincoln's Inn Fields. 'Non-character' me thinks this is a foregone conclusion – I'm twenty-eight and sprightly, and Derrick is forty-four and looks like a cigarette that's already been smoked and stubbed out – but in the end we have to rig the race because halfway through the first take I get tunnel vision and have to stop. I'm really quite unwell. I don't have a disease as such, I just can't breathe.

I'm still emotionally nuts when I first meet Jennifer. We are both with other people at the time but I'm besotted with her. It takes three or four years of us each having overlapping relationships with other people for her to recognize that I am in love with her, but eventually she does. We've known each other for so long before we get together that she seems to have already accepted my idiosyncrasies.

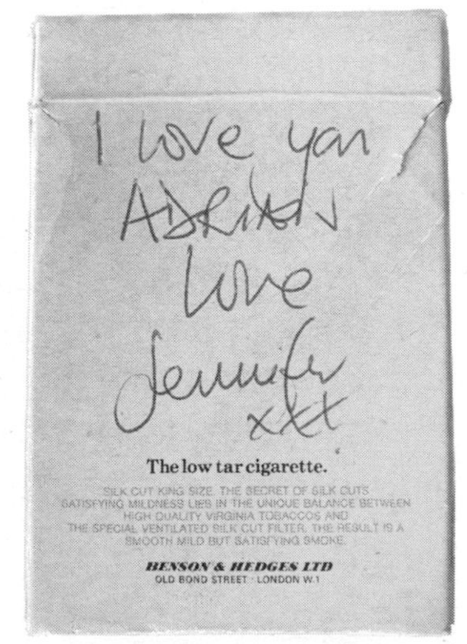

Our relationship is confirmed when she leaves an empty Silk Cut packet under the windscreen wiper of my car on which she's written 'I Love You'. We decide to get married and have children. And it's whilst she's pregnant with the first of three that she develops a fierce aversion to cigarette smoke, and

I just stop. I stop. In one day. In one moment. It's remarkably easy.

Because, I think, cigarettes were just a replacement for everything that was missing in my life. And I no longer feel like an outsider, no longer feel the need to be hard slash cool, I'm no longer bored, and no longer feel abandoned.

And I haven't had a cigarette since.

You see, I got to her in the end.

I'll get to everything in the end . . .

20th Century Coyote at The Band on the Wall in Manchester, 1976.
Left to right: Lloyd Peters, Mark Dewison, me, Mike Redfearn, Rik (in a cape, naturally).

The only photograph in existence of Coyote performing. Mark, Rik, Lloyd, me.
Everyone in bikinis except for Rik (in a cassock, naturally).

At Rik's parents' house in 1979. Out of Uni and straight into . . . ah . . . well . . . just four paid gigs in the first year.

Performing at the Fringe Club in Edinburgh, 1979.

In the Comic Strip Club dressing room, wearing the sweaty plastic suits. Something funny is going on.

Another relaxed performance by the Dangerous Brothers.

Me and Dawn touring Australia with the Comic Strip in 1981.
I believe the rest of the gang went by coach.

The Comic Strip Presents . . . Pete Richens, me, Robbie Coltrane, Sophie Richardson, Pete Richardson and Pete Richardson's shorts. We filmed nearly everything on the Devon coast . . .

. . . except for 'Mr Jolly Lives Next Door', which we filmed partly outside 10 Downing Street in 1987. Glynn Purcell, me, Stephen Frears, Rik, Basil Ho Yen. No permit, we just turned up very early and told the coppers we were 'with the film crew'.

• = Rik's choice
X = Ade's choice.

Choosing a photo from the contact sheet for the *Bottom Live* tour. Rik has four choices, I have one – this was generally the way of things.

The Bonzos in 2006: including Vernon Dudley Bohay-Nowell, Sam Spoons, Rodney Slater and Neil Innes – with me, out front! ME! WITH THE BONZOS!

Me and Troy as the Bad Shepherds. Not a sheep in sight.
That's how bad we were.

The Idiot Bastards: me, Phill Jupitus, Rowland Rivron's hand and Neil Innes.

Trying to impress Jennifer at a party in the eighties.

Success!

Our last photo together. We've just had one of our lunches.
He still doesn't understand. And neither do I.

In Paris with David,
enjoying the best that life
has to offer.

*'"O Oysters," said the
carpenter . . . but answer
came there none—'*

The Young Ones

Surely enough's been said about this over the years.

The Young Ones

Oh, all right then . . .

It's just odd trying to write about *The Young Ones*. I find it very difficult. It's almost too big to get my head around. I know I'm in danger of wanging on about it, but I'll say it again: *The Young Ones* takes up precisely fourteen weeks of my life, but looms over everything else I ever do in a very disproportionate way.

It's not that I don't like it – I'm incredibly proud of it, and of my part in it – but it takes up too much space. I've been asked so many questions about it, and given so many answers, that I've probably talked about it for more than fourteen weeks.

Anyone talking about something for longer than they spend making it is either a) making stuff up, or b) nuts.

I might be both.

The Young Ones is also a cult, and this is another problem, because its devoted fans have a very fixed idea of what the programme is, why it's brilliant, and what everyone should think about it.

Cults are weird. I know this from being in the cult of The

Bonzo Dog Doo-Dah Band. It's like a secret society. We don't have masonic handshakes but we have the ability to drop small sentences into the conversation if we suspect another member is in the room.

'Hey, you have the same trouble with your trousers as I do,' we might say, or 'Yes, brr, it is a bit chilly.' And these phrases might alert the other follower, and we'll smile at each other, move to a corner, and begin to reminisce.

When I say reminisce I mean repeat wholesale.

I once played Captain Hook in panto in Canterbury and there's a tradition that the Archbishop always comes to a performance and meets the cast afterwards. As a devout atheist I wasn't particularly bothered, and was perhaps looking a bit unconvinced as Rowan Williams came down the line. He was being introduced to each member of the cast by our producer but as he reached me he jumped in before the introduction and said: '"And looking very relaxed . . ." Adrian Edmondson as Captain Hook.' The first phrase being a line from 'The Intro and the Outro'; he knew; we immediately shared a bond; I fell in love with him; we chatted Bonzos, and could easily have gone on all night if Smee and the rest of the pirates hadn't been waiting so impatiently.

I'm aware there's a society like this for *The Young Ones* but I'm not a member of it. People often quote a bit of the show at me, they'll offer me lines of dialogue, like feed-lines, and expect me to come in with the famous rejoinder – a line that I said in the programme forty years ago. But I haven't watched it since it was first on TV, and I always disappoint by not knowing the answer. Every *Young Ones* fan I meet knows the programme better than I do.

Why don't you watch it?

Because I don't watch repeats of any of the shows I've made. I watch them first time out and then I'm done.

Why?

Because it just seems a weird thing to do. It's so backward-looking. I'd feel like Norma Desmond in *Sunset Boulevard* sadly watching her past glories, with the obvious insinuation that there will be no more. Well, I'm still of the mind that my best is yet to come.

Ha ha ha ha ha!

It's true.

Ha ha ha.

I'm still looking forward!

Ha . . .

Shut up, and let me tell you what I know about *The Young Ones*.

The programme is born in the crossfire between the birth of *The Comic Strip Presents* on Channel 4 and the BBC trying to persuade the same group of people to work for them. The BBC are very worried about losing young viewers to the new channel. It's also a tussle between the *Comic Strip*'s leader, Pete, and *The Young Ones* chief instigator, Rik. There's no animosity between the two, and indeed they end up living half a mile from each other in Devon, but there's a definite . . . jostling.

Nigel and I are happy to go along with both. We're going to be on telly. *Twice*.

Another bit of grit in the oyster is that *The Young Ones* contains at least two characters that already exist before writing begins, maybe even all four: Rik's character, Rick the Poet, has been his solo act for a couple of years; Nigel's character, Neil the Hippy, has been in existence even longer; Vyvyan the Punk is basically a version of Sir Adrian Dangerous, or is that just my inability to create a new character? Either way, I'm definitely hired as the berserker, a role I've been playing for a while; and Mike the Cool Person is very similar to a style and presence of character Pete Richardson plays in his double act with Nigel, and the original intention is that Pete will play him. Pete's very cool, I mean for God's sake – sometimes he wears his sunglasses indoors!

However . . .

The Young Ones producer, Paul Jackson, is cut from the same sort of cloth as Pete, in that they both like to be in charge – but there's an antipathy between them that comes from somewhere else.

Paul's another red-brick alumnus – Exeter – and he joined the BBC ten years before *The Young Ones.* He's worked his way up from assistant floor manager to producer and comes to us having just produced the last two series of *The Two Ronnies.* He's very good at his job, and he's genuine in his desire to produce something more anarchic than *The Two Ronnies* – not just because the BBC wants to keep young audiences on side, but because it's his sense of humour and he likes the 'danger' of *The Young Ones.* He's very enthusiastic about it – but he's definitely attached to the mainstream when we meet him, like everyone at the BBC he's a part of the 'corporation', and I think Pete views this with suspicion.

And to be honest Pete's just not a 'telly' person. He's not at home in the world of multi-camera sitcom. He likes film.

In the early days of *The Comic Strip* the *Monty Python* producer John Goldstone lends us a basement room in his suite of offices in Soho. There's a large U-matic video machine in there along with John's film library, and instead of writing we spend most of our time watching John Waters' early films, like *Pink Flamingos* and *Female Trouble.* They all star Divine and a little repertory company of the same actors – a very similar concept to *The Comic Strip Presents.* This is Pete's world.

So Pete and Paul are from two different wings of comedy, in the same way that the RAF and the navy are two different wings of the armed forces. They might have the same objective, but they're coming at it from different angles, and the upshot is that Pete withdraws from *The Young Ones*.

Does he withdraw? Or is he pushed? I think there are ultimatums on both sides. I'm not involved in the fracas because, along with Nigel, I'm simply hired as an actor. It's the first time in my career as an accidental comedian that I'm not involved on the writing side. Not that I feel too excluded, because I'm creating 'Bad News Tour' for *The Comic Strip* at the time, but it's the reason my involvement with the show is so short.

The Young Ones is written by Ben Elton, Rik and his then girlfriend Lise Mayer. I know from personal experience that writing with more than two people in the room can be difficult. At the time Ben's already a proven stand-up comic and writer with more than ten plays to his name; Rik is a practising comic genius, but has only created stuff through improvisation up to this point; and Lise is new to the game. They end up writing two separate versions of each episode, Ben on his own, Rik and Lise together, and then squash the two scripts together, but when I see the draft for the pilot it's mostly in Ben's scribbly handwriting.

There's also some kind of struggle between Ben, Rik, Lise and Paul as to who should replace Pete. Ben himself is in the running for a while, as I think is Chris Ellis from 20th Century Coyote days, but these are shenanigans I'm not party to. In the end they hold auditions and Chris Ryan, who's being hysterically funny in the Dario Fo farce *Can't Pay, Won't Pay* in the West End, gets the part.

In the long run Chris is not treated well by the programme makers, the press or the general public. Once Pete removes himself from the equation, the three writers struggle to agree on what Mike the Cool Person is, the writing for him is generally quite confused, and the character becomes slightly neglected.

There's a scene in one episode where we all come downstairs playing each other's characters, Nigel is Rick, Rik is Vyv, Chris is Neil and I'm playing Mike, and it's one of the most difficult things I ever do – it's hard to get a handle on this character from what's on the page. Chris's comic skills are without question – he goes on to create the brilliant Dave Hedgehog in *Bottom*, and Marshall, Edina's ex-husband, in *Absolutely Fabulous*.

He's also one of the funniest impressionists I've ever heard – he does impressions within impressions: he'll do the American crooner Andy Williams being Sid Vicious, or Orson Welles being Ken Dodd. Some of my favourite memories of making the programme are doing the location filming in Bristol and spending the evenings in restaurants and pubs laughing at Chris.

It's difficult to appreciate now because we've all seen it, and because so many other programmes 'pay homage' to it, and because in the world of TV trailers the word 'revolution' has become just another marketing term – but *The Young Ones* is truly different.

It's couched in the familiar language of all the television that's gone before: multi-camera, sitcom set, live audience. It uses the same basic grammar as *Terry & June*, and we've already had scatological leaps in *Monty Python*, and Spike Milligan breaking the fourth wall at the end of every sketch in the *Q* series.

But what no other comedy show has had before is this:

1. Four completely bloody horrible unsympathetic main characters: venal, selfish, irresponsible, violent, petty and insanitary. Rik and I have a competition before every show to see who can get the most disgusting spots on his face, much to the chagrin of our make-up artist Viv Riley, who yearns to work

on costume drama and do 'pretty ringlets'. There's never been a sitcom before where all the main characters are meant to be so unlikeable. We're used to going 'ahh' at Felicity Kendal in *The Good Life*. We love Pike in *Dad's Army* and want to take him home. We're on Manuel's side in *Fawlty Towers*.

2. For a lot of young people it's the first sitcom they can see themselves reflected in. Despite the characters being so nasty they're completely relatable in a way that many sitcom characters aren't, even the good ones. I love *Steptoe & Son* but I don't know anyone like Harold or Albert. I love *Hancock's Half Hour* but I don't know a Tony or a Sid. But if you've been to school or university you will know a Rick, a Vyv, a Neil or a Mike. In fact the chances are you probably are one, or an amalgam of two or more of them. Their meanness, their pettiness, their going behind each other's backs – that's you, that is.
3. It talks about things no other comedy programme has before: periods (no one has seen a tampon on telly before), masturbation, Thatcher, bogies. It looks surreal on the surface but it's about grubby realities. There's a level of crud and filth that goes way beyond anything in *Steptoe & Son* but it's totally recognizable to anyone who's lived in a student house. And there's a political attitude that's also quite novel. If not exactly red, it's very red-brick. We are Scumbag College – which is where most people go.
4. It has a level of slapstick and violent stunts that haven't been seen since the days of *Laurel & Hardy* and *Buster Keaton*. I make my first proper entrance into the public consciousness crashing through the

wall into *The Young Ones* kitchen. In the same episode I bite a brick which explodes – it's made of Ryvita biscuits which makes it sound harmless, but it contains a small explosive device that's detonated by the offscreen SFX (Special Effects) team. The healthy wholegrain crispbread may be low in saturated fat but it cuts me quite badly and leaves me deaf for a week, but I don't complain because it's a great gag. And I'm a berserker. The SFX team love me because I make it clear from day one that I'm never going to sue. When they 'slightly' overcharge the cooker with explosives it blows up and the flames lick all around the set – the heat is so incredible that the plastic clock on the opposite wall melts. You don't get this kind of thing on *Don't Wait Up* or *To the Manor Born*. SFX fill their boots when we arrive. One of the joys of the whole process is going to the SFX department – a kind of Nissen hut on the outer reaches of the BBC compound – like in those war films where they go to see what 'specials' the mad boffins might have come up with to fool Jerry. There's an array of Heath Robinson machines: gas tanks firing dirty laundry out of washing machines – it comes out so fast in the actual episode that Rik cuts his eye; explosions, rubber cricket bats, frying pans, breakable bottles and plates; giant sandwiches and eclairs; people working out how to get a wrecking ball through the set wall or blow up a bus. *Terry & June* never ask for this kind of thing, so they absolutely adore us, and when it comes to me kicking my own head down the railway track – obviously I can't be in the same shot with my own head because they've dug a hole, stuck me in it, and backfilled me with ballast – so the SFX designer Dave Barton steps in as the headless body because he has the unique ability to lower his head to such an extent that if you look at him from behind he looks like he has no head. And because he's SFX-trained he manages to keep the blood spurting out of his own open wound at the same time. Hero. Later, when we do the Dangerous Brothers on Channel 4 the SFX team aren't quite as knowledgeable. There's a sketch in which we're doing an impression of *The Towering Inferno* – the SFX people smear my lower legs with glue and tell me the flames will come up to my waist. I'm wearing fireproof long johns and they say they'll stand by with extinguishers. I'm conscious that my dialogue is something like 'Help! Help! I'm on fire!' And I don't want them to misinterpret this for an actual cry for help so we agree on a codeword that I will shout if things get too much. We start recording, Rik sets fire to me, and the flames immediately engulf my entire body, burning my eyebrows off and scorching the inside of my throat. In the surprise of this unanticipated scale of conflagration I immediately forget the codeword. 'Help! Help!' I cry. 'No, really – I'm properly on fire!' Everyone watching is laughing, thinking that this is brilliant, that I'm improvising, that I'm perfectly OK because I haven't uttered the codeword. I bluster on, genuinely crying out for help as they continue pissing themselves and it's only Rik – who notices something different in the frequency of my voice – that calls for them to put me out. Thanks, you bastard, though you could have spotted it a bit sooner.

5. There's a live band every week. Admittedly this is partly a lucky accident because it's a requirement of being commissioned by the Variety Department rather than the Comedy Department. But Paul takes it to the Variety Department because they have bigger budgets, which means more special effects and two days in the studio every week – one to pre-record, and one in front of a live audience. And we love our audience. Paul's mantra is 'If you've got a big joke do it in front of an audience.' Which is why Rik and I are dropped 20 foot from above the studio into the kitchen on a double bed. There is *some* protection – the bed is basically a disguised tray holding collapsible cardboard boxes – but in reality we're doing the work of proper stuntmen. In front of a live audience. If you look closely you can see how winded and shocked we are as we struggle out of the crushed boxes and continue fighting.
6. It's full of ideas. Rammed in fact. John Chapman, a successful writer of Whitehall farces, was one of the writers of the seventies sitcom *Happy Ever After*, starring Terry Scott and June Whitfield. I have to make it clear that I love and admire Terry Scott and June Whitfield. However, John Chapman's on record as saying the show had 'run out of ideas' by 1979 and had to come to an end. But the executives were so keen to continue the show they simply changed the name to *Terry & June* and employed new writers. Essentially between 1979 and 1987 they made nine series of a show which had 'run out of ideas'. Despite the odd jewel like *Fawlty Towers* and

> *Yes Minister* this was the state of a lot of sitcoms at the time. Compare the plot of the *Terry & June* episode 'New Doors for Old', in which Terry and June buy a new front door only to discover it's two inches too short but they've already thrown the old door away – that's the entire plot – with the plot of *The Young Ones* episode 'Oil', in which: Buddy Holly is found singing in the attic; Vyv sets fire to Rick's bed; a genie appears from the kettle; Neil gets eight arms; Mike has to dispose of a dead body; the oven explodes; two men are living on a raft in some kind of weird hallucination; Mike opens a Roller Disco in Rick's bedroom; Neil finds a moose's head in his bed; Vyv discovers oil in the cellar; there's a parody of *Upstairs Downstairs* in the broom cupboard; Neil sneezes so violently the broom cupboard explodes; a dictatorship emerges with Mike as El Presidente and Vyv as his brutal police force; there's a prescient gag about Arab potentates chopping up people they don't like; Neil accidentally puts a pickaxe through Vyv's head; and there's a failed revolution which includes a very badly attended benefit concert.

You've got a very good memory for someone who never watches the programme.

Tough luck, buster! I had my fingers crossed behind my back all along!

No, in truth, in trying to explain my point about how crammed full of ideas it was, I had to watch an episode – I reclined on my chaise longue like Norma Desmond and had my eccentric butler lace up the old projector.

I was surprised by how good a lot of it still looked, though some bits are just as dreadful as I remember – the two men on the raft in the cellar. What's that about? It was deadly boring at the time but now it looks insane, and not in a 'zany' funny way. It looks plain wrong, like it's from another show. A really crap show. I was so mesmerized by the horror of it that I had to go back and time it – it's over two minutes long. And I counted the jokes – none.

I was never particularly keen on all the puppets either. For all the 'anything can happen' vibe I'd have been happier with just the four boys, that's where all the best jokes are.

But watching it also reminded me of the sheer exhilaration of studio nights, and the joy of playing to a live audience.

There's one laugh I can hear that crops up all the time, it's a constant at every show we do, including every studio night for *Bottom*, and that's Rik's brother Ant. He's such a brilliant supporter of all our endeavours. He's not a plant, his laugh is genuine, but he's always slightly ahead of everyone else, and he's infectious. Every audience needs a 'seed' laugher – someone who shows them it's all right to laugh – and Ant is our man. His laugh is just a beautiful and innocent expression of joy and delight, and he's what we call a 'jazzer' in that he's the first to pick up on the more esoteric material. I think it's a word Rik and I invent, or at least a meaning we invent – where in jazz you might have an aficionado who recognizes all the subtle variations and changes in pitch and tempo, we use it in our world to mean someone who recognizes all the jokes, not just the obvious ones. If there's a joke we struggle over when writing *Bottom*, and worry about keeping it in, if Ant laughs then we know we were right.

Watching the episode I'm also reminded of the pressure of studio night, the worry of getting it done in time. We'll have recorded some bits the day before – the boring bloody raft, the dull puppets etc. – but the second day is camera rehearsals until 6 p.m., then audience in at 7 p.m., and start recording at 7.30. It's basically a theatre show with cameras, but there're lots of very technical elements that mean a lot of stops and starts, and multiple takes to make sure we get it right. And we have to get it done by 10.00, a) because the audience start to get really bored, and b) because after 10.00 the whole caboodle swings into expensive overtime and Paul starts breaking pencils, throwing things at the monitors, and shouting at everyone.

Paul is a lovely man and he's our true champion – he's the man who gets *The Young Ones*, *Filthy Rich & Catflap*, the Dangerous Brothers and *Bottom* on to the telly – but he can also be a very angry man. There's a depiction of a comically angry director in an episode of *Filthy Rich & Catflap* played by Chris Barrie, which is basically an impression of Paul at five to ten on a studio night.

Ed Bye, who is the assistant floor manager on the first series, our floor manager on the second, and who will go on to direct *Bottom*, is comically diplomatic through it all. Paul will be in the control room, Ed will be on the studio floor relaying Paul's messages. Ed's a very affable and courteous man, and the more apoplectic Paul becomes, the more Ed manages to exude an air of absolute calm. The BBC headphones of the era leak very badly and we'll be able to hear Paul ranting and raving, effing and jeffing at the top of his voice, and when the tirade finally ends Ed will say: 'Paul wonders if you wouldn't mind, very kindly, moving a little to the left.' Or: 'Paul thinks we should perhaps try it the way we rehearsed it.'

Ed's also in charge of collecting the money after the post-show group meals: every show is like a first night and a last night rolled into one, and is therefore an excuse to party big time. The release of nervous energy is off the scale as we inveigle our way into the BBC Club at TV Centre to get a few pints in before going to one of the Indian restaurants on Westbourne Grove. It'll be a huge party – the cast plus partners and family, the band and hangers-on, people from production – there's generally thirty to forty people all fairly shit-faced and ordering freely. It's Ed's job at the end of the meal to check the bill and start collecting . . . it's sometimes funnier than the show.

'Er, Mr Sensible,' he'll say as Captain Sensible walks up and down on the table tops, handing out Tony Benn's latest pamphlet. 'I think you had the lamb bhuna and . . . four pints, does that sound right?' 'Ah, Lemmy from Motörhead, you're back from the toilets, good – there's just the little matter of the bill . . .'

'Five Go Mad in Dorset', the first episode of *The Comic Strip Presents*, goes out on the first night of Channel 4 – 2 November 1982. Culture Club are top of the charts with 'Do You Really Want to Hurt Me?' Turns out the BBC do want to hurt us because the first episode of *The Young Ones* goes out exactly one week later. We think we're lucky to get two very different comedy products onto the telly in the same year but the broadcasters obviously see it as a cut-throat competition. We're in competition with ourselves!

• • •

We make twelve episodes and that's it. Rik's very impressed by John Cleese only making twelve episodes of *Fawlty Towers* and thinks if we copy him *The Young Ones* will be just as iconic. And Rik's very keen to be a legend. Besides, the writing room has collapsed: Rik and Lise split up, Rik and Ben start to write *Filthy Rich & Catflap* together, but in the end Rik leaves all the writing duties to Ben.

The success of *The Young Ones* changes the lives of everyone involved, but changes Rik more than anyone else. He loses the uncomplicated charm of his student days and becomes much more complicatoratory, as George W. Bush might say. He falls in love with his fame.

Just going down the street with him becomes a trial, because he walks around as if every passer-by is a future biographer in search of an amusing anecdote that will prove how off the wall he is. He gurns at people until they recognize him, eyes swivelling to attract attention, then he'll do something 'outrageous' like pretend to pick his nose and wipe the bogie on their coats.

This excites some passers-by who will then ask for an autograph, and it will take for ever to find paper and pen, and if they are female it might entail a hug, a kiss, and a squeeze.

I alluded earlier to a shared idea we once had of what happiness was: being in a cosy boozer with a pool table and a jukebox full of seventies hits. It feels like Rik has now re-entered this dream as a jack-the-lad, flashy pools winner.

It's exhausting, and the weird thing is that he's completely aware of how ludicrous he's being. Once we get back into a private space he'll become old Rik again, making jokes about how vain and preening he is, and about the very people he's just been trying to impress, who he calls 'the ghastly ordinaries'.

• • •

Of course I'm lying when I say *The Young Ones* only takes up fourteen weeks of my life because in 1986 we make the 'Living Doll' single with Cliff Richard for Comic Relief. It's a day to record, about two minutes to make the rather shambolic video in a dreary park in north London, and three nights doing the Comic Relief live show. So make that fifteen weeks. It stays at number one in the UK for three weeks, keeping Bowie's 'Absolute Beginners' off the top spot, which is a travesty.

Cult hero

For fifteen weeks' work *The Young Ones* packs a big punch. The zenith of my cult notoriety comes somewhere during the broadcasting of the second series. I still have Vyvyan's orange hair (it takes a while for the dye to wash out) and I'm walking along Shaftesbury Avenue thinking about – I dunno – wah wah pedals, or lunch, when I hear a teenage girl's voice proclaim: 'It's him!' I look round with mild interest to see who she's talking about, there must be someone famous in the vicinity, and immediately deduce it is me. She is looking at me, and I am 'him'.

She's with a group of friends and they suddenly start running across the busy road towards me, a couple of them let out little squeals of delight and these sounds alert other teenagers who, like hyenas, take up the clarion call and join in. It isn't quite The Beatles at Paddington Station, I'm talking around a dozen people, mostly girls, running towards me. But they run pell-mell. And I have to tell you, it's not a nice feeling. It makes you quite panicky. I imagine it's how the fox feels. My instinct, like his, is to run. And that's what I do.

I dart into Soho, where I figure my superior knowledge of the back alleys will give me an advantage, and the fact that they reek so strongly of urine will surely help put them off the scent: up Dean Street I shoot, down Bourchier Street, which looks like a dead end but isn't, a quick right onto Wardour, down Meard, left back onto Dean, sneaky left into Richmond Mews and then into the multi-storey car park where the current Soho Hotel now stands and hide behind a Ford Cortina. And I lose them. Gone to ground.

I can hear 'Two Tribes' by Frankie Goes to Hollywood playing on some car radio, and whilst my situation isn't quite Reagan v Chernenko, I'm glad to have escaped.

And that's my one brush with 'screamers'. I don't envy The Beatles, or The Bay City Rollers or David Cassidy.

A few years later I'm cast in a four-part series called *If You See God Tell Him* with Richard Briers and Imelda Staunton.

Richard Briers is a witty and self-deprecating bloke who likes to remind everyone that he won the silver medal at RADA in his year. He does this not to brag, but because he likes pretending to be bitter about not winning gold. Or is he pretending? Whichever, he likes the joke of casting himself as second rate.

'I could probably do this scene better if I wasn't just a simple silver medal winner.'

He treats me with suspicion when I turn up. And quite rightly. Anyone watching series two of *The Young Ones* will have seen Vyvyan's rant about *The Good Life*:

'NO, NO, NO, NO! WE ARE NOT WATCHING THE BLOODY *GOOD LIFE*! BLOODY, BLOODY, BLOODY! I HATE IT! IT'S SO BLOODY NICE! FELICITY "TREACLE" KENDAL, AND RICHARD "SUGAR-FLAVOURED SNOT" BRIERS! WHAT DO THEY DO KNOW? CHOCOLATE BLOODY BUTTON ADS, THAT'S WHAT! THEY'RE NOTHING BUT A COUPLE OF REACTIONARY STEREOTYPES, CONFIRMING THE

MYTH THAT EVERYONE IN BRITAIN IS A LOVABLE MIDDLE-CLASS ECCENTRIC, AND I! HATE! THEM!'

On our first meeting Richard quotes it to me more or less verbatim.

It takes quite a lot of reversing out of. I tell him I wasn't the writer, I was just the actor – but that sounds a bit like the Nazi guard saying he was 'only following orders'. I tell him that *The Good Life* has stood the test of time much better than *The Young Ones* which is already looking a bit dated, and that the scene on the raft wasn't funny, and the puppets were a bit crap. He likes that.

But mostly I get through because it's the very early days of 'trailers' on film sets. Indeed our 'trailer' – and it's just the one trailer for the three of us – is just a small touring caravan, the type an elderly couple might tow to Bridlington for the weekend. Richard, myself and Imelda are wedged in around the tiny dining table. There's nowhere to escape to.

This is one of the most delightful parts of being an actor – the way you suddenly find yourself living cheek by jowl with other people for as much as twelve hours a day. There's nowhere to hide, and you either bond or fall out big time. Luckily with Richard, I bond. Mostly because we have something in common – like me he's famous for sitcom, but talking to him it becomes clear he often feels like an actor stuck in a comedian's body.

The most bizarre *Young Ones*-related event takes place in Los Angeles in 1989. I'm out there working as a director, shooting a video for a band called The Innocence Mission, for a song called 'Black Sheep Wall'. It's their debut album and the record company have thrown a lot of money at the first single: they want a video, a posh video, and my posh video for 'Hourglass' by Squeeze has just won two MTV awards, so I get the call. Hollywood here I come.

Never been asked back . . .

We're filming away on the Chaplin stage – to be honest it's not my best work, the singer plays a child's piano as she remembers scenes from her childhood – when there's a kerfuffle in the far corner of the studio. Though kerfuffle is perhaps the wrong word. There's no noise, it's just a kind of psychic wave. Perhaps this is what communication between trees feels like – because without anything being said, without any pointing or gesticulating, everyone in the vast studio is suddenly aware that someone unexpected has come in, and what's more, everyone is in awe of this person. And the person is Joni Mitchell. I know it's her, a) because I know it's her, and b) because my wife absolutely bloody loves Joni Mitchell. If Jennifer had been there instead of me she might have had an attack of the vapours. And it's not that I don't like Joni Mitchell. I love Joni Mitchell, I'm just not as obsessive a fan as my wife; I regard Joni as a Naiad or a Muse rather than an Olympian, and these very different levels of worship make what happens next all the more surprising.

Because, as I'm looking over to see who it is, and I see it's Joni Mitchell, she catches me looking at her. We're about fifty yards apart and, to be fair, everyone in the studio is looking at her, however surreptitiously, but our eyes seem to have locked onto each other. Like a tractor beam in *Star Trek*. And I don't know what the etiquette is here – how did I get caught up in this? Should I break eye contact first, or would that be rude? Would that be dismissing her, dishonouring her? Would that be ranking the icon who's sold 15 million albums below the young ingenue currently playing a kid's piano in front of me?

But while I'm trying to work this out, I am of course still staring at her, and she, whilst maintaining her gaze, begins to stride towards me, a stride that breaks into a run. It's quite a big studio, the Charlie Chaplin stage. And I'm thinking, this is an alarming turn of events, I've obviously broken some unspoken law and she's gonna hit me!

And she's closing in. And I'm bracing myself. But when she reaches me she throws her arms around me and hugs me. So tightly. And then – this is true – she pulls back and kisses me. On the lips. A platonic kiss, no tongues, she's not a sex pest or anything, an affectionate kiss. And I'm thinking, she's got the wrong bloke, this could go to court when she finds out. And then she holds me at arm's length, so she can get a good look at me, and she says, 'Adrian [Adrian! I'm suddenly thinking maybe it's not such a bad name after all], Adrian, I'm so happy to meet you, whenever we have *Young Ones* parties I always play Vyvyan.'

That is the exact sentence. 'Whenever we have *Young Ones* parties I always play Vyvyan.' Which means that *Young Ones* parties in the Mitchell household have happened more than two or three times, don't you think? So they have regular *Young Ones* parties, AND they all dress up, and Joni Mitchell, well-known hippy and wearer of floaty dresses – she dresses up as the punk Vyvyan. I'm imagining Dave Crosby as Rik, Steve Stills as Mike, and Neil Young as Neil.

My feelings about being recognized in the street are different to Rik's. They're not better or worse – this isn't a value judgement – they're just different. To be blunt, I don't enjoy it, it makes me uncomfortable. I find it awkward, and it's generally such a one-sided transaction.

And once you get sucked into believing you're 'famous' you can be instantly disappointed because, of course, most people don't know who you are.

In the early eighties I do a charity gala at the Victoria Palace Theatre and The Police – the band, not the rozzers – are on the same bill. It's during a time when I've allowed my hair to return to its natural blond, and when I come to leave the theatre after the show the stage door swings open to an alarming shriek of excitement, and a frightening surge forward. A large throng of teenage girls see my shock of blond hair as the door opens and mistake me, however briefly (stop laughing), for Sting or Stewart Copeland or Andy Summers. They all have blond hair. *We* all have blond hair. Then they see my stupid glasses and spotty face and the surge recedes as if from a medieval leper ringing a bell, the crowd opens like the Red Sea and I walk the gauntlet of disappointment. I can hear them tutting. To be mis-recognized is almost more embarrassing than being recognized. It's as if I've broken their trust.

Conversely, when you mix with the incredibly famous you sometimes get the ability to go incognito, it's like wearing an invisibility cloak.

By the late nineties Jennifer's show *Absolutely Fabulous* is in its pomp and plans are afoot to remake it in America for an American audience. The British version is already very popular in America, so why anyone thinks this is a good idea is beyond nearly everyone involved, but Jerry Hall gets wind of it, and as our children go to the same school she buttonholes Jennifer at the school gate and declares her interest in playing Patsy. Jennifer is non-committal but Jerry invites us round to dinner to 'talk further' about it.

I want to go, and I don't want to go. It will involve meeting Mick Jagger. I loved Mick Jagger as a teenager. I loved The Rolling Stones. As you know, *Gimme Shelter* was the first album I ever bought – the way I chose to define myself at school. To be honest, I stopped listening after *Exile on Main Street*, but I know the early albums inside out – they were a significant part of my early teenage rebellion. As far as I'm concerned, now that Presley is dead, Mick is the King of Rock 'n' Roll, and I fear this might be a hard standard to live up to. I am not wrong.

Turning up at the Jagger/Hall house Jerry opens the door dressed as Patsy from *AbFab*. She's basically auditioning, so it's awkward from the start. She tells us Mick is upstairs having his eyebrows dyed because he's about to go on tour, and we sit making stuttering small talk until a Filipino maid calls us for dinner.

We sit down in a dingy basement dining area and Mick deigns to join us. His eyebrows look fabulous, if slightly incongruous on his wrinkly old face. I don't think he's seen *AbFab* but he seems aware that Jennifer is a writer or something, and that Jerry wants to impress her, though it's obvious he'd rather be somewhere else, that this is a duty, and his behaviour borders on sulky teenager. I really enjoy this about him – this is the surly revolutionary I was hoping for.

He thinks I'm Jennifer's manager and calls me Andrew. Jerry corrects him, saying my name is Adam. I roll with it – perhaps this is going to be more fun if I don't have to explain myself. The maid serves what looks like a school dinner. And at this point Mick notices there is no wine on the table. Now, you don't get to be a knight of the realm without understanding some basic dinner party etiquette so he says he doesn't drink wine but asks Jennifer if she would like some. Jennifer, a keen imbiber, says 'yes', and Jerry looks worried and leaves the room. She comes back a couple of minutes later with a bottle of plonk; it's half full and has a wrap of clingfilm around the top.

'Does wine like kinda go off?' she asks.

It becomes evident that this is the only bottle of wine in the King of Rock 'n' Roll's house. The man was a byword for debauchery in the sixties but there is no booze. We assure Jerry that good wine has a shelf life of hundreds of years and eagerly drink a glass each of cooking sherry. And that is the end of the 'wine'. And more or less the end of the evening. And the end of my absolute hero worship. Come on, Mick, there are standards.

Jerry doesn't get the part. Acting is a tough business.

Dear boy, why not try acting?

But what is an actor? What do they do? And why would Jerry want to be one? More to the point, why would *I* want to be one? In fact am I being one in *The Young Ones*? Or am I being a comedian? Is there a difference?

I have some shared character traits with Vyvyan – I am the man who tried to drive his motorbike up the stairs at a student party – but Vyvyan is not exactly me. There's a photo of me on the set of *The Young Ones*, obviously taken between takes or in rehearsal, in which I'm dressed as Vyvyan with the spiky hair and the spots and the stars on my forehead – but I've got my glasses on. It immediately makes me not Vyvyan, so something's going on.

Acting is lying. And the best acting is the most convincing form of lying. If you can lie really, really well, they give you a small statuette of a naked man holding a sword.

Konstantin Stanislavski, born in Russia in 1863, is the father of modern 'method' acting. His acting theories were formed partly to accommodate the new writing style of people like Anton Chekhov, which needed actors to tease out the interior life of characters. It was very different to the histrionic style that had gone before: legs wide apart, chin thrust forward, shouting into the dark. After the melodrama of the nineteenth century it was suddenly all about subtext. (This is the only chapter in which my degree in drama comes in handy.)

Some others – notably Lee Strasberg and Sandford Meisner – refined the technique, but they all had the same intent: they wanted actors to achieve a form of reality, an emotional authenticity. *Truth* is the word they like to use.

Stanislavski was keen on actors finding something within their personal lives or the people they knew that resonated with what the character was going through. Meisner went the whole hog and suggested you should treat the other actors around you as real – and that you don't do something 'as the character', you 'are' the character.

Of course you then have to ask yourself why you're in a room with a film crew and one of the walls missing. Or standing on a stage with a thousand people looking on, eating Maltesers and coughing. It's all about different levels of deception, and a lot of it is about deceiving yourself.

There's a famous story about Dustin Hoffman and Laurence Olivier on the set of *Marathon Man* which supposedly demonstrates the clash of acting styles. Hoffman's playing a scene in which his character has had no sleep for three days and he decides not to go to bed for seventy-two hours so that he can play the *truth* of the scene. Olivier arrives in make-up, spots a tired-looking Hoffman, and asks why he looks so rough. Hoffman explains, and Olivier says: 'Dear boy, why not try acting?'

In early 1985, when Elaine Paige and Barbara Dickson are top of the pops with 'I Know Him So Well', I audition for the director Les Blair and get cast in his film *Honest, Decent & True* – part of the *Screen Two* series on BBC2, the strand that took over from *Play for Today*. Les is looking for someone to play a shit-stirrer, and something in *The Young Ones* or *The Comic Strip Presents* catches his eye. Les is a genial soul with a warm Salford accent and a friendly face. There's something of the teddy bear in his demeanour and the twinkle in his eye is the only hint that he's an anarchist too. He and Mike Leigh were childhood friends and Les produced Mike's first film *Bleak Moments*. They share a similar film-making technique and call it 'devising'.

Devising goes something like this:

1. Les chooses a subject matter. In this case a satirical swipe at the advertising industry.
2. Les chooses a group of actors: me, Derrick O'Connor, Richard E. Grant, Gary Oldman, Arabella Weir and a few others.
3. Each actor chooses someone they know well from their own life and bases the character they're going to play on this person. I choose a bolshy comedian I know who likes to fuck things up for the fun of it. *I know him so well.* I call him Alun.
4. Les works one-on-one with me to determine what kind of person Alun is. This involves improvising something as mundane as how Alun gets up in the morning, and what he has for breakfast. When we were at uni we used to use the question 'What did your character have for breakfast?' as a kind of jokey shorthand to imply that someone was taking this acting lark far too seriously. Now I'm taking it this seriously.
5. Les gives Alun a job – advertising copywriter. To this end I spend a week in an advertising agency shadowing a creative team. The one I shadow likes to secretly incorporate Masonic symbols into their

ad campaigns. It's a quiet and pointless level of anarchy that I integrate into Alun – more a symptom of impotence than of real revolution.

6. Les brings the characters together in pairs. I first meet Richard E. Grant in a pub when I'm pretending to be Alun and he's pretending to be Moonie, an advertising art director. I first meet Gary Oldman in a cafe when he's pretending to be my flatmate, Derek. You couldn't get more Meisner. I'm not sure I've ever met Gary when he wasn't in character. Have I indeed met Gary, or have I only met Derek?
7. Les develops a palette of a dozen or so actor/characters, gives them all jobs – mostly in the advertising agency – and then throws various spanners in the works to see what happens.
8. Les generally hides himself away behind a pillar or the sofa while all this improvising takes place, like a little gnome with a pad of paper, and takes copious notes.
9. He devises a story based on all these improvisations.
10. We set about filming it: for each scene he reminds us of attitudes we've expressed in rehearsals, and after an hour or so's improvising on the set we generally agree on the shape of the conversation and bring in the cameras.

The rehearsal/devising period takes about three months, and the filming takes about two months.

Nearly everything of worth I've learned in life has come to me outside formal education. Working with Les is my version of drama school. It's basically a five-month training in the 'method'.

In fact I enjoy *Honest, Decent & True* so much that I go on to make another film with Les in 1990 called *News Hounds* – a satirical swipe at tabloid journalism. In preparation for playing someone who works on the news desk of a tabloid I get a placement for a week on the news desk of the *Daily Star*. I sit in on editorial meetings, listen to everything that's going on around me, and make mental notes about how deeply unhappy everyone seems. There's a moment when I'm sitting on the news desk and someone at the back of the room pipes up: 'Greenpeace on the line!' And the news editor barks back: 'Tell 'em to fuck off!'

This is the kind of research Stanislavski would have loved – using real life experience to feed a character.

News Hounds also features the brilliant Alison Steadman, and it goes on to win a BAFTA in 1991 for Best Single Drama. It's a wonder to me that it turns out so well because, as a major fan of *Nuts in May* – the comedy she made with Mike Leigh, co-starring Roger Sloman, about a husband and wife having an appalling camping holiday on the Isle of Purbeck – I spend the entire five months trying not to sing Alison's songs to her: '*cigarette smoke, it makes me choke, litter makes me quiver.*'

The BAFTA doesn't launch me into the world of straight acting in the way you might think it would. Or perhaps in the way I hoped it would.

It would be nice if my life fell into neat compartments – or would it? Either way it never happens, so I'll never know. During the period I'm making these two films with Les I'm still heavily involved in the world of television comedy, and directly after *News Hounds* I start on the first series of *Bottom* – a project that will stretch over the next decade and beyond.

Part 8

The life and death of a double act

Getting to the bottom of it

A lot of our early stage material is improvised and then honed on stage – it gets better the more we perform it – but this ends up being a bit of a problem. We do the well-honed stuff, which just gets better and better, but whenever we try new gear it doesn't immediately get the big laughs we've got used to, so we get frightened and scuttle back to the tried and tested routines. The incentive to try out new material diminishes because we're addicted to the big laughs, and consequently the range of our material ends up being fairly small. In a year of shows at the Comic Strip Club, a tour of England, and a tour of Australia, we basically end up doing the Dangerous Brothers and a Sam Beckett piss take.

It's frustrating because we know we've created some great comedy but don't know exactly how we got there, or how to do it again, and we struggle to write ten long sketches for the Dangerous Brothers on *Saturday Live* in the mid-eighties.

Our method is to think of the single most exciting thing that can happen, then try to top it. As you can imagine this gets difficult once you're half a page into a sketch. Once you've written 'there is an enormous explosion' at the top of the page it becomes difficult to think how to top it other than to write 'there is an even bigger explosion'. And then you're quickly onto 'there is an even more biggerer explosion' and you've kind of shot your bolt.

The sketches are seven minutes long – generally the same length as a *Road Runner* cartoon – but have twice as many stunts. And these are live action stunts: there's a lot of punching, nipple tweaking, explosions, cannons, hammers, dynamite, being set on fire, smashing through windows, being shot in the head, a siege engine and even a live crocodile. I'm surprised they work as well as they do because the writing process is torturous, and when we finish we feel quite spent. We put absolutely everything we can think of into them and turn down the second series because we think there's nothing left.

Saturday Live broadcasts in 1986. *Bottom* doesn't appear until 1991 – a five-year gap. There's never any conscious decision to stop the double act, but we both get very busy with other projects – quite a few of them together, like *Bad News* and *Filthy Rich & Catflap* – but the double act, or more specifically the writing part of the double act, goes into hibernation.

Alongside doing more *Comic Strip Presents* and the films with Les, I do a couple of projects written by Ben: *Happy Families* – in which Jennifer plays all four of my sisters and I play her imbecilic brother; together with Nige and Rik I do *Filthy Rich & Catflap*, also written by Ben; and Rik also works on *Blackadder II* which is a much funnier proposition to the first series now that Ben has joined Richard Curtis as co-writer.

Obviously we've already done *The Young Ones* too, so we're basically learning a lot about the way Ben writes. Creativity is mostly subconscious theft – and not always your own subconscious. Once you become a writer it's hard not to look at other writing from the other writer's point of view. As a writer who's also a performer you get to examine another writer's work even more closely. And being in the rehearsal room with Ben as opposed to just watching, for example, another brilliant sitcom like *Desmond's*, is a great learning experience.

Essentially he teaches us one of the fundamental truths of sitcom: you don't have to start from square one every time. You don't need to start with the big explosion. It is the characters that are funny. Take great care over creating your characters, and if they have conflicting desires, and the audience knows the characters well enough to anticipate those desires, hilarity should prevail. A lot of it is giving the audience what they're expecting and making them feel clever about it at the same time.

By 1990 Rik gets a little bored with *The New Statesman* – a sitcom he's been making since 1987 about a scurrilous MP, Alan B'Stard. It's a great character but Rik knows he's the only attraction in the show, and though that flatters his ego, I think he's a bit lonely, creativity-wise. And I miss the old bastard too. We go for a drink, it feels like old times, and we decide to write something together.

When I think of *Bottom* I generally picture the little office where Rik and I used to write opposite the entrance to the Hole in the Wall pub in Richmond, and I think mostly of us laughing.

And laughing.

And laughing and laughing and laughing.

There was such a joy in it all. It felt untrammelled, unconstrained and vaguely unbelievable. There we were earning a sizeable wedge for just sitting on our arses trying to make each other laugh. It's exactly what we'd been doing at university, but now we were getting paid.

Everything we did before *Bottom* felt like it was leading towards it, and, according to my Numskulls, or my interpretation of Sturgeon's Law, it's the best thing we ever do together.

Our initial idea is to call it *My Bottom*. We want the

continuity announcer to say: 'And next on BBC2 tonight – my bottom.' We want people at work to be saying to each other: 'Did you see my bottom on telly last night?'

The title is frowned upon by Alan Yentob, the controller of BBC2 at the time, and we reach a compromise by calling it simply *Bottom*. BBC2 is the home of new comedy throughout the eighties and nineties but there's still a kind of intellectual snobbery against pure 'childish' humour.

As a small act of defiance in the face of this snootiness, instead of writing 'THE END' at the end of all our scripts we write 'FIN' as if they're scripts from the Nouvelle Vague of French cinema and we are as intellectually highfalutin' as Jean-Luc Godard or François Truffaut.

Being bottom becomes our theme anyway, so maybe Alan was right. It becomes about two sad losers at the bottom of the pile. It borrows heavily from *Waiting for Godot* – the two tramps waiting for some improvement in their unexplained lives. It borrows from *Steptoe & Son* – Harold the man yearning to climb out of the gutter, Albert doggedly holding him back. It borrows from *Hancock's Half Hour* – Tony thinking himself a cut above, Sid recognizing they're more likely a cut below. It borrows from *Laurel & Hardy* – two losers who only have each other. And it borrows from the Dangerous Brothers in its commitment to find ever more ingenious ways to beat the living daylights out of each other, but this time with a little more context.

We've finally sussed how to write without painting ourselves into a corner at the top of page one: we have two characters, based on hyper exaggerations of our own personas – one reaching for the stars but hopelessly inadequate, the other a bluntly philosophical berserker who's prone to violence – and our writing days consist of 'filling the larder', as we call it, with material about how they would each react in certain situations: a library, famine, debt, love, police, death.

It is the characters that become honed. Imagine the Angel Gabriel – a character everyone knows, and whose behaviour is predictable – but take him out of the Nativity and think about how he would fare on a golf course, or doing his tax return, or trying to buy porn at a petrol station.

It's a fairly unique process, making *Bottom*. The only sitcom before it written entirely by the main performers is *Fawlty Towers*. So we don't have a map. I suppose we could ask John Cleese, but he's a rather daunting individual.

In 1989, at the Amnesty fundraiser *The Secret Policeman's Biggest Ball*, I do the *Python* sketch in which Michelangelo argues with the Pope about his painting of the Last Supper (Michelangelo has painted twenty-eight disciples, three Christs, some jellies and a kangaroo – the Pope wants a more conventional image). I'm playing Michelangelo, John's playing the Pope. We convene at a cafe in Greenwich to read it through.

I'm frankly overwhelmed to meet one of my absolute heroes, but he is a very, very intense man. It's like meeting the headmaster of comedy. I feel like I'm in Guybrow's study. I begin to wish I was wearing two pairs of underpants. I have to put my script on the table, otherwise he'll see how much it's shaking in my hands. Obviously he's done the sketch before, so he knows how to do it, but he delivers a long set of rules about the timing, and the playing of it, in an extraordinarily serious way. He takes his comedy very seriously. It's like Latin – it's full of rules.

I go away and learn the lines more thoroughly than I've ever learned my lines before, we get one more bash at it in the dress rehearsal, and then we're on . . . and it goes down extremely well. We do it very well. Every joke lands. I don't copy Eric Idle, I do my own Michelangelo, and it feels great. And John is brilliant as the Pope, but I'm not sure I'd want to work with him on a sitcom, because I can't treat it as scientifically as he does.

He's obviously a much more successful comedian than I am, and I'm not saying his method is wrong – it's right for him – but I want to laugh all the time, I want it to be fun.

So we're on our own. Again. We have to come up with our own methods, and the one we develop is this:

We meet at 10.00 a.m.

We make coffee and spend the first forty-five minutes talking about the world; about what's happening with our families; about schools; about being annoyed at a supermarket checkout; about the news headlines; about different types of sandwiches; about what we've seen on the telly; about some behaviour we've seen on a bus; about where we're going on holiday; about some gossip we've heard; about how to fix a dripping tap; about how to get hold of an actual gun; etc., etc. And somewhere within this jumble of ideas about the world in general something will eventually ping out. Usually after about forty-five minutes. Don't lose your nerve.

'Where would Richie and Eddie go on holiday? They've got no money, have they? Where's the nearest holiday destination to Hammersmith? What's the cheapest kind of holiday? What kind of holiday causes the most friction? What's the worst kind of holiday?'

We then try and answer these questions, which invariably throws up more questions, and we start to fill the larder with ideas.

'All right, suppose they're camping. Whose idea is it? Why would they go camping? Is it an escape? Is it a bet? Who would be the best prepared? Have they got any equipment?'

Some of you might recognize that I'm describing the origins of the episode 'Bottom's Out', in which Richie and Eddie go camping on Wimbledon Common. They basically camp in the dog toilet, they've remembered the can opener but forgotten the cans, there's a tussle over a packet of chocolate Hobnobs and they land in the fetid pond, Richie falls in the fire, they hunt for Wombles with Eddie's darts, using a tent pole to make a rudimentary blow pipe – Richie gets a dart in the head, a dart in the hand, and another in his arse – their tent is called a Stormbuster Mk IV (named after my own teenage tent) but is little more than a bivouac, Richie gets trapped in his sleeping bag, Eddie doesn't have one, there's a thunderstorm and the nudey flasher of Wimbledon Common gets his pubes caught in the zip of their tent and runs off with it . . .

I think my favourite bit is when Richie, trapped in his sleeping bag like an angry caterpillar, takes the peg mallet in his mouth and repeatedly hits Eddie with it. It's deliciously insane.

It might sound easier than it is. In truth each episode takes about three weeks to write. Mostly because we have a burst of creativity after the initial ideas session and then go to the pub for lunch, after which we're not much good for anything except what we call 'secretarial work' – arranging the ideas into some kind of order. So basically, a script is fifteen times two-and-a-bit hours.

But that little period, between around 10.45 and one o'clock, is the good bit. That's when we offer up lines and laugh at each other. That's the sparky bit. That's when it feels like the lightning strikes. When we laugh like drains.

Some of the writing happens when you're not thinking about it. You can be making the kids' tea and you'll suddenly think of how to solve a tricky link between lighting the gas stove and drying out the Hobnobs, or getting ready for bed and think about using a vest as a fishing net. Writing is a permanent state of mind, but the big bit, the fun bit, the bit that happens together, is that morning session.

Nearly everyone I meet who isn't in the business imagines that the programmes must be improvised; that crazy stuff must just happen, that it must be wild, it must be mayhem, it must be chaos. I'll admit some ideas are added to in rehearsal but the real mayhem and chaos takes place inside our heads during the writing period.

Once we get to the studio, and the pre-record of the trickier stunts, it's about helping the SFX team and the technicians make that imaginary mayhem into reality. You can't suddenly improvise when you're pushing Rik's head into a campfire. Ed Bye, *The Young Ones*' floor manager who's now our director, will have discussed the procedure for weeks: it's a mixture of real fire that is extinguished quickly, smoke delivered through a tube, and an old Victorian magician's trick called Pepper's Ghost in which an angled pane of glass in front of the camera records a flame effect to the side at the same time as Rik leans into the fire. The two images combine.

Anarchy must be organized.

Ed is the best director we ever have and camera rehearsals are so intricate that they take a long time. There's a lot of to-ing and fro-ing, getting the angles and the sizes right. I hate to burst the bubble of people imagining constant mayhem and chaos but I spend most of the camera rehearsals doing the crossword. It's one of the calmest points of the whole process. I sit there on the bench on the set of Wimbledon Common, and happily work out my anagrams and cryptic definitions. It's like a holiday – the calm before the storm of the recording in front of an audience.

Unfortunately the episode 'Bottom's Out' doesn't go out when planned. A fatal sexual assault takes place on Wimbledon Common just before the transmission date and it's considered insensitive to show the nudey flasher shagging our tent.

When the next series goes out it's tagged onto the end of the run but is pulled again when one of the suspects in the case goes on trial. It eventually goes out three years after its scheduled broadcast.

We don't win prizes for *Bottom* but we do win an enormously loyal fan base who can quote our scripts at us in the same way that I can quote Laurel & Hardy. The first series gets the best viewing figures for a comedy on BBC2 until *Absolutely Fabulous* steals our crown a year later. Ed tells us with an amused grin that whenever ITV put on some crowd-pleasing special the BBC repeat an episode of *Bottom* against it to dent ITV's viewing figures.

I think it's one of the few times in our lives when we know exactly what we're doing. But looking back at the dates I'm shocked by how much we get done in such a short time, it's a real burst of energy: between 1991 and 1995 we create three TV series – eighteen episodes – and the first two live *Bottom* stage shows.

It's made more extraordinary by the fact that we're doing so many other things at the same time. I play Brad in *The Rocky Horror Show* in the West End; together we do *Waiting for Godot* (directed by Les Blair); I do another play, *Grave Plots*, in Nottingham; I shoot the series *If You See God, Tell Him*; *The Comic Strip Presents* makes *The Pope Must Die* and the special 'Red Nose of Courage' that goes out after the polls have closed on election night in 1992 – in which I play John Major as a clown who runs away from the circus, lured by the world of stationery. I write a novel, *The Gobbler*. All this while having three young children born in 1986, 1987 and 1990.

If Picasso had his blue period, this is definitely my purple patch. I can't imagine how I could create that amount of material now. It's taken me a year to write this book.

The Starcraft years

It's after the second TV series that our promoter Phil McIntyre, the man who organizes and produces all our live work, says we should take it out on the road as a 'live sitcom'. This hasn't been done before. Rab C. Nesbitt has taken a version of his TV show on the road but it's not exactly what the show looks like on the telly. We say we'll do it if the production values are high enough: we want the set to look identical, we want the same stunts and slapstick, we want explosions, and sound effects for the fights.

This is in the days before easily programmable sequencers and our 'spot FX' man has to constantly load floppy discs in and out of machines to play the various noises we want. But this attention to detail pays off well – when the theme tune plays and the curtain rises on the first show of the first tour to reveal the exact set, the cheer goes on for several minutes because people realize we're going to give them the real thing. We're not doing *Bottom*-like routines in front of a black cloth, we're giving them the proper show. With added rude words.

• • •

Phil comes to rehearsals at the Dominion in central London one day and takes us outside to present us with . . . 'The Starcraft'. It's a converted Dodge camper van. It has no toilet or kitchen area, and there's nowhere to play 'one leg', but it has two enormous seats like La-Z-Boy recliners, and behind them a double bed. This might be taking the Laurel & Hardy reference too far but we often find ourselves lying down together in our double bed.

We both have young families and we like to get home as much as we can. The double bed helps make this possible. We live in London and only start staying in hotels once we get as far as the arc that takes in Bristol, Birmingham and Nottingham. Any closer and the routine is to step off the stage straight into the Starcraft and get going. Once underway we change out of our sweaty stage gear and bung it in a bin bag to seal in as much of the stink as possible. It's not ideal, but it means we get home to our own beds.

It also saves me from the boredom of wandering around town looking for something to do during the day and getting constantly bothered for autographs, which is what a lot of touring is about.

Oh! Spoilsport.

Let me try and explain.

We're your fans!

I know, and that's lovely, but being a fan is odd. And having fans is even odder.

I am a fan. I understand what it's like being a fan. As a teenager I see Tom Baker – who in the mid-seventies is the current Doctor Who – walking in the street in York. It's Tom Baker. It's definitely Tom Baker. What do I do? I've seen him on telly. I know it's him. He probably doesn't know that I know he's Tom Baker. He might think I haven't recognized him. I ought to correct this. Plus, I could then tell all my mates that I'd met

Tom Baker. I need to get him to sign something, to prove it's him. Obviously he knows he's Tom Baker, but I need the proof. What have I got for him to sign? The back of my bus ticket? My fag packet? I haven't got a pen. Surely he's got a pen? He must do autographs all the time, he's bound to have a pen. 'Tom,' I shout, but he's sloping away, quite quickly. He's too far away now. It would seem odd to run a hundred yards to ask him if it's really him, if I can have an autograph, and if he has a pen . . . and some paper. So I watch him go. But, from what I know now, he knows that I'm watching him, he knows he's been recognized.

By the late nineties the *Bottom Live* show is doing very well and when Rik and I go touring we spend the full week in each town. And I'm not criticizing the noble towns of, for example, Newcastle, Leeds or Birmingham, but when you're touring, and every day is just a slow preparation for the impending battle of wits that evening, filling in the time can be difficult.

You can't work on other things because your mind is already occupied. It's even hard to read when you're keeping two hours' worth of crowd control in your head. Hotel rooms soon lose their appeal – ironing the towels and making the bed immaculately to fool housekeeping is a game of diminishing returns – so you eventually head out onto the street to wander about, maybe take in the art gallery, the local beauty spot, the shops.

But of course, walking down the street undetected is more difficult than usual, because there're posters everywhere, with your face on, which makes it easier for people to spot you, and to constantly interrupt your walk with requests for an autograph. This is perfectly lovely and very flattering . . . until you've done it a few times too many. And it's hard to actually get anywhere.

So you learn to walk around looking at the pavement. Wearing a hat. You develop a sixth sense which understands when people have spotted you, and you scuttle off in the opposite direction before they can pluck up the courage to shout out. This is how I know Tom Baker must have known I was watching him. And that's why he kept his head down. And wore a hat. And scuttled off in the opposite direction.

Things get more time-consuming when the mobile phone arrives. 'Can I have a selfie?' Watching for all the interminable minutes as people fumble their way round bits of technology which have suddenly become completely alien to them.

'How do you switch it on? Oh, that's looking the wrong way, oh, can you hold my bag a minute, you must get really bored of people doing this?'

Yes.

They co-opt another passer-by to take the photo – how is this a 'selfie'? – then that person takes the opportunity to ask for their own selfie, and suddenly the self-perpetuating horror grows exponentially, until you have to be rude and more or less run away.

And none of them want you. Really. They have hardly any interest in *you* at all. What they want is to prove to their friends and family that they've met you.

Years later I try a different tack; I say, 'Let's not do the selfie/autograph thing, let's just have a chat. What are you up to today? Where have you come from? What's your day like? Do you live round here?' And they don't like it, they don't want interaction, they only want the proof.

In the early 2000s, back in London, I'm in the French House in Soho when my sixth sense is alerted and I look up to see Tom Baker at the other end of the bar. And he's looking at me. And I look back. He gives me the tiniest nod of the head, and goes back to his drink.

There's very little music we agree on in the van. The only artists we *both* like are Little Richard, Dr Feelgood and Mott the Hoople. What am I saying – these are the *only* bands that Rik likes, plus 'Brown Eyed Girl' by Van Morrison. We listen to Mott's greatest hits a lot. We particularly like 'Saturday Gigs'. It's brilliantly triumphant but rather sad and wistful at the same time, and it talks about the successes and failures the band had, and we relate to that. It contrasts the fun and apparent ease of success – no one really knows how they got there, it just happens – with the pressure to keep it up.

Mott happen ten years before us and we really appreciate the feeling of striving in the song. It's very easy to look at any apparently successful act and wonder why they should ever doubt themselves, but we're riddled with it. Especially when touring. We do five major tours, and, unlike a band, we can't just play our hits, people want new material.

I'm accosted in the street by someone in Nottingham who'd come to see our show two nights running and is pissed off that we did the same stuff. That's how much people want something new in comedy, whereas a band will be harangued if they don't play the old hits. Like me with Procol Harum.

Every time we come up with a brand-new two-hour show we'll be so worried that THIS TIME it won't work. The live show happens every two years from 1993 to 2003 – with a break in 1999 to make our feature film *Guest House Paradiso* – and we live in constant fear of not delivering. Rik and I are almost catatonic before every first night of a new live show. The recurring thought being – 'is this the one where we get found out?' We've both had dreams of opening a new show and simply getting no laughs at all. Of some lone voice shouting out from the back: 'But . . . it's just not funny!' Like the little boy who hadn't heard about the magic suit in *The Emperor's New Clothes*.

We're both just accidental comedians.

• • •

Every time we tour we film the show to make a video. We usually do this two-thirds of the way through the run in a town where we feel confident of the audience response. On the second tour we do this at the Oxford Apollo, but the week before, the director comes to see the show in Bristol to write a camera script. We're playing the Colston Halls – named after the slave trader Edward Colston whose statue was more recently tipped into the river. It's worth rewatching footage of the event because the statue's facial expression is precisely that of a man who's resigned to being tipped into the river. It's as if the sculptor knew.

The hall has since been renamed the Bristol Beacon and it's a building that's been through many changes. Its original purpose was as a concert platform and the backstage area is notoriously cramped and irregular.

Having seen the show, the director turns up the next afternoon and asks us to 'walk through' the more technical bits so that he can organize his script. 'Walking it through' is doing it at half the speed and stopping to explain the trickier moments.

At one point I'm explaining how Eddie runs across the whole width of the stage and dives through a closed window to avoid cleaning the toilet, smashing through the glass and the frame as he goes. I walk it through.

'I run across here,' I say. 'And I dive through this window.'

By this point I've reached the window. It's made of sugar glass, which breaks very easily but can scratch you quite badly. It's more opaque than actual glass. I peer through it. Our set reaches the edges of the Victorian concert platform and my landing spot is down the narrow stairs that lead up to the stage. It's a drop of about six feet. There are a couple of mattresses there to break my fall and the grinning figure of our tour manager, Ian Day, who's there to catch me if I 'overshoot' – he's a rugby player, which is why he's chosen for the job.

During a live show I do this with consummate ease and a fair degree of relish. It always gets a good cheer. Looking at it in the cold light of the walk-through, I can see why – it's absolute bloody madness. They're laughing because you'd have to be clinically insane to do this.

Every Christmas after a tour the video of the show competes with Billy Connolly and Roy Chubby Brown for top spot in the video charts. We sell millions of them. People think you can earn big money from being on the telly, but it doesn't compare to the money on offer from live touring and video sales.

Glory days.

So where does it all go wrong?

The Jacobite Rebellion

It's 1745 and Bonnie Prince Charlie lands at Glenfinnan on the shores of Loch Shiel in Scotland. He hangs around for a couple of days until a few Highland chums arrive, then sets off on a tour of Britain, taking in the sights of Edinburgh, Carlisle, Preston and Manchester, and getting as far south as Derby, before heading back the way he came, escaping on a small boat to Skye disguised as a washerwoman, and fleeing to Italy to become an alcoholic.

History calls it the Second Jacobite Rebellion, or more simply, the '45.

In that ten-year period between 1993 and 2003 Rik and I do pretty much the same thing. We take in the sights of Edinburgh and Manchester etc., but we do a lot better than Bonnie Prince Charlie and penetrate much further south than Derby; oh yes, we put Brighton, Bournemouth, Exeter and Plymouth to the comedic sword, not to mention the capitals of England, Scotland, Wales, Northern Ireland and Ireland. Yet the similarity is striking – a long slog interrupted by moments of blind terror.

Of course nit-pickers will say we're not engaged in deadly

combat on a regular basis, but as anyone who's done live comedy will testify, we come pretty damn close.

And the actual battles of the '45 are all very short: Culloden lasts an hour, Falkirk Muir about the same, and the Battle of Prestonpans is over in twenty minutes – we've had difficult spells at the Sunderland Empire that have lasted longer.

The casualties in the Clifton Moor Skirmish are about a dozen killed and wounded on each side. Thanks to the slapstick violence of our live show – sledgehammers, frying pans, explosions etc. – we've spilled almost as much blood in an evening. Without the benefit of camera angles to disguise the gap between our heads and the cricket bats and pickaxes with which we 'pretend' to hit each other, distances are tight and can often be misjudged, and the results see us getting stitched up fairly frequently.

The difference between reality and make-believe is surprisingly thin. One night at Sheffield City Hall I accidentally catch Rik with a large metal milk jug. It opens up his eyebrow. Perhaps Rik's 'rubbery-faced intensity' means he has more blood vessels there than most, because it fairly cascades down his face. Though he's such a sweaty performer – his costume is wringing wet after the first five minutes – that he doesn't notice he's bleeding, and carries on. He's a trooper, after all, and this is showbiz, darling. I'm game, and carry on too, though I find it hard not to laugh as he begins to look more and more like some bloodied devil in a painting by Hieronymus Bosch.

I've always wanted to do a study on the performer's heart rate during a live show. I feel mine rising every night before I go on. I don't particularly feel nerves after the first couple of weeks, but I still feel the increased heart rate. It must be a natural preparation for the fight ahead – maybe the MacDonalds and the Camerons felt the same as they ran headlong down the hill through the wind and sleet to overrun Hawley's left flank at Falkirk Muir.

I'm pretty confident Rik's heart is beating fast because the blood keeps pumping and pumping, and starts to soak into his white shirt . . . and it's the audience that make him aware of it, because they stop laughing. We look at them and their faces are drained and worried, like children who've seen their parents arguing. Rik wipes the blood away with one of the towels we've placed around the set for the sweat problem. He tells them it doesn't hurt, it's just a flesh wound, and we try to resume the show, but the audience are still in a state of shock. They simply won't laugh any more. We have to cut to the interval and get a medic in to stitch him up.

And this is the paradox: they've come out for the evening to watch two blokes knock chunks out of each other; the harder we hit each other, the more they laugh; but the moment we actually connect, they throw up their hands in horror – like the dignitaries of Falkirk who came out to 'watch the battle' from the sidelines, and ended up getting overrun themselves. Imagine their faces – well, that's the audience at Sheffield City Hall.

Why do I keep mentioning the Jacobite Rebellion? I'll tell you why: because touring is ultimately very boring.

During our first tour in 1993 we drink copiously. Too copiously. There's a strict rule that we don't drink *before* a show – because we need our wits about us – but *afterwards*, well, the end of each and every show is a cause for enormous celebration, the relief is overwhelming and we drink for the sheer joy of conquering the panic. A lot of people drink to celebrate the end of their exams – we get meticulously examined every single night.

It turns out, in the long run, that Rik isn't very good at drinking. As students, lack of funds severely constrained our drinking habits – we couldn't afford more than four pints of cheap lager of an evening, and four pints made Rik amiable and fun to be with. But now we're earning good money, we can drink as much as we like, of anything, even spirits, which had seemed an unaffordable luxury – and half a bottle of Scotch makes Rik, by turns, belligerent, morose, and then unconscious. It's no fun for either of us.

As I've said, our office overlooks the front door of a pub, and as we're writing the second show in 1995, Rik turns up increasingly late, and I often see him nip into the pub first thing before we start writing. He thinks I can't see him, and that vodka doesn't smell – he's wrong on both counts.

We've often wished that we could write drunk, what a life that would be, and don't think we haven't tried: many's the time we've taken a notepad on a lovely pub crawl, but reading it back the next day we've confirmed the universal truth that drunks are not as funny as they think they are. And the same is true now as he sits in front of me, secretly half cut. I eventually challenge him. He swears he hasn't touched a drop, but annoyingly for Rik, his lazy eye wanders further to the left the more he drinks, and right now it's practically looking backwards. We finally have a friendly, truthful and rather tearful discussion. Rik doesn't appear for a week, and when he finally returns he says he's come to accept that he has a problem with booze.

So from the second tour onwards Rik doesn't drink at all, and to make it easier for him, and because drinking alone is a bit sad, I stop drinking too. It helps Rik with his problem, but gives us another – what the bloody hell are we going to do instead of drinking?

Instead of drinking wine I read a lot about it, and my cellar back home becomes an ever-growing thing of wonder – stocked floor to ceiling with French and Italian wines that I will drink when the tour ends. I'm no expert but I can name-drop and bullshit my way round any wine list, and over the course of the tour I order so much wine that I'm still drinking some of it today.

Then, wandering around a second-hand bookshop in Leeds,

I find two enormous tomes: *The History of England* and *The History of Scotland*. They were published in the 1930s and are full of articles about where to go to follow the history of these two countries. As we're heading to Edinburgh we take a look at *The History of Scotland* and decide to fill in our time following the events of the Jacobite Rebellion. We settle on the 1745 rather than the 1715 because that was the big one.

Food is our other distraction, and now, after every show, we go back to our hotel – having carefully ordered a slap-up meal from the menu and had it kept warm – so that we can eat late. And as we munch we watch *Newsnight* on the telly, and discuss where we might go the following day.

We wake, refreshed and un-befuddled by hangovers, I borrow the keys to the Starcraft from Ian, and we drive out to see the historical sites. A slight disappointment is that often there's not much to see. In later years these places will grow visitor centres and informative notice boards, but right now there is mostly nothing.

At Prestonpans (or as we call it, Not-very-well-pressed-on-pants), just outside Edinburgh, there's a small cairn on a triangle of grass sandwiched between the busy B1361 and the road to Meadowmill. It has the number 1745 carved into it, but nothing else. We climb what passes for the largest hill thereabouts, which may just be a slag heap from the nearby coalmine, and get a really good view of . . . a power station. However, the guide book directs us to a somewhat larger memorial to Colonel Gardiner (a Scotsman fighting for the British), and tells us Bankton House, just beyond, was where he lived – he was a career soldier and fought major battles all over Europe but died just outside his own front door, in the one that lasted twenty minutes. This is the kind of thing that amuses us, and we drive away contented. Who needs booze when you've got the Jacobites?

Colonel Gardiner with his house in the background

A field near Falkirk offers another monument on which is helpfully written: 'The Battle of Falkirk was fought around here 17th Jan 1746', and that's it. There's no more information. Which is just as well because the book relates that the battle was such a confusing mess of bloody hand-to-hand combat fought in storm-force winds and torrential rain, that at the end of it neither side knew who'd won. Which is another striking similarity to our live show, on occasion.

The Battle of Inverurie is just a sheep field outside Aberdeen.

And Culloden is similarly unspectacular. It's a piece of scrub the size of two football pitches covered in thistles, and the book tells us the Scots would divest themselves of their cumbersome kilts and charge bollock-naked at the English ranks. We don't know if the thistles were as high then as they are now, but we laugh hysterically for nearly an hour at the thought of it.

There's nothing to see in Carlisle either. The local militia, a handful of old codgers, just opened the gates because they hadn't been paid for months. But we have some good fish and chips, and look at the castle walls without getting out of the van, because it's raining.

Following the '45 is one of the most enjoyable touring experiences we ever share, but, much as the wheels fell off for Bonnie Prince Charlie halfway through his tour, things start to fall apart for us too. And it isn't drink, like you might imagine, it's a kind of vanity.

Charles Edward Louis John Casimir Sylvester Severino Maria Stuart is an undoubted claimant to the throne, he's the grandson of James II. He's also a figurehead, both for Catholics and for nationalist sentiment in Scotland. He promises his supporters a French invasion force is on its way to join them and that they will attack London together. Trouble strikes when he reaches Derby; his promises are found to be wishful thinking, the French are nowhere to be seen, his supporters lose faith in him, and in a room over a pub in the town centre his generals say they should turn back.

Richard Michael Mayall is an undoubted comic genius, he is a cult hero riding the crest of a very successful wave, and he's equally successful with the ladies. Richie Richard, the character he plays, is definitely not a genius, and is not at all successful, especially with the ladies. Trouble strikes a few weeks into the tour, when we hit the Derby Assembly Rooms and the line between Rik and the character Richie starts to blur. This is when the audience stop laughing quite as hard, and when Rik wants to turn back.

It's hard to explain the difference between a good laugh and a diminishing laugh. The audience will not be aware of it, but all performers, not just comedians, will occasionally come off stage saying, 'What a shit audience they were tonight.' Of course, the opposite is usually the truth – that the performers haven't been on top of their game – and it's not really a problem until . . . you start to recognize the same feeling every night.

Once you start thinking the audience are shit every night, you're in trouble.

The writing is fun – we enjoy the writing – it's where we get to hear the jokes for the first time, and we enjoy making each other laugh.

In rehearsals the crew laugh at every line. They're not paid to laugh, they just do because they find it funny. That's partly why they like to tour with us.

It starts to be less fun when Rik stops playing the character and begins to believe the laughter. I see it on his face. He starts to think that the crowd are not laughing because Richie is a funny character but because Rik is a comic god. And it's complicated, because it's both, but he starts being more Rik than Richie. Unfortunately, Rik the comic god isn't quite as funny as the character. The character is humble, nervous, insecure, scared and desperate. The comic is none of these things.

Don't get me wrong – Rik is a comic genius. But he delivers his comedy through characters. That's when he's funniest.

And then sex begins to rear its ugly head.

Richie the character isn't confident of his sexuality because he's never had it off. Rik is very sure of his sexuality and has had it off a lot. Playing one or the other of these makes the show very different. In fact he now has a choice of three: Richie, Rik the comic genius, and Rik the sex god. The more the sex god prevails the weaker the laughs become. There's always a point a few weeks into every tour when he'll say: 'None of the stuff I have is funny, let's cut all my lines.' And I'll try to point out that if he stayed in character the laughs might come back. If I had a penny for every time I said 'just play the character' I'd have £5.42.

Nothing wrong with being a sex god – well, I wouldn't know, but I'm imagining it must be lovely – however, the jokes are written for the exact opposite. The character is wailing that he's destined to be a virgin his entire life, whilst the sex god playing him is winking at a girl in the fifth row.

Our audience is probably only a third female at best, but occasionally Rik starts to shout 'Scream, Girls!' apropos of nothing, like he's a Beatle, or a Monkee – he loves the girlie shriek that comes back at him. I respond by looking very confused and shouting 'Scream, Boys!' as if it's some kind of experiment, and it gets a good laugh.

And this is basically the choice – shrieking or laughing. It doesn't seem possible to have both.

He cuts huge sections of carefully written jokes which only he at his manic and sexually inadequate best can perform, and the show gradually loses any complexity it might have had and becomes a race to the next fight.

We usually save the Hammersmith Odeon in London for the end of the tour. The accepted wisdom is that Londoners get so much entertainment that we need our show to be at its well-honed, tip-top best to sate their jaded palates. Unfortunately this turns out to be the point in our tours when we're basically doing the Chuckle Brothers version, and by the end of each tour, especially the later ones, I'm thinking, 'I don't want to do this again.'

No one's sure whether women forget the pain of childbirth enough to consider doing it again because of time or hormones, but we forget the pain of touring through time and the rather more sordid promise of enormous financial reward. However, even that palls over the years, and everything comes to an end.

The Jacobite Rebellion ends in defeat at the Battle of Culloden in 1746. It's a confusing situation and basically the end of a fight for the throne that's been going since 1688. The Duke of Cumberland's force is mainly English but includes a lot of Scots lowlanders; Charlie's army is mostly Scottish but includes a lot of English Jacobites. Charlie's men are knackered, they haven't eaten for two days. The battlefield suits the Duke's artillery and dragoons. It doesn't suit the Jacobites, whose chief tactic is to charge at the enemy front on. Bollock-naked. Over the thistles.

Our Culloden in 2003 is the Watford Colosseum. Nothing specific happens – it's just the last day of another 120-date tour, but it turns out to be the last time we do the live show. It's the end of the road. The sex god within Rik has been fighting for supremacy since 1976. We've done five tours, more than 600 gigs, around 1,000 if you include our work before *Bottom*. We're still pretty much charging front on, we put up a better fight than the Jacobites, and we aren't exactly overrun, but I've had enough. I suppose the specific thing that happens is that I decide not to do it again – like Charlie, I want to run away to Italy and drink everything I've read about, and that's more or less what I do.

And I know the 2003 show is possibly not as good as the 2001 show. It's like being an investor in stocks and shares – you have to judge when the stock is at its peak and then bail out. To my mind we've reached that peak. We're at the top of the mountain, there is nowhere higher to go, and we're now looking down.

We all know comedy acts that have gone on beyond their sell-by dates. They can still be funny but look slightly damaged and increasingly desperate. Only by degrees, but it adds up over the years until they look like sad acts.

I don't want to be one of those.

The end of the road

Some people find it extraordinary that I bail out of a successful partnership, one that makes a lot of money too, but I feel trapped and unsatisfied. I am, after all, only an accidental comedian. I don't want to be just 'that bloke from *Bottom*'. I want to do other things. I'm not quite sure what they are, but I'm sure I want to do them.

Rik never gets his head around the decision. For the next decade, whenever I ring him up to suggest we have lunch, just to chew the fat, just to be friends rather than colleagues, he always assumes this is going to be the time I suggest we get the act back together again.

Things aren't helped by his head. His head that suffered badly in the late nineties when he fell off his quad bike onto a concrete slab. He recovers well initially – we make a feature film and do two tours after it – but despite his ongoing medication he has the occasional seizure and it feels like something is deteriorating, that his memory isn't what it was.

Every time we have lunch I have to explain my reasons all over again. It becomes our Groundhog Day. He arrives bright and chirpy, thinking this will be the day we start working together again, and every time I have to explain that I just wanted to see him, to be friends, and he looks sad and confused. I start to dread our lunches.

Nearly ten years after we stop working together we have lunch and he asks again whether I've arranged to meet because I want to get the act back together again. I try a different tack. I say the executives at the BBC have all changed and that they wouldn't even want us any more. This is not entirely disingenuous – we were never offered a fourth series of *Bottom*.

'But we don't know that unless we try, do we?' says Rik.

I hit upon a way to put the idea to bed once and for all.

'OK,' I say. 'Let's write an episode of something, give it to the BBC, and see if they want it.'

I'm confident they won't. The beauty of the plan is that now it will be the BBC's fault that we are no longer a double act, not mine.

We meet up and talk through ideas. It's hard to avoid the personas of our previous incarnation. We put them in a few different situations: as janitors at an office block; as two old codgers in an old people's home; and eventually settle on stealing an idea from one of our live shows – *Hooligan's Island*.

Hooligan's Island is basically Richie and Eddie marooned on a desert island after being thrown off a cruise ship for misbehaving. We dash off a script. And I mean dash. It is all very slapdash. I have no interest in prolonging this futile exercise, I just want to get the script written, to hand it in, to get a firm refusal, and get on with my life.

We hand it in . . . and it's accepted. They offer us a series. Christ Almighty.

So in the summer of 2012 we start writing episodes of *Hooligan's Island*. It's not unfunny, but it's not our very best stuff. We write two episodes. In the second one they run out of home-made booze and it turns out that Eddie, when sober, when not berserk, is highly intelligent and knowledgeable, someone who even knows the difference between a gerund and a gerundive – Richie is faced with the task of keeping him drunk enough in order to be on a par.

The way we always check back on material is that I read it out, playing both parts, and Rik listens to get an overview. I'm reading out a scene from the second episode when I notice out of the corner of my eye that Rik is counting things off on his fingers. It doesn't make much sense, he's using each hand to count something different; what can he be counting?

'What are you counting?' I ask.

'Jokes,' he says.

'On two different hands?'

'I'm counting your jokes and my jokes,' he says. 'And you've got more jokes than me.'

I go quiet. I'm aware that my breathing is strained. I get that tell-tale pain in my neck that I get when I'm hyperventilating.

If you watch any of our programmes – not *The Young Ones*, because I didn't have a hand in writing that, but *Bottom*, the Dangerous Brothers, *Guest House Paradiso* or 'Mr Jolly Lives Next Door' – I defy you to come to the conclusion that either of our characters has any more 'jokes' than the other.

There's an old actor's joke where one actor says to the other, 'I'll trip you up, you fall flat on your face, and we'll share the laugh.' The conceit being that the one who's talking isn't really contributing much.

But our stuff isn't like that, the tripping is as carefully considered as the falling over, the tripping is part of the falling over, it's always about the pair of us, we're constantly struggling, as a pair, to make it as funny as possible. This is why so much of our material is framed in a two-shot, because you need to watch both of us at the same time to enjoy what's going on. The reaction to a punch is as funny as the punch. This is Comedy 101 for double acts from Laurel & Hardy onwards.

'I thought they were *our* jokes,' I say. 'We're a double act.'

I'll admit that some double acts appear more lopsided than ours. Morecambe and Wise, for instance. Everyone thinks Eric is the really funny one and that Ernie is more of a stooge. But there's a video of a live *Morecambe & Wise Show* I've seen where at one point Eric has a solo spot. This is more than a bridging moment between two sketches, it's him on his own for some minutes. It's by far the least funny part of the show. Eric needs Ernie to give him the world in which to do his shtick. The same goes for Little & Large and Cannon & Ball.

Most double acts play it straight down the middle; The Two Ronnies, French & Saunders, Vic & Bob, The Mighty Boosh, Fry & Laurie, Mitchell & Webb, Smith & Jones.

I try to make this point to Rik but I'm too angry to get my thoughts in line. His seizures mean he can't drive any more so I've come to his house. I suggest we call it a day, that I leave, and that we reconvene in the morning.

The next day I pitch up at his house again and we have a friendly cup of coffee and talk through what has upset me. He's very apologetic, but in that way a child apologizes without knowing what they're apologizing for. He just wants to get the apology out of the way and get on with something else.

We start writing again. I read it back, playing both parts. And I can see his fingers going again. Counting. Two tallies. I don't think he's doing it to provoke me, in fact he's trying to do it without me seeing.

I challenge him and we go through the script sitting side by side. He points at it and provides a judgement on each line.

'See, that's your joke. That's my joke. That's your joke . . .'

And I realize that the double act is properly over. There's no trust any more. We're just two individuals. He's fighting for himself, not for us.

It's a relief in a way because it's no longer simply my fault that the act has reached the end – like a frost-bitten vine, it has withered and died. It was glorious when it was alive, I'm immensely proud of everything we did together, it still makes me laugh, but I'm glad we didn't do a dodgy final series.

Things come to an end.

Not this book, by the look of things – how much more can there be?

Steady on, Tiger. You can always bail out like Bonnie Prince Charlie if you like.

It's been noted by some that *if* Bonnie Prince Charlie had managed to persuade his comrades in that little room over the pub in Derby to carry on, that George II *might* have run away. And *if* Charlie had become king, being an ally of the French, he wouldn't have been at almost continual war with them for the next seventy years. And therefore Britain wouldn't have had to squeeze the new colonies in America for the tax revenue to fight these wars. In which case there might not have been an American war of independence. And possibly no French Revolution.

If is a big concept.

In 1985 I made a TV film with a young Gary Oldman and a young Richard E. Grant. Two of us went on to be major Hollywood stars but neither of them was me.

If I'd stopped being an accidental comedian could I have joined them?

If my schoolboy band Peace of Thorn had tried a bit harder could I have been an international rock god?

Part 9

International rock god pt 2

Some bad news

I have to take you back to 1987.

1987?

Yes. It's 1987 and I'm standing on stage at the Guildhall in Portsmouth with the rest of Bad News, my spoof metal band.

We've made two documentaries of the band as part of *The Comic Strip Presents*, and just to be clear, we are not the 'British Spinal Tap', chiefly because we appeared a year before them.

It's a monumental pisser when someone else covers the same subject matter with a bigger budget a year after you've done it, but heigh ho. And anyway The Rutles had come out in the late seventies so we're all thieves. There's nothing new. Inspiration is 90 per cent theft, and the creativity is often in how well you hide it.

But we've made an album for EMI on the back of the documentaries, and now we're out on tour supporting the album release. The tour starts the day after the violent extratropical cyclone of 15 October – the one Michael Fish said was nothing to worry about – the one that felled 15 million trees and left twenty-two people dead. It's not a good omen for the tour.

There have been highlights in the history of Bad News. We've supported Iron Maiden at the Hammersmith Apollo and we've done benefit gigs where Brian May, Jimmy Page and Jeff Beck have come on as guests – I've swapped lead breaks with the guitar heroes of my youth. We've jammed with Motörhead and their guitarist Würzel gave me his skull ring in recognition of the fact that I can 'play a bit'.

But in truth it all started to go wrong at the second gig we ever played. The first gig was quite literally to two men and a dog – a common expression made into a proper joke in 'Bad News Tour'. The second was to 100,000 people at the Monsters of Rock Festival in Castle Donnington. It was filmed as part of the second documentary 'More Bad News'.

We had cameras picking up audience shots throughout the day and constructed a narrative in the editing room to make it look like people were chucking stuff at us the whole time we were on stage. In truth they threw as much at Warlock and The

Scorpions. Tommy Vance, the compère, wisely wore a baseball helmet to protect himself from the constant missile attack.

We also had an audience participation song called 'Hey Hey Bad News', which my character – Vim Fuego (named after a cleaning product and a Renault sport hatchback that came out in 1980) – took great pains to explain was definitely 'hey hey Bad News' not 'fuck off Bad News', which of course meant the audience only ever sang 'fuck off Bad News'.

Audiences can be so easily led.

But back to the Portsmouth Guildhall.

I'm playing a specially modified guitar with a super-charged pre-amp inside it. The man who sold it to me said it emits the loudest signal of any guitar in the world. It delivers what I call 'amazing crunch', and along with an array of distortion pedals I'm making an extraordinary racket. I'm dressed like Joe from Def Leppard – Union Jack singlet under a leather biker's jacket. My long blond hair flounces around like the girl flicking her hair about in the Timotei advert. We've got a light show. I've got an actual Marshall stack. I've even got an actual roadie for God's sake, who will come and swap out my guitar whenever it goes out of tune. The gig is rammed. I am living the rock dream of my teenage years.

So why isn't it as much fun as I thought?

Partly because I've just been hit in the face with a sheep's eyeball. Some wags in the crowd were listening to us on the radio this morning riffing about the band's leanings towards Satanism. They've heard us inventing comedic nonsense about the rituals we do with offal to summon the devil, who then helps us write the lyrics.

These wags, who probably work in a butcher's shop, have decided it will add to the 'fun' of the event if they pelt us with bits of dead sheep. They keep chucking bits of liver, kidney, lung, duodenum, digestive tract, and sundry less identifiable body parts.

Pete tilts his cymbals up as a rudimentary barrier and manages to avoid the worst of it. Nige on rhythm guitar and Rik on bass are free to roam around – they can see the incoming organs flash by in the lights and take avoiding action. But unfortunately, because I'm playing and singing, I'm stuck at the microphone front and centre and therefore I'm the easiest target. Though to be honest, the barrage of offal isn't as bad as the gang of youths at the very front of the crowd who are trying to spit in my mouth. Trying and occasionally succeeding.

It's not what I thought life as a rock god would be.

The problem is that once you've led the audience to wherever it is you want it's hard to take them back. We've made a rod for our own backs, and the audience are basically coming to throw stuff and shout at us. It's like a violent, sweary panto.

There's only so much of other people's spittle you can swallow without becoming bad tempered. It's only a short tour but it's hard work. And this infects the mood in the band. We almost split over 'musical differences'. . . We've made a Christmas single, 'Cashing in on Christmas', and Pete gets so angry about the way I've mixed it that we have a stand-up row in a hotel bar in Birmingham. He throws a pint of beer at me, I duck, and it hits the barman. Only the timely intervention of our tour manager Ian Day saves the day – smoothing out the problems with the soggy barman, and coaxing Pete to sleep on it and decide whether to quit or not in the morning when he's sober.

The next summer we play Reading Festival. The crowd are slightly further away and there are no butcher's shops on the site, making meat-based missiles less of a problem, but this doesn't dim their ardour. They piss into empty two-litre plastic bottles and chuck them instead. Although one enterprising young festivalgoer has managed to throw up into his bottle – no mean feat given the size of the opening – and this crashes onto the stage and bursts with alarming olfactory consequences.

Rik, whose joke for Reading is to pretend to have a broken leg and be pushed around the stage by a roadie in a wheelchair, finds that once he's driven through the vomit his wheels are covered in the stuff. The roadie abandons him as the barrage increases and Rik becomes marooned in a sea of piss-filled bottles – a sitting target whose only escape is to grab the puke-covered wheels and try to manoeuvre himself away. It's the wrong day to have your leg in a fake plaster cast.

It's the last gig we do.

Wow! You got so close to achieving your teenage fantasy of being an international rock god but it all went a bit Pete Tong.

Exactly! Except that . . .

The third reunion

Neil Innes is an exceptionally kind human being and doesn't realize that I am basically his stalker.

It's 2006. The Bonzo Dog Doo-Dah Band are having a reunion gig at the Astoria Theatre (sadly no longer with us). Viv Stanshall (also sadly no longer with us) has been dead for ten years and Neil has hit upon the idea of asking several acknowledged fans to fill in for Viv, who was the lead singer of the band.

The Bonzos have a history of splitting up and getting back together, in fact their post-break-up contractual obligation album of 1972 is called *Let's Make Up and Be Friendly*. There have always been tensions in the band.

The third reunion show is in two halves – in the first the original band minus Viv will play the old jazz and novelty records they used to cover in the early days, and in the second the band plus myself, Stephen Fry, Paul Merton, Phill Jupitus and Bill Bailey will perform their more modern, more rocky, self-penned numbers.

Consequently I find myself in the front row of the circle with Stephen, Paul, Phill and Bill watching the first half run through. I'm mouthing every word of every song and I look along the line and see that we all are. We're all über fans.

I get to hang out with the people I've idolized all my life: Neil, Legs Larry Smith, Sam Spoons, Vernon Dudley Bohay-Nowell, Rodney Slater, Roger Ruskin Spear. And none of them disappoint because not only am I hanging out with them, I'm performing with them – performing the songs they have imprinted on my psyche over the previous thirty-six years. This is a different level of fandom altogether.

The crowd are as pleased to be there as I am and it all goes very well. Though my favourite part of the show is backstage afterwards when the tannoy blares out: 'Calling Mr Spoons – Mrs Spoons is at the stage door with several of the teaspoons.'

The show goes so well that they decide to take it out on tour. They ask us all if we will join in and carry on filling in for Viv. Myself and Phill immediately say yes. The others are too busy. Too busy to tour with the Bonzos? Perhaps they're not über fans after all. Or perhaps they're just more successful than we are.

But Phill and I have a blast. A lot of Phill's comedy has a particularly cruel and vicious streak to it but I learn it's just a protective shield against the many slings and arrows that come his way, and that underneath he's a delightfully gentle soul. We share the Viv filling-in duties between us. I sing and I play kazoo, triangle, ukulele and the coconuts. I also get to play the trumpet in 'Jazz Delicious Hot Disgusting Cold'. This is a track from the beloved *Gorilla* album, the track Rik and I put on the end of *Guest House Paradiso*, the track I want played at my funeral. It was made in a hurry when they'd run out of studio time. As a kind of Dadaist experiment they simply passed their instruments to the person on their left and set to on an up-tempo jazz instrumental. It's about the triumph of enthusiasm over ability. So I'm supposed to sound like I've never played it before but that I'm playing with gusto, and, boy, do I succeed. It's the instrument Viv played on the track and I feel like I'm channelling him. It's heaven.

I'm also given the role of the parrot during 'Mr Slater's Parrot' and find myself in a large parrot costume saying 'hello' repeatedly. On stage at the Shepherd's Bush Empire I spot a sign on the wall that reads 'No Crowdsurfing'. As the parrot I look at the sign, then at the audience, then back at the sign . . . the audience get it and roar their approval at the idea.

Bearing in mind that the average age of a Bonzo fan is quite advanced I gingerly lower myself onto a group of geriatrics. The costume is like a large plastic cocoon, and I find myself gently moving around the auditorium until I hear someone cry out: 'Oh Christ, my hip's come out!'

It's a sublime thing being on tour with a lot of elderly art students, they have a different appreciation of the world. Amongst the Sanatogen and prescriptions for age-related ailments the tour bus is an absurdist's dream in which we play games like inventing a word for the crack in a sailor's wooden leg. 'Queech' is the winner. Sam Spoons makes little paper models of Phill and me. And as we drive north up the A1 we become aware that they're increasingly anxious as we pass Chester-le-Street, and then, as the Angel of the North swings into view, they all stand and applaud. Artists celebrating another artist. One or two of them have tears in their eyes.

After the tour, in a private dining room in Elena's L'Etoile in Charlotte Street, they discuss plans for a new album and Neil says the most extraordinary words:

'And now that we have two new Bonzos.'

He means us. He means Phill and me. Phill and I look at each other open-mouthed. We are no longer stalkers. We are part of the band. We have gone from the kind of people who try to crowbar Bonzos' lines into every conversation: 'A man's not dressed unless he's got a nice shirt on, guv'nor, is he?' To the kind of people who might deliver such lines for Bonzos' fans of the future.

We make another album – *Pour L'Amour des Chiens*. It's a bit Sturgeon's Law, though 'Wire People' is a good song, and another tour is planned. But remember those tensions I mentioned? Well, they resurface. We find ourselves rehearsing at the Bisley shooting range in Surrey – is this some kind of absurdist decision? It's like an ancient village cricket pavilion – and old disagreements, some seemingly festering since the late sixties, raise their ugly heads.

I hear Roger Ruskin Spear shout, 'You're not my father, Neil!'

I see Neil, the only real musician besides Rodney Slater, voted out of arranging the songs. 'Well, you just tell *me* what to play then.'

I watch Sam Spoons assume leadership of the morning rehearsal, and find myself walking round the room in line with the rest of them banging dustbin lids together – no one knows what's going on, and Sam bursts into tears because he can't explain what it is he wants to achieve.

They're such a lovely bunch of men, but it's over, again. It's such a sad thing to see.

But I have another string to my bow. Or should I say mandolin.

A mandolin

For several years in the early 2000s, myself and a small group of friends would meet for a pre-Christmas booze-up in Soho – a joyous pub crawl that would start in the basement bar of Black's at around 11 a.m. and finish in the basement bar of Black's around five hours later. Having gone nowhere. We'd start the crawl with good intentions but the thing about the basement bar of Black's at the time is that, despite it being part of a member's club, it's actually the cosiest little hostelry in the middle of London – a convivial spot with long trestle tables and a hatch-like bar. It's like that little bit of a Breughel painting where a group of merry peasants seem to be having more fun than everyone else.

It's not there any more, obviously, because entrepreneurs don't seem to be able to make money out of nice things.

However, the biggest danger of the yearly revels is not incipient cirrhosis of the liver, but that it invariably ends with a trip to Denmark Street on the north-east fringe of Soho. This is the world epicentre of guitar shops: Regent Sounds, Hank's Guitars, Macari's, Rhodes Music, Rose-Morris and many more, most of which I've been familiar with from ads in the back of *Melody*

Maker since the seventies. I know very few people who've ever picked up a guitar who can enter these shops without losing their minds and, quite frequently, their wallets – they're like an Aladdin's cave of potential rock stardom.

Every guitar is a dream of another life. How many Sunday supplement articles have you seen where the backdrop of someone's living room has a guitar hung neatly on the wall like a religious icon? The walls of these shops are where this idea comes from, but it's not just the odd guitar, it's literally thousands – you can't see the walls. Some of the shops are four storeys high. Maybe twenty shops, at an average of three storeys, with perhaps 150 guitars per floor – that's 9,000 guitars! 9,000 dreams. How can you not buy *one* of them?

I've fallen for its charms many times but one year I'm in the 'classic' department of one of these shops when I spot a guitar with only four strings. I ask about it: it's a tenor guitar, tuned like a tenor banjo or a viola, and made by the very reputable American firm Martin's in 1945. It's an antique. I get it down and try to play it. Some people think that instruments get better with age because the wood has somehow absorbed every note it's ever heard, and this may be true because it sounds absolutely beautiful. I mess around on it for a few minutes but I don't know how to form any chords for this kind of tuning, C G D A, and put it back.

The next morning I go down for breakfast and see it lying on the kitchen table. Apparently, I bought it.

I pick it up, I look up some basic chords on the internet, and start painstakingly working out the songs I normally play to myself on a six string – mostly seventies with a lot of punk and new wave: The Sex Pistols, The Clash, XTC, The Members. They sound instantly different with this new tuning – the chords are the same but the voicing is different. It's a eureka moment. One of the things all wannabe musicians want is to be able to make their 'own' versions of existing brilliant songs.

There's something 'folky' about the sound and I'm reminded of The Ducie, the Irish pub behind the university, and the excitement of the trad tunes they used to play. I look them up and they're all written for the fiddle – it's a similar tuning to the tenor guitar, but half an octave higher. If I want to play the fiddle tunes I'll have to learn the fiddle, or . . . get a mandolin, which I learn has the same tuning as a fiddle.

It's amazing how many times in your life as a middle-class dilettante musician you discover you 'need' another instrument. I 'need' to buy a mandolin, and so I do. I bring it home, I work out how to play some of the songs, I twiddle about with some of the fiddle tunes, and . . . I think I've got something.

I tell a friend about it and he introduces me to Troy Donockley. Troy is a multi-instrumentalist, he plays guitars, the bouzouki, and various whistles, but he's mostly recognized for being a virtuoso on the uilleann pipes, a mellifluous kind of bagpipe on which the air bag is pumped up with the elbow rather than blown into – uilleann being Gaelic for 'of the elbow'. That's him you can hear on the soundtrack of Ridley Scott's *Robin Hood*. He's been in a lot of folk bands, he's done sessions with almost every folk artist of note, and he lives . . . IN POCKLINGTON.

WHAT?

Yes, I know, that's exactly what I thought.

We arrange to meet, in Pocklington, and we get on like a house on fire that firemen are mistakenly spraying with petrol rather than water. He's got the same dream of a cosy pub with a seventies jukebox and a pool table, in fact he's got one . . . IN HIS HOUSE.

WHAT?

I know.

It's an instant and incredibly close friendship and we form a band on the spot – The Bad Shepherds. We play punk songs on folk instruments – not as a gag, but because we like how it sounds – and we interlace them with jigs and reels which have all the energy of pogo dancing. A lot of folk and punk songs are very similar, they're often protest songs, or songs about real life. They're not as self-centred as most pop music and are mainly about he or she rather than I or me.

We co-opt the Mancunian Andy Dinan, the first UK-based player to win the All Ireland Fiddle Championship, and it turns out . . . HE USED TO PLAY AT THE DUCIE.

NO WAY.

Yes way. (In fact, I already told you that in a previous chapter – I hope you aren't just 'skimming'?)

It's like that film *Sliding Doors* which keeps swapping between two different storylines on the basis of whichever tube train

Gwyneth Paltrow gets on, except in my version I get to live both lives.

Troy is a couple of years younger than me and was brought up in Cumbria but we share an extraordinary range of references: we can both sing every Gram Parsons song, we know the lyrics to every cheesy seventies and eighties number one from Ray Stevens's 'The Streak' to Bonnie Tyler's 'Total Eclipse of the Heart', and he's a Laurel & Hardy fan. In fact he's a bigger fan than I am, he knows every single word of every single episode.

Troy is also an excellent sleight-of-hand magician and looks like a trainee wizard who might have escaped from Middle-Earth, while Andy looks like a bricklayer who's just been in a fight. The three of us make an interesting dynamic.

We tour relentlessly for seven years, and though I say it myself we're a bloody good live act. The punk songs we play take on a more plaintive air with the folk treatment. The punters often comment: 'It's the first time I've really heard the lyrics and understood what the songs are about.' JC Carroll from The Members joins us on the Avalon stage at Glastonbury, playing accordion, and says he prefers our version of his song 'Sound of the Suburbs'. 'We only played it fast because we were desperate to impress the girls,' he says. But we puncture that mood with the jigs and reels, which are more punk than punk. It's a neat trick.

I never quite make international rock god – even though we tour Australia a couple of times and play festivals in Belgium and the Netherlands – but I thoroughly enjoy these years of touring, playing everywhere from scuzzy rock pubs to massive festivals. We're crammed into one van like in 'Bad News Tour' and go through a succession of bass players, percussionists and road crew, each of whom we develop nicknames for: The Oompah Loompah, Balou the Bear, The Hawk, The Throat

Puncher, The Trumpeter (so called for his relentless farting rather than his musical prowess).

'I'll stay until you find out I'm a cunt,' says one of the bass players. It takes us three years to find out, but he was right. It's a funny thing, touring. Turns out 'Bad News Tour' was more accurate than I thought when I was writing it.

But mostly what I learn is that a real band is a spark between people, like in a double act. The sum is better than the parts. It's an expression of a connection, and the person I connect with is Troy. There are moments on stage when we're playing intricate parts that build together into something that's on a different plane. It's the sort of thing that can infect an audience and you build a kind of communion with several hundred people that can become slightly overwhelming, that makes the hairs stand up on the back of your neck. This is very different to my teenage dreams of rock stardom, which centred more on strutting and adulation, and it's ten times more fulfilling.

Troy and I love to get to the festivals a day early and 'wobble about' as we call it, watching all the bands and consuming 'malty drinks' – our word for beer. It's like having a second go at being a teenager. A truly blissful period.

When I see it all coming to an end I'm better prepared, because I've done it before. Around the sixth year we stop adding to our catalogue of songs. We've made three albums' worth of material but it feels like the idea has come to an end and we've started repeating ourselves. It's weird that the one thing that always made me jealous of bands when I was a comedian – being able to do your hits rather than constantly coming up with new stuff – turns out to be a turn-off. I can understand why Procol Harum waited until the third encore to play 'Whiter Shade of Pale'. I'm sorry for shouting at them back in York that time.

Troy agrees, and in any case, the band he's been guesting with for many years, Nightwish – a 'symphonic metal' band from Finland who like his uilleann pipes ('I Want My Tears Back' is a good introduction) – have asked him to join the band full time.

And I too have another band that's been going alongside The Bad Shepherds, but it's a much smaller commitment, and there's no 'symphonic' about it.

After the demise of The Bonzos, Neil, Phill and myself, along with Simon Brint and Rowland Rivron, form The Idiot Bastard Band – a band devoted to the comic song. We have a residency at the Wilmington Arms in Clerkenwell. We do what we call 'live rehearsals' – we have a rough idea of what we want to do, and we might have practised separately, but the fun of the evening is in the surprises and the genuine confusion. It's kind of Dadaist in that we reject logic and reason and put a heavy accent on the nonsensical. But there's enough musical talent in the band for the music to transcend the idiocy on occasion.

Simon does a brilliant version of George Formby's 'Swimmin' with the Wimmin'' but in the languid style of Tom Waits; we do the Flanagan and Allen song 'Nice People'; we cover Jake Thackray, The Flight of the Conchords and They Might Be Giants; and we write new songs too, and have guests like Nigel Planer, Barry Cryer and Paul Whitehouse. It's a splendidly relaxed evening.

If only we'd stayed at the Wilmington – that's when it was at its Dadaist best – but ambitions grow and we end up on tour and eventually get a commission from Radio 4 for a series. It's all a bit too serious for me. I liked it as a hobby. I liked it as a ramshackle off-the-cuff experience. But the radio idea needs scripts, and everything has to be planned and 'defined'. It's not the way I want to go, and very apologetically I tell the rest of them that I don't want to do it, and the project ends. Our producer Steve Doherty says it's the only time in his life he's handed back a commission.

Everything comes to an end.

Part 10

Where's the berserker?

Cold turkey

Trying to stop being an accidental comedian is like trying to lose weight, or stop drinking, or come off heroin.

Heroin?

I've never been on heroin. I'm just being dramatic.

Right.

But there's a withdrawal period where the lines are blurred. There are relapses. There are moments when you wonder if you're doing the right thing.

In 2003, almost as soon as I stop working with Rik, I get offered a part in *Doctors & Nurses*, a sitcom written by Nigel Smith and Phil Hammond. Despite having David Mitchell, Joanna Scanlan, Abigail Cruttenden and Mina Anwar in the cast it doesn't catch fire. It's the last programme to be made in the Carlton TV Studios in Nottingham, and we quickly become aware that the crew are working out the last few weeks before they're all made redundant. Everyone in the building is monumentally depressed. It's like spending six weeks talking someone off a window ledge – and the comedy turns sour in the miserable atmosphere of constant goodbye parties and tearful cake-eating.

I get on really well with Nigel though – this is the cheerful, glass-half-full Nigel whose immune system attacked him and who has to get pissed through a tube – and after *Doctors & Nurses* gets lost in a miasma of indifference we settle down to write another sitcom together, about a dad who's sofa-surfing in his daughter's student flat, partly because he's broke and badly divorced, but mostly because he wants to feel young and anarchic again. It's called *Teenage Kicks*. We make it as a radio programme first, but then Paul Jackson – yes, Paul Jackson again, who's now head of comedy at ITV – picks it up for television.

And so it comes to pass one day that I'm sitting at home waiting for the viewing figures to come in. Paul texts the figures to me every Saturday morning. The first week it gets 3.6 million, the second week 3.8 million. ITV works on a very straightforward principle – viewing figures – and Paul tells me that if we keep above 3.5 million we'll get a second series.

I didn't catch the show when it went out the night before so I'm watching it on catch-up. It's an episode called 'Sorry' – my favourite of the series. I particularly enjoyed writing and shooting the final scene in the caravan. It's a funny show. It's well written. It's well performed. It's technically very accomplished. But I realize as I'm watching that it's just not 'it'.

Why isn't it 'it'? Vernon's a great character, the situation is ripe, the script is full of jokes, the studio audience is laughing. Why isn't it 'it'? I can see it's funny, and I'm ticking off the gags, but sometimes things can be joke-shaped without being the real thing.

I'm not trying to compare myself to Spike Milligan, but as I sit there I'm reminded of watching the last few iterations of the *Q* series. I remember thinking at the time, 'This man is a genius, and these shows have all the right things in place . . . but they're just not really funny any more. He should have stopped before he did this. They're just not "it".'

And then an extraordinary feeling engulfs me – I don't have to do this any more, do I?

The text comes through from Paul – slight dip to 3.4 million, but still with a 17 per cent audience share – he's very happy with the result.

But I can't take it in. I'm feeling such elation at the thought of not having to do it any more that I feel dizzy. It's a feeling of such profound relief. It's unfathomable. Imagine not having to prove that you were funny any more. Comedy is the only art form that demands instant and constant proof – if they're not laughing, you're not funny. It's an enormous pressure. For thirty-three years I've lived with the pressure, and I've just realized I don't have to live with it any more. I don't have to be a comedian.

Brilliant.

But what do I do now? How do I tell Paul? Luckily I don't have to. It's a series of eight and the numbers continue to dip. It scrapes along in the low threes for the rest of the run.

My friend and producer Lucy Ansbro rings to say there's a conversation to be had with ITV since the average figures were close to the mark but I tell her I don't want to pursue it, I tell her I'm done, and to her immense credit she immediately understands. Lucy's been the producer on all the *Bottom Live* tours and videos, we've worked a lot together, we've sat in a lot of hotel bars, we get on very well, and she gets it. Maybe I've already let it slip out that I'm an accidental comedian. Maybe she's been expecting it? It adds to the sense of relief.

I am free.

Brilliant.

What do I do now?

Brave (and rather confusing) new world

I want to do what I set out to do when I went to Manchester. I want to be an actor. In fact, now, actors don't even have to be members of Equity any more – oh, the irony. But now I'm too old to play Hamlet at the RSC, or be the new Malcolm McDowell – and the baggage of having been a comedian keeps getting in the way.

Casting agents see me as a comedian. Writers see me as a comedian. Producers see me as a comedian. People in the street see me as a comedian.

In the world of straight drama, the distrust of people who have identified as comedians is very strong. They fear some kind of latent anarchy – that I won't take it seriously enough. But as grotesque as many of my creations have been, they were all fundamentally acting jobs. They were all as carefully constructed – Baron von Richthofen, Eddie Hitler, Dick from The Famous Five – the programmes they were in just had a different goal in mind.

• • •

I set about being a non-comedian.

Except that it's hard not to fall back into it sometimes. How could I resist the pull of The Bonzos? Or the joy of The Idiot Bastards? Although in my defence I'd say The Bonzos were beyond comedy, they were more like art. And The Idiots at their best were so relaxed that the pressure to perform, to be some kind of berserker, was practically non-existent.

There are some false dawns.

I audition for a director called Nick Murphy who casts me in a programme he's making called 'Chernobyl Nuclear Disaster'. This is in 2006, and it shouldn't be confused with the 2019 series *Chernobyl* – though anyone watching them both couldn't fail to recognize the spookily similar approaches to the story.

Nick is a delightful human being who takes his work very seriously but is not unaware of the pomposity of people who take things very seriously – he keeps pricking his own bubble. He's come from the world of documentaries, is moving into drama, and our programme is a halfway house, a docudrama.

I'm trying to move from comedy into drama. We get each other.

The camerawork is purposefully scruffy, as if struggling to keep up with real events. There's a script, but he wants us to treat it as a guide and roughen up the edges to add to the authenticity – no one in the real world talks in proper sentences. We're shooting in Lithuania in Soviet-era locations. Everything is about realism. The finished programme is cut with real footage from the time and it's hard to see the joins.

I'm in my element: I understand cameras, I know where I am in the shot, I know what he's going for, I've researched my character – an actual historical person called Valery Legasov – it feels like it's real, and I'm good at improvising. Look at me, Sandford Meisner! Look at what I'm doing. It's one of the best things I ever do.

Unfortunately it goes out as part of a series called *Surviving Disaster* and the other episodes, made by other people, about other disasters, are . . . a disaster. No, that's harsh, but they're a different style – strange confections of sugary melodrama and tabloid journalism. So 'Chernobyl' gets lost. You win some, you lose some.

I lose myself in a couple of presenting jobs. I make thirty-six episodes of *The Dales* – which is me wandering round the Yorkshire Dales looking at things and talking to people. I make fifty episodes of a daytime series called *Ade in Britain* – a pun on 'Made in Britain' – in which I wander round Britain looking at things and talking to people. I make a primetime series called *Ade at Sea* in which I wander round the coast of Britain looking at things and talking to people and prove that I'm all at sea.

As I've said before, it would be nice if my life fell into neat compartments, but it just won't. Life after comedy is frankly a complete bloody mess: 'Chernobyl'; the presenting jobs; The Bonzos, The Bad Shepherds, and The Idiot Bastards; forays into reality TV; *Hell's Kitchen* (who would have thought the final would be between Crystal Carrington from *Dynasty* and Vyvyan from *The Young Ones*); *Celebrity MasterChef* (winner 2013 – take that, Janet Street-Porter and Les Dennis); *Comic Relief does Fame Academy*.

I'm a man without a focus.

But one thing all this floundering around does is confuse people – and this is probably the best thing I can do – because now they don't know what I am at all, which is marginally better than just being an ex-comedian. There's quite a lot of 'me' in that furious list above, and 'me' is very different to Vyvyan or Eddie Hitler; 'me' has started to look less like a berserker, and more like . . . a human being?

I slowly become what some people call a 'jobbing actor': forty-six episodes of *Holby City*, playing a doctor who wears his heart on his sleeve (which as any doctor knows is the wrong place for it to be); *Miss Austen Regrets*, a period drama in which I play Jane Austen's brother, while Greta Scacchi plays my other sister Cassandra; *War and Peace*, in which Greta is now my wife – is this incest?

Even *Star Wars* – though I discover this has roots in my comedic past.

My first thought when my agent calls to say they're offering me the part is, *Imagine what Fred and Bert would think!* Fred and Bert are my grandsons and they've got the Top Trumps version of *Star Wars* – imagine if I suddenly turned up in the next pack of cards. (I do actually become a collectible trading card.)

It turns out I've been hired for a similar reason. The director, Rian Johnson, was a fan of *Bottom* in his student days. He tells me he first became aware of *Bottom* as a book of scripts, rather than as a TV programme, and shot one of the episodes as a film while at film school. He's basically done what I did with *The Goon Show* scripts, only with better equipment and actual actors. But we're both getting something else out of this experience.

Filming schedules in the modern era generally don't allow the time to go down the full Meisner route. A friend who worked with Keanu Reeves in the nineties says he places a towel over his head in between set-ups to keep the outside world at bay, which obviously works for Keanu, but sounds a bit unsociable. I develop a method that works for me: I just learn my lines to death.

You may have seen me in Hyde Park doing my four-mile stomp around the perimeter with pages of script in hand, chuntering at the trees. Luckily the park is so full of nutters I don't look too eccentric.

I repeat them over and over again. By the time I say them in front of camera I'll have said them a minimum of 500 times. The lines go on a weird journey of their own: they start off being an exercise in memorizing; then, as a kind of muscle memory begins to work in my mouth, they become almost meaningless; then the meaning slowly drifts back, but by this point the thoughts and the words are no longer two separate processes and it hopefully sounds like I'm actually thinking them.

On the set of *A Spy Among Friends*, Damian Lewis remarks that I turn up 'camera-ready', but that's not quite the aim: I want to be so completely prepared that I can spend my time off-camera having a laugh and swapping stories – which is what the filming day is mostly about in my view. Keanu doesn't know what he's missing.

Though my line-learning method fails when I do *Star Wars*. It's hard to learn your lines to death when they won't tell you what they are.

My friendship with Rian doesn't open the security level that would permit me to read the whole script. The production is obsessed with secrecy. I'm allowed a brief read of some of my lines, in a locked room with a production assistant looking on, a week before filming, but I'm not allowed to take a script home. And when I show up to film each day I'm given the relevant scene with all the other characters' lines redacted.

You can't see what the other characters are saying?

That's right.

But that's insane.

I always knew my readers would be wise.

It's only at rehearsal on set that I find out what the others are saying. It's hilarious. Imagine my surprise when I turn up at the premiere and find I have the first line in the film. This might be why most of the minor characters in *Star Wars* seem so 'spaced out' – they really don't know what's happening.

• • •

Over recent years I've been involved in several programmes that are labelled comedies: Sara Pascoe's *Out of Her Mind*; Daisy Haggard's *Back to Life*; and Cash Carraway's *Rain Dogs*. I've seen them variously described as a sitcom, a dark comedy-drama, and a black comedy. I had to think very hard about doing them (even though I went through two rounds of auditions for *Rain Dogs* – two rounds of a scene in which I had to simulate masturbation – life can seem pretty unedifying at times).

Sara's *Out of Her Mind* is largely autobiographical and I play a version of her actual dad, and what drew me in was the emotional content. There's a scene where her dad is apologizing to his ex-wife, played by Juliet Stevenson (the second time we've played a divorced couple). They're preparing for their daughter's wedding and he apologizes for not having been there, and it just broke my heart.

In Daisy's *Back to Life* I play a rather gruesome character, John Boback, someone who had sex with his daughter's best friend. But Daisy writes so brilliantly about what it is to be human, about how messy and complicated it is, and she gives Boback a great escape from being a two-dimensional 'wrong 'un' – his genuine grief for his dead daughter. There's a scene where he visits her grave and sings a song she liked, and he loses control and can't get through it.

In Cash's *Rain Dogs* I'm playing a scurrilous letch called Lenny. He's a pervert and a sex pest, but in amongst the sordid world Cash creates, he emerges as a complicated man with a heart, a man who cares for Daisy May Cooper's character – a kind of father figure.

None of these can be described as comic turns, even if they have some humour in them. The truth is that a lot of real life is bleakly amusing. Sometimes the tragedy is funny. This is what has always drawn me to *Waiting for Godot*.

It's a long way from the world of the berserker though.

• • •

The older my own children become, the more I connect with playing fathers. It's a privileged role, and perhaps because I had such a strained relationship with my own dad I find exploring fatherhood irresistible.

In *War and Peace* I play the jolly patriarch of the Rostov family, Count Rostov. Once I'd got through the audition and landed the part I read the book for the first time. I had to keep reading bits out to Jennifer because the descriptions of the count sounded just like her dad – the soul of the party, the generous host, the man who hated snobs. Tom Harper, the director, does a brilliant thing in the early rehearsal period, and makes us have a couple of 'family' meals together to increase the familial bond between us. So pretending these people are my family becomes second nature: Lily James becomes my daughter, and Jack Lowden becomes my son. And . . . the love I develop for them feels genuine. Is that mad?

It still feels genuine now, years later. I'll see them on screen doing other things and I'll be willing them to be brilliant just like I do with my own children. This happens with all my fictional children: Morfydd Clark from *Interlude in Prague*; Molly Windsor from *Cheat* – even though the fictional relationship is combative, I still feel paternal towards her off-camera. My actual daughter Beattie appears with Lily in *The Pursuit of Love* and I'm filled to bursting watching them on the screen together.

Where's the berserker gone? This bloke's in tears most of the time.

This is like a berserker who's hacked his way through 1,000 Anglo-Saxons and once he's killed the final one, he looks round at the trail of devastation, and weeps.

I finally get to the RSC. It only takes forty-two years, but I get there. Twice. First as Malvolio in *Twelfth Night* and more recently as Scrooge in *A Christmas Carol*.

In *A Christmas Carol* there's a scene in which the Ghost of Christmas Past takes Scrooge back to his schooldays and shows him the lonely schoolboy all on his own when the other boys have all gone home. In my time at school I was often left there during the twice termly 'exeat' when all the other boys went home for the weekend.

During every performance it's always a triggering moment for me, this reliving of a similar experience. A kind of catharsis. It's a similar idea to blues music, which is often about misery, but isn't miserable in itself – singing the misery through can be an uplifting experience.

It's practising being human.

On the other hand, I find myself playing a lot of complete bastards these days, probably because I'm a white, middle-class, middle-aged man, and we're pretty much to blame for everything that's gone wrong in the world. These parts mark me out as the villain: I'm an absent father in *One of Us* and *Out of Her Mind*, a bullying dad in *Cheat*, a bullying husband in *The Pact*, a sexual-abuser type father in *Back to Life*, a member of an actual paedophile ring in *Save Me*, and a captain of the First Order in *Star Wars*, and we all know they're complete bastards.

Though, incidentally, I have a little trick when I play Captain Peavey. His lines are fairly formulaic – he's Admiral Hux's second in command, a minor baddie on the bridge of the Resurgent-class Star Destroyer *Finaliser* – but I invent an internal monologue for him: he doesn't agree with everything the Empire is up to. He isn't a rebel, he doesn't have an alternative plan, he's no revolutionary, but before every take I make him think about oranges.

It's a childhood memory about a planet that had oranges. He can still remember the smell of the zest, the taste of the juice, and the deep colour of the skin. That planet has, of course, been destroyed, and he's never seen an orange since.

Of course we feel no sympathy for him, because he's an officer in the First Order, and therefore just a self-pitying complete bastard.

Over the last five years I've been fatally run over by a lorry on the A1, I've been stabbed to death twice, I've been killed with a blow from a Breville sandwich toaster, I've shot myself in the mouth, I've died of cancer, and I've been incinerated on a spaceship.

So what are the writers trying to tell me?

It's obviously part of the re-balancing, after centuries of white, middle-class, middle-aged men having everything their own way, and I'm all for it, but that doesn't stop it feeling weird.

At school I once played The Logician in Ionesco's play *Rhinoceros*, and he has the following exchange:

> *Logician*: Here is an example of a syllogism. The cat has four paws. Isidore and Fricot both have four paws. Therefore Isidore and Fricot are cats.
> *Old Gentleman*: My dog has got four paws.
> *Logician*: Then it's a cat.

It's the kind of joke that drew me to the Theatre of the Absurd in the first place, and I always thought that syllogisms were essentially jokes, that they would always throw up something logically preposterous. And funny.

But the current syllogism is this: white, middle-class, middle-aged men are responsible for most of the iniquity in modern Britain; I am a white, middle-class, middle-aged man; therefore I am responsible for most of the iniquity in modern Britain. It's not quite as funny, is it? Well, not to me.

When I'm not being slaughtered for the sins of my age, race and gender I've started playing authority figures. I'm a deputy chief constable in *Prey*, I'm another deputy chief constable in *Bancroft*, and more recently I've been promoted to head of MI5 in *A Spy Among Friends*. These aren't berserker roles.

In *The Trick* I'm the vice-chancellor of a university – he probably knows Latin, probably knows how to conjugate and decline, and what the words *pluperfect* and *transitive* mean. This is the establishment. I have become the establishment. Some people think this is a stretch from Vyvyan, but you have to remember he was a medical student – a lot of the medical students we met at uni were similarly unstable in their youth but they all grow up to be consultants, magistrates and general pillars of the community.

The berserker is nowhere to be seen.

Part 11
Endings

A different kind of father

Love and death are inextricable. If you don't love you won't notice death. The first death to have a considerable effect on me is that of my father-in-law, Tom Saunders.

Tom is one of the most delightful human beings I ever meet. He's ex-RAF. He taught the King of Jordan to fly. He was also part of the Meteor Aerobatic Team – a precursor to the Red Arrows – and there are numerous photographs in our house of him flying with them. In most of these photos his aeroplane is upside down. And if you look carefully with a magnifying glass you can just about make out his face and see that he is grinning.

When he left the RAF he joined British Aerospace and constantly jetted around the world selling commercial airliners. The family joke is that this was cover for his real job as a spy. His work involved selling to the national airlines of various countries, so I'm sure he formed relationships with many government ministers around the world, and being an ex-serviceman I'm equally sure he was 'debriefed' whenever he returned home – a sort of 'soft' intelligence-gathering operation.

But we prefer to think of him as a proper spy. He always

delighted in telling stories of flashing his American Express card or Marriott Hotel key card to gain entry into various government buildings around the world, of bringing back huge tins of caviar from Iran, or eating monkey brains to keep in with some foreign potentate.

At home he was equally eccentric: he had an enormous jar which contained the 'toys' from every Christmas cracker that had ever been opened in the house, and he was famous for cooking eggs in the kettle when Jane, my mother-in-law, was away – more than one of which exploded, leaving the tea permanently tainted with a slight flavour of scrambled egg.

He was very much anti snobbery and had a particular dislike for ex-servicemen using their rank after they'd left the service. A local neighbour made an annual visit for Christmas drinks, and when he appeared at the door Tom would welcome him in and shout to the rest of the house: 'Everybody – the *Commander* is here! *Commander* Crill! You must come and welcome the *Commander*.'

He was always so positive towards me and what I did in a way that my own father found impossible.

'What are you up to?' he would ask.

'I'm doing a voice over for the Peperami sausage on Tuesday, then at the end of the week I'm shooting a pop video for Zodiac Mindwarp and the Love Reaction. And then Rik and I have had an idea for a sitcom about two losers living in a flat in Hammersmith.'

'How absolutely splendid. You are a clever chap. That's marvellous. Well done.'

The way it comes across on the written page makes it sound fake or affected, but he was always very genuine. I like to imagine that he used this positivity to inspire the men under his command in the RAF.

It's a stark contrast to my own father, who would wince and

say: 'Will there be a lot of bad language in it?'

In 1992 I'm in a production of a play called *Grave Plots* at the Nottingham Playhouse. It is not the best thing I ever do. In fact it's what you might call a flop. We play for three weeks and then it comes off and the hoped-for West End transfer never materializes. But my mum and dad come to see it and afterwards Dad says he's pleased to see me in something 'proper' at last. By 'proper' he means a) a play with no swearing in it, and b) a show where the audience aren't hyped up and hysterical, because he finds that uncomfortable and unseemly. He likes his theatre to be reverential. Culture is something to sit through patiently, and at its best should never be fully understood.

In 1993 when Rik and I are playing the Hammersmith Apollo with *Bottom* I look into the audience to see Tom laughing so hard that he is sliding off his chair onto the floor and I genuinely fear that he might be having a heart attack. Dad never comes to a *Bottom* show.

Why are you being so hard on your dad, he's your dad!

But fatherhood is active, you have to constantly earn it, it's not as simple as sharing a bloodline. There's a very simplistic view of fatherhood promoted on today's soaps – that the bond is automatic and cannot be messed with.

'But he's my son,' some long-lost character will wail, as if biology trumps everything else.

I felt a lot happier in my own mind when I stopped expecting anything from my dad. Obviously it's a deep scar, as this book testifies, but practising Stoicism I've learned to see it more objectively. Not with complete success, but with enough to let me live a happier life with fewer panic attacks and marginally better sleep.

Checking out early

In the early 2010s I struggle when two of my top ten friends kill themselves. Not least because I discover that I only have about ten close friends, so it's a 20 per cent loss. It's like losing two fingers – you can carry on, but life is different.

It's rare that you put your friends in order. Do you ever rank your friends? You might be able to identify your best friend, but what about your fifth best friend? Or your seventh? What's the difference between the eighth and the ninth?

I never think about ranking them until I'm writing about them for *The Essay* on Radio 3 in an episode about being nuts. I mention them in the earlier chapter 'A bit nuts'. When I hand it in my editor suggests we avoid any complications or complaints by not naming them. So I write about 'my close friend' blowing his brains out with a shotgun, and when I come to talk about a second friend who's hung himself I find I can't just write 'another close friend' because it somehow makes them indistinguishable, so I write 'an even closer friend'. And that's when I realize that I've ranked them, and that he's a closer friend than the other, possibly by dint of how much longer we've known each other, and by sharing more formative experiences when we were finding our place in the world.

We knew each other before we became successful. He's in that small group of friends who make the move from obscurity to some degree of fame at the same time: Dawn, Jennifer, Pete, Nige, Rik, Ben and Simon. This is a useful control group to have. We all know what we were like *before* the change. We have no airs and graces with each other. We know the actual truth. Not that this is sensational in any way, it's just more accurate if more mundane than the press version. It's about all the minor incidents which make up a human being, not the big leaps: Dawn's much regretted perm; Jennifer's obsession with VPL (visible panty line); Pete's joy at finding cheap Ray-Bans in a chemist's on Wardour Street; Nige's worry that his new jacket makes him look like an undercover policeman; and Ben's insatiable desire to beat me at squash, to the extent that if I've played someone else in between our matches he accuses me of cheating.

I think the ranking changes depending on which friend I'm with at the time, but Simon Brint is definitely in the top three, often in the top spot, especially when we spend lots of time together in the recording studio, or on shared holidays, of which we have many. Russell, who I meet in my mid-thirties, and with whom I share a love of pubs, Exeter City FC and walking on Dartmoor, is further down the batting order but nevertheless a solid fixture in the team.

I can use their names now because I've shown this chapter to people who might be affected and they've given me the OK.

I meet Simon at the Comic Strip Club in 1980, he's in the house band which plays the opening music, the intros to each act and the backing to all the songs throughout the evening. Whenever people need musical accompaniment they turn to Simon.

The Comic Strip Club sees a lot of new comedians pass

through its doors, and when that group of comedians starts breaking into television, Simon is the natural choice to create the music for them. He has a phenomenal gift for interpreting mood through music, and an innate sense of humour which never lets the music intrude on any jokes. He's particularly brilliant at pastiche – he can effortlessly emulate every musical style from Abba to Guns'n'Roses.

He becomes the composer for a long list of shows, including *The Comic Strip Presents . . .*, *French & Saunders*, *Bottom*, *Absolutely Fabulous*, *Alexei Sayle's Stuff*, *The Lenny Henry Show*, *The Ruby Wax Show*, *The Mary Whitehouse Experience* and *A Bit of Fry & Laurie*; even reworking the *Blue Peter* theme tune in the early nineties.

Some people find him a little aloof but he's really just a bit shy and if you become his friend he's very loyal, very good company, and very amusing. We do lots of tours together in the early days, he's so civilized and convivial, so well read, and has such phenomenal taste – this is a man who saw the first Hendrix gig in Britain when less than fifty people turned up to a club in Hythe – and he introduces me to so many things that I still enjoy to this day: the Pina Bausch dance company, the country singer Gillian Welch, and the sixties psychedelic folk group The Holy Modal Rounders. We cover their track 'Flop Eared Mule' in The Idiot Bastard Band: idiotic lyrics delivered with high intensity, scant musical talent, and an over-abundance of enthusiasm. The essence of punk really, but from sixties New York, and on acid.

In his personal life Simon's an exquisite minimalist, and lives in spaces that are painted several barely perceptibly different shades of grey. However, although everything looks clean and ordered, all the cupboards are bursting with stuff; absolutely chock-full of multitrack tapes, gizmos, instruments and recording equipment, and a million different leads, wires and transformers.

Open a door too quickly and it all falls out – and perhaps this is a metaphor for Simon himself.

He confides in me when he begins to struggle with his mental health. As you may have gathered, I'm of the opinion that 'being sane' is quite subjective, and I don't think Simon is any more or less 'sane' than anyone else. We are all a bit nuts. But as his thoughts become more confused they seem to proliferate, each new turmoil sowing further disorientation; bad thoughts building upon each other at an alarming rate until they threaten to burst the seams of his brain.

By the time he's in his late fifties most of the people he works for stop making their own shows, and the new generation of programme makers tend to bring along their own composers. He loses his place in the world and finds it increasingly difficult to deal with.

The trouble with spiralling thoughts of self-destruction is that it gets harder and harder to press the reset button. You might think it through and retrieve some kind of equilibrium but you never get all the way back to zero. You've already been where you've been.

He moves back to a small town in Somerset, the town where he was born. Alarm bells should have been ringing then really, because in hindsight it feels like he was already trying to complete the cycle – to get back to the beginning.

It's shocking listening to someone describe how they might do it. It's incredibly unnerving. I feel powerless, and useless, and not a good enough friend.

His wife Amanda is brilliant with him and they get professional help. He takes the drugs they prescribe, but they just make him feel less and less himself, which is part of the problem in the first place.

I'm on tour with The Bad Shepherds, and I'm just refuelling the van in a petrol station in Penrith when Jennifer calls.

'It's about Simon,' she says.

And I know what's happened before she says it. I know because it's exactly the same tone of voice my friend Pete Wood uses the year before.

'It's about Russell,' he says, as I sit on the bed in a Birmingham hotel room after a gig.

I first meet Russell when I move to Devon in 1995. We both turn out for the village cricket team – for the knockabout mid-week team, not the serious Saturday League team. It pretty much defines the kind of people we are: we don't take sport too seriously, but we like some kind of diversion before we hit the bar. We find a similar attitude to sailing: we sail out of Dartmouth in a sixteen-foot boat, which is little more than a dinghy, we drink merrily while we are aboard, and even more merrily when we get back to shore. In supporting Exeter City FC we like to go to all the home matches and the local derbies in Plymouth, Torquay and Yeovil, then settle down into a lovely session in a pub once we get home.

This sounds like all we do is drink, but we're not alcoholics, we're just living out the fantasy that was denied us as schoolboys: we share a bond in wanting to prove how unfettered we are, and going to the pub seems to prove this. We're aided and abetted by the fact that most of the pubs around us are bloody gorgeous.

We're also helped by the fact that Jennifer and Cindy, his partner, have struck up their own friendship, so we become a quartet, regularly trying out all the eating establishments within a thirty-mile radius. We occasionally do this with another couple, Pete and Jo Wood, and we like to squash into one car and have a designated driver.

Russell works in the dark art of marketing and is forever glad-handing potential clients in every restaurant we go to. One evening we go to the Agaric in Ashburton and as we leave

Russell does that thing of spotting a client on the way out. He spends ten minutes playing the big 'I am' and schmoozing.

Outside, we're just getting into the car, and Russell is getting into the 'short straw' seat for the ride home, when, unbeknown to us, the client follows us out of the restaurant with his wife.

'He's getting into the boot!' she cries out in alarm just as I close it and Russell's head pops out through the parcel shelf. Market your way out of that, sunshine! We laugh all the way home.

Some years later things go awry between Russell and Cindy and they split up. I make the fatal error of trying to be on both sides, or is it trying to be on neither? Whichever, it's not a good choice as, understandably, they both want loyalty to their cause. My bond with both of them becomes strained.

Russell starts other relationships, mostly with younger women, but they don't work out. He becomes a bit belligerent and makes a few enemies in the pubs we like to frequent. It later transpires that the man in Ashburton isn't the only client he's lost, and that he's in serious debt.

Russell doesn't seek me out as much as he did, but we still go to the football together. One day we're coming back and he says he's got things to do and doesn't fancy the pub. He gets out of the car.

'Goodbye,' he says.

This is two weeks before I get the phone call sitting on the bed in the Birmingham hotel room. It's only then that I recognize how oddly Russell said 'Goodbye' a fortnight before. It haunts me. He knew then. He knew he was going to do it. He was planning it. He was actually saying 'Goodbye' for ever. With a smile on his face.

It becomes obvious he'd been planning it for months. Clearing his house, it doesn't take Sherlock Holmes to deduce he's been emptying his freezer over the last few months, to the point where there's not a single thing left in it. My daughter Ella remembers having a peculiar meal there some weeks before: kippers, broad beans, and Alphabites followed by a Viennetta.

He thinks he's being heroic. He thinks he's tidied up all the loose ends. He leaves a note insisting we play The Jam's 'Going Underground' as his coffin is carried out of the church. It's all so unspeakably sad because there's nothing heroic about devastating all your friends and acquaintances, and traumatizing all the children who looked up to you as their jolly honorary uncle. His freezer might be empty and the suicide note left neatly on the table as he goes out onto the moor to blow his brains out with a shotgun, but his life is actually a mess of debt and disorder and in a small rural community many of the emergency service people know him personally and have to deal with his body.

But he just couldn't face it any more. He'd had enough. He didn't see enough happiness on the horizon.

I find both suicides very hard to deal with. It's impossible not to feel that if I'd applied myself more, if I'd been more vigilant, more present, more helpful, that I might be sipping cold dry sherry in a tapas bar in Madrid with Simon, or rocking back with laughter in a country pub with Russell.

On the other hand, I have considered helping someone to die.

Dad

It's 2014. Dad was first diagnosed with dementia some three years before. His first symptoms are merely an annoyance to Mum – forgetting simple things, getting confused. Things become more serious when he starts asking when they might go home.

'But you're already home!' Mum says.

'But this isn't Liversedge, is it?' he asks.

This man in his eighties thinks he still lives in his childhood home, a place he hasn't seen in over seventy-five years. And there's no reasoning with people who've got dementia, there's no longer a rational base level to appeal to. He's still making understandable contributions to the conversation but they're based on shifting sands and can quickly become scatological or completely unintelligible – sometimes hilarious, sometimes distressing.

There's a steady decline: he drives away in the car and doesn't know where he's going, returning hours later not knowing where he's been, everyone's frightened; he becomes a liability around the house, fiddling with the electrics, forgetting where the bathroom is; he becomes a danger to himself and Mum. She's also in her eighties and can't look after him any more, she can't physically manhandle him, and eventually she makes the painful decision to move him into a home.

The first time I visit him in the home I take along the latest copy of *National Geographic*, his favourite magazine.

'I got you this,' I say.

He looks at it without taking it from my hand and I see a look of deep sorrow flash across his face.

'It's no use, Adrian,' he says. 'I can't . . . understand it any more. I can't . . . read any more.'

And that's when I know he's a goner.

He starts in the more open part of the home but imagines he's being held captive and keeps setting off the fire alarm and trying to escape. They move him to the more secure part of the building.

I live in London; the nursing home is between Selby and York. Each time I go I notice the scale of the decline in a way my mum's daily visits probably don't. There's a terrible period when he's almost completely unresponsive but as I talk to him – a one-sided conversation – some sliver of what I'm saying connects and I see a panic in his eyes, as if for that brief second he understands the full horror of his situation.

The last time I see this flicker of comprehension he's lying in his bed like one of the twisted bodies on display in Pompeii – his mouth hangs open, he's wearing a nappy, I don't know if he can even hear me, let alone understand anything I say. He looks to be in abject misery. I'm alone in the room with him and it crosses my mind that I could gently take the spare pillow and press it against his mouth and nose. He's barely breathing anyway, and he wouldn't have the strength to resist. I wouldn't have to apply much pressure. How long would it take for his weak lungs to stop altogether?

I don't do it, but I often wish I had. He hangs on for another month or so of torment.

I'd want people to do it for me. In fact, if this book could count as a living will I'd like it to be known that at the first sign of terminal distress I would like to leave this world on a cloud of morphine. At the *National Geographic* stage.

Given our uncertain relationship I feel strangely relieved in the week leading up to the funeral. Relieved for both of us. I can't believe he didn't find it difficult either. We will have no more ponderous pauses. No more of those shuffling handshakes that threaten to turn into a hug in later life but that wither on the vine in an awkward dance of arm movements. I will never know if he loved me or not, but now he can't tell me either way, and that's a kind of closure.

Yet inside the church I become aware that I'm bawling my eyes out and that my face is stuck into the shape of a howler monkey's. Mum has put 'Abide with Me' into the service. Even at FA Cup finals I can never get through the first verse without weeping.

'It always gets me, that song,' I say, as I walk Mum to the graveside to throw clods of earth onto the coffin.

'I know,' says Mum.

The People's Poet

Less than two months later, Rik drops dead at his home in Barnes. I'm in Devon at the time. I live on the edge of Dartmoor and the phone signal is very weak. I'm working in the garden and I'm passing the sweet spot between the pond and the apple tree where the mobile signal is sometimes as much as one bar strong, when the audiobook I'm listening to is interrupted by a phone call.

'I'm so sorry, it must be awful for you, I know there isn't but if there's anything I can do to help,' says my friend Nick.

'What about?' I ask.

'Oh my God – you don't know, do you?'

Apparently it's some time since Rik's death was flashed across the airwaves. Almost everyone in Britain knows except me. People have been trying to reach me but the signal is so weak they haven't got through.

Bizarrely, between the pond and the apple tree is exactly the same spot where I stood in 1998 when Rik's brother Ant rang me to say that he'd had a serious accident on his quad bike.

But this time it's more serious. The people's poet is dead.

> I feel sorry for you, you zeros, you nobodies. What's going to live on after you die? Nothing, that's what. This house will become a shrine, and punks and skins and rastas will all gather round and hold their hands in sorrow for their fallen leader. And all the grown-ups will say: 'But why are the kids crying?' And the kids will say: 'Haven't you heard? Rick is dead! The People's Poet is dead!'
>
> Rik's character Rick in *The Young Ones* in 1981 after eating too many laxatives

In the same way that Rik is only different to Rick by one letter, the character of Rick was not too far removed from his own. The above speech was pretty much Rik's own idea of the kind of youth icon he thought he actually was. He's making fun of the idea in the speech, but he's simultaneously enjoying it. He was vain, but saw the comedy in it. He would have been over the moon to be on the front page of every newspaper, to make all the major news bulletins, and to be the subject of a segment on *Newsnight* as Jeremy Paxman questioned Caitlin Moran about his cultural importance.

His death is a dreadful shock to the world, and to me.

My head fills with a kind of white noise. It's difficult to comprehend that he's dead. We drive back to London and go round to his house to see Barbara and the kids.

The house is full. Family and friends have gathered round. Bottles have been opened and . . . it's like a party, but it's the oddest party I ever go to. The alcohol serves both to anaesthetize the pain and to release inhibitions. I find myself talking to people and suddenly the howler monkey in me will appear and I'll be wailing in their faces, then he'll subside, only to return a few minutes later. Rik's posthumous son-in-law Red, with whom Rik shared a lot of laughs, seems similarly stricken, and we find ourselves howling at each other, not commenting on it, recovering, and carrying on.

Whereas death brings closure to my difficult relationship with Dad, Rik's death leaves an open wound. I'm sad that he never understood why I wanted to stop doing *Bottom* and do other stuff. I don't miss having to repeat it every time we meet, but I wish he could have settled it in his own mind. I wish we could have got back to simply enjoying each other's company and laughing at stuff. To be the way we were when we first met. The *Hooligan's Island* business ended on such a sour note – a mixture of incomprehension and bad blood – and our friendship suffered as a result in those final two years. I wish it hadn't.

I write a letter to his mum, Gillian, and she replies and says the sweetest thing. She says she has an abiding memory of standing in her kitchen listening to us as we sat in two deckchairs in her garden just laughing and laughing and laughing. She says it was hard to understand how anything could be so funny.

It's not a hard and fast rule, but in the writing room I wrote more of his character Richie than he did, and similarly he wrote more of my character Eddie than I did. Our characters are grossly exaggerated versions of ourselves, and we were in love with each other's characters. When he dies I feel that I've lost my champion.

At least I get to read a bit of *Waiting for Godot* out in the church at his funeral, his favourite line:

'They give birth astride of a grave, the light gleams an instant, then it's night once more.'

He would have enjoyed that.

Le Venerable

But the death that affects me most is yet to come and takes me very much by surprise.

We meet Betty and David in the early nineties; Betty is a designer and David, who is French, runs the business side of the operation. Betty designs a stage jacket for Jennifer, there's a spark between them, and we go round for Sunday lunch. We have three young children, they have two – the five of them span only five years in age and they mesh together instantly into a playful unit.

As do we adults.

In the early nineties we've got to a similar point in our lives. The four of us are all successful, we're not afraid to enjoy ourselves, we eat well, and we drink well. We understand each other, and we really enjoy each other's company. We spend practically every Sunday together, we go on holiday together, and the kids play so well, they're closer than cousins. The Cohens and the Edmondsons become closer than blood family because we've actually *chosen* each other. When the Cohen children become adults we're talking one day about there being no godparents in the Jewish tradition and between ourselves we instantly decide that I will be their godfather and they my godchildren. Although we've since changed it to Oddfather and Oddchildren.

The same thing happens with Ben's children – brought up in an atheist household with Jewish roots – we're discussing their lack of godparents, and the fact that I've never been deemed suitable by any parents, and we simply declare ourselves Godfather and Godchildren. I treasure these relationships.

David and I play a lot of chess, smoke fat cigars until we're frankly a bit green, and drink far too much eau de vie. He's an extremely generous host, but his kindest act is to teach me everything he knows about food and wine. My favourite trips are going with David to the shops when we're on holiday in Provence. He's a witty, lovable, talkative epicurean: every shopkeeper is engaged in a lengthy conversation to determine the best month to eat figs, where to get the best burrata, or how to cook a cardoon; and he introduces me to them as if I am the chef-patron of a Michelin-starred restaurant.

Obviously his French is very good, and though his English is perfectly intelligible it's full of humorous mistakes and, to be frank, seems to get worse rather than better over the years. But then my French is equally laughable, so who cares? We understand each other completely and make each other laugh.

But we also enjoy a more philosophical side. Of all the men in my life David is the only one I feel confident to talk to about some of the things that trouble me. He's Jewish by birth but also a Buddhist, and not a notional one – he has a mentor, a monk he calls 'le venerable'.

David's story supports my theory that we are all nuts. He has had personal struggles in his life and he needs to constantly question himself, and his mentor, to find equilibrium. He works at it very hard. As I've explained, my mental health has not always been particularly robust and I work away at Stoicism, which is not a million miles away from Buddhism: they both help by defining what you can and cannot control. But in many ways David is my personal monk, my 'venerable' – it's never a formal relationship, but he gives me a lot of good advice, and a lot of comfort.

Slightly older than us, Betty and David retire in 2019, intent on travelling around Europe on a more or less permanent holiday, but almost as soon as they stop working David has a medical check-up and discovers he's got cancer. These days we tend to think cancer isn't as frightening as it once was, there are so many stories of successful treatment and recovery – Jennifer being a case in point – but David has got it everywhere and they can't treat it. They give him six months. He dies in three.

We have one of our philosophical chats shortly after the diagnosis. He lays on some delicious pastries. We drink good coffee. Our talk is at the same temperature and level as usual except this time we have tears streaming down our faces. He looks so healthy, but he's dying right in front of me.

When I see him a couple of days before he dies he's gaunt and emaciated, a shadow of himself. I can't tell if he's listening or not, he's certainly not contributing much to the conversation, but I think he knows I'm there. I have an idea to give him a problem, the kind of problem he likes to solve: I tell him about some trouble I'm having with an actor on the project I'm currently filming. His eyes light up and he immediately becomes more animated. He uses all his acquired wisdom to provide me with a solution to the blockage. He's brilliant. Then he retreats back into himself and I leave.

He dies on my daughter Ella's birthday and is buried on mine. I know dates are just numbers but it feels special to me that there's some connection through these.

How many fingers?

To return to the metaphor of my top ten friends being like the fingers on my hands, I've now lost four fingers. I've got a thumb and two fingers on each hand. Better than none. Reasonably serviceable. Django Reinhardt managed to become a celebrated jazz guitarist with only two functioning fingers on his left hand. Emotionally I'm very good at making the 'devil's horns' sign with both hands, though I'm not as keen on heavy metal as I was.

Those berserkers must have lost a few fingers, literally and metaphorically. I wonder how many of them survived into their sixties like me.

What did those old berserkers do? Surely the looting, pillaging, and killing with a wild and senseless abandon had to stop at some point? You can't be off your tits on henbane and alcohol your entire life? Surely they were allowed to go home? Maybe they got a little smallholding, raised some chickens, grew some prize vegetables? Lived in the warm glow of a family – a wife, children, grandchildren.

This isn't me wanting to retire, far from it, I think I would literally die of boredom if I didn't work, and my best work is still to come (stop laughing), but I think I've finally come to terms with what made me a berserker. Becoming a berserker was a reaction to the situation I found myself in, a defence mechanism. It became a way of life, and a way of expressing myself. I found the fun in it, even though it was essentially quite damaging. But the years of being a practising Stoic have made me more at ease with myself. I'm not as angry. I feel more secure. I'm a lot happier. I feel I don't have to prove anything. I've got it in perspective, and writing it down has helped me do that.

The Japanese have a tradition called *kintsugi* in which they mend broken pots with a gold-coloured pigment so you can see where the damage was. They're proud of the repair. Part of the process of coming to terms with the damage is to show it off, and not be ashamed. The berserker in me feels like one of those pots – you can see my cracks, but I've been repaired, and I'm more or less fully functional. I could probably hold a pint of miso soup without leaking. (This is my second attempt at Pseuds Corner.)

And where are you?

You've probably learned enough biographical material to access my old post office savings account – good luck with that, because I can't get into it – but have you recognized bits of yourself in any of this? I don't mean directly of course, but we're all connected to other people, we all have dreams, we all have difficulties, we all meet with success and failure, life is very rarely linear, we can all take a little introspection on occasion, and we all have to make peace with our pasts.

And yet, we also have to bear in mind what the noted psychologist Carl Jung once said:

'I am not what happened to me, I am what I choose to become.'

So maybe it's all bollocks.

FIN

Acknowledgements

Deepest thanks to Caroline Raphael, who first commissioned me to write a piece entitled 'The Funniest Thing I Ever Saw' for the Radio 3 strand *The Essay,* and then commissioned me to write five more, and then a further five after that. She nurtured an autobiographical urge within me and helped me find a way of writing about myself that I found enjoyable – and a voice that was possibly less self-obsessed than it might have been. An autobiography that isn't self-obsessed? Who am I kidding? I hope you know what I mean. Caroline certainly does, because she also edited this book. During moments when I struggled with structure, content and tone she was always on the end of the phone offering great advice and encouragement, and, very kindly, making things seem less difficult. The book wouldn't exist without her. Thank you.

Picture acknowledgements

Page 4, Ade portrait © Iain McKell.
Page 20, Adrian Street © Dennis Hutchinson/Mirrorpix/Getty Images.
Page 25, Chess piece © National Museums of Scotland.
Page 56, *if . . .* film poster © Retro AdArchives/Alamy.
Page 82, Sonja Kristina © Keystone Press/Alamy.
Page 260, 'True Humility' cartoon © Punch Cartoon Library/TopFoto.

PLATES ONE

All images courtesy of the author.

PLATES TWO

All images courtesy of the author, with the exception of:

Page 1, 20th Century Coyote images © Lloyd Peters.
Page 2, Rik's parents' house 1979 © John Mayall; Fringe Club 1979 © Caroline Raphael; Comic Strip Club dressing room © David Johnson/shapersofthe80s.com.

Page 5, *Bottom Live* tour contact sheet © Phil McIntyre.
Page 6, The Bonzos 2006 © Phill Jupitus; The Bad Shepherds © Christie Goodwin/Getty Images; The Idiot Bastards © Andy Hale/Wallasey Amateur Photographic Society.
Page 7, Jennifer at a party in the eighties © Chris Dorley-Brown; Edmondson family portrait © Chris Chapman.

About the author

Adrian Charles Edmondson is an English actor, comedian, musician, writer and television presenter. He studied drama at Manchester University, where he met his comedy partner Rik Mayall. The influence of the absurdist dramatists he studied and his early love for The Goons, The Muppets and Monty Python are all reflected in his comedy practice. He and Rik were part of the first wave of alternative comedy, where their glorious pursuit of laughter and anarchic performances changed the comedic landscape forever.

He starred as Vyvyan in *The Young Ones*, a series that blasted its way onto our screens and tore into our preconceptions of what television comedy could be. In later years, Edmondson's career has also taken him into 'straight' acting – including at the RSC and in the BBC's *War and Peace* and *EastEnders* – and into writing books for adults and children. He has also had an award-winning music career with his band The Bad Shepherds, which fused punk and folk to great acclaim.